Adorno and "A Writing of the Ruins"

Essays on Modern Aesthetics and Anglo-American Literature and Culture

James Martin Harding

State University of New York Press

Cover photo "Frankfurt, 1954" by Fritz K. Sautter

Published by
State University of New York Press, Albany

Printed in the United States of America

For information, address State University of New York Press,
State University Plaza, Albany, N.Y. 12246

Production by M. R. Mulholland
Marketing by Fran Keneston

Library of Congress Cataloging-in-Publication Data

Harding, James M. (James Martin), 1958–
Adorno and "A writing of the ruins" : essays on modern aesthetics and Anglo-American literature and culture / James M. Harding.
p. cm.
Includes bibliographical references and index.
ISBN 0-7914-3269-6 (hardcover : alk. paper). — ISBN 0-7914-3270-X (pbk. : alk. paper)
1. American literature—20th century—History and criticism—Theory, etc. 2. Beckett, Samuel, 1906– En attendant Godot. 3. Adorno, Theodor W., 1903–1969—Aesthetics. 4. Aesthetics, Modern—20th century. 5. Postmodernism (Literature) 6. Modernism (Literature) I. Title.
PS221.H353 1997
810.9'005—dc20 96-15951
CIP

10 9 8 7 6 5 4 3 2 1

Adorno and
"A Writing of the Ruins"

Contents

Acknowledgments vii

Introduction 1

I. Adorno, Dialectics, and Aesthetic Theory

1. Historical Dialectics and the Autonomy of Art in Adorno's *Aesthetic Theory* 11
2. *Aesthetic Theory* and Fragmenting the Unities of Negation 27

II. Adorno, Literature, and the Conceptual Forms of Historical Reflection

3. Trying to Understand Godot: Adorno, Beckett, and the Senility of Dialectics 51
4. The Lexicon of Music: Adorno, the Philosophy of Music, and Eliot's *Four Quartets* 65

III. Adorno, Folk Culture, Commodification and National Identity in Literature and Music

5. Adorno, Ellison, and the Critique of Jazz 97
6. Cultural Identities, Commodities, and Myth: Adorno and Baraka on Wagner and the Flying Dutchman 117

Notes 149

Bibliography 179

Index 191

Acknowledgments

I want to thank the editors of *The Journal of Aesthetics and Art Criticism*, *Clio* and *Cultural Critique* for their kind permission to reprint articles that originally appeared in their journals: Chapter one, "Historical Dialectics and the Autonomy of Art in Adorno's *Ästhetische Theorie*," appeared in *JAAC* 50.3 (1992); Chapter three, "Trying to Understand *Godot*: Adorno, Beckett, and the Senility of Historical Dialectics," appeared in *Clio* 23.1 (1993); and chapter five, "Adorno, Ellison and the Critique of Jazz," appeared in *Cultural Critique* 31 (1995).

Discussion with friends and colleagues has been invaluable to this project. I want to express my thanks to those who have been sources of advice, criticism and insight as I put this book together. Foremost, I want to thank Friederike Eigler who discussed every stage of this book's evolution with me. I also want to thank Peter Baker and Francisco LaRubia-Prado, both of whom were always willing to give my work a hearing. Joe Sitterson's comments on chapters three and five were indispensable. Comments made by Ralph Heyndels, Deborah Chaffin and Billy O'Brien gave the book direction when it was first beginning as a project, and the support of Marcia Dalbey and my colleagues in the English Department at Eastern Michigan made it possible to finish it. Finally, I would like to thank Carola Sautter and Megeen Mulholland at SUNY Press for the assistance they provided in seeing the manuscript through its final stages. A special note of thanks goes to Carola Sautter for permission to use the photograph on the book's cover. Thanks also to Marilyn McCabe who worked as the copy editor on this project.

Introduction

When Theodor W. Adorno died in 1969 after over thirty years with the Institute for Social Research, he, together with his fellow members of the Frankfurt School, had established a tradition of critical thought that has proven to be an almost inexhaustible source for subsequent scholars. Widely acclaimed in Europe as one of the twentieth century's most important critics and philosophers of modernism, Adorno has nonetheless received isolated attention in the United States. This is in part due to a density in his writing that has thwarted adequate translation, even of seminal works like *Dialectic of Enlightenment*.[1] Yet in the last three years, seven titles have been added to the list of his translated works, and several books pertaining to Adorno's cultural criticism, modernist aesthetics, and philosophy have appeared in English. The increasing accessibility of Adorno's writings to readers of English has created a new audience for Adorno's thought. My book speaks to both the historical and cultural dimensions of this audience.

As far as the historical dimension is concerned, my interests are with the consequences of Adorno's rather belated reception in the United States. I am less interested in further crystallizing the rivalry between modernism and postmodernism than I am in exploring the fragments of Adorno's thought whose critical force has survived a growing distrust of philosophical systems—a distrust which Adorno ironically shares with those critical of him. Unlike David Robert's *Art and Enlightenment* (1991) which, for example, opposes Adorno's modernism to postmodernism and seeks a postmodern art that is post- or "after Adorno," my work seeks to understand the relevance of Adorno after the advent of the postmodern. The postmodern has not rendered Adorno obsolete; it has shifted the bearings on the course and scope of his relevance. In this respect, I would argue that Adorno's modernist aesthetics fall under Albrecht Wellmer's more general assertion in *The Persistence of Modernity* that "modernity is . . . an unsurpassable horizon" and that postmodernism, rather than seeking to surpass modernity, redirects its critique:

> With postmodernism, ironically enough, it becomes obvious that the critique of the modern, inasmuch as it knows its own parameters, can only aim at expanding the interior space of modernity, not at surpassing it. For it is the very gesture of radical surpassing—romantic utopianism—that postmodernism has called into question.[2]

It is the wide dissemination of this notion of "an unsurpassable horizon" that, it seems to me, characterizes the attitudes of Adorno's audience and that demands a redirection in the reading of his texts. The modernism/postmodernism debate has so shifted the critical paradigms of Adorno's audience that his work can best be assessed in terms of its relevance in specific localized contexts.

The book's title correlates this argument with Jean-François Lyotard's revision of Adorno's philosophy: "Philosophy as architecture is ruined, but a writing of the ruins, micrologies, graffiti can still be done."[3] I take Lyotard's elliptical embrace of a "writing of the ruins" to be a postmodern tactic that preserves Adorno's opposition to hegemonic programs and that heeds his cultural critiques but that is also wary of Adorno's own (negative) penchant for totalizing concepts. The book does not—as Habermas accuses the post-modernists of doing—give "up modernity and its project as a lost cause." Rather it aims "at expanding the interior space of modernity" and at taking seriously the potential rewards of "a writing of the ruins." As I understand such "a writing," it presumes that the critical validity of Adorno's thought can partially survive the collapse of the implicit system which he constructed. "A writing of the ruins" would then scrutinize the structure of contexts—however limited, fragmented, or localized they might be—in which Adorno's arguments still offer critical insight. Inasmuch as Habermas argues that the project of modernity is "to release the cognitive potentials" of "aesthetic-expressive rationality" and of art "from their esoteric forms," a careful examination of the interior spaces of modernity offers the possibility for a release that does not increase the (post) modern divide.[4]

The emphasis on the interior spaces or viable ruins of Adorno's thought distinguishes my project from other works like Lambert Zuidervaart's *Adorno's Aesthetic Theory* (1991) and Max Paddison's *Adorno's Aesthetics of Music* (1993), both of which aim at a comprehensive synthesis of Adorno's writings.[5] Though their books are arguably the best works on Adorno in recent years, my emphasis on the interior spaces of Adorno's thought attempts to circumvent the bind that Paddison produces in two competing observations. He notes, on the one hand, Adorno's belief "that to systematize is to impose a unity upon the dissimilar, a false totality which betrays difference in the interests of equivalence and exchangeabilty." On the other hand, he argues that "Adorno's writings demand a systematic . . . reading, and anything less is to betray them equally effectively through fetishizing their complexity as poetic obscurity."[6] Paddison thus justifies his own synthesis of Adorno's writings by narrowly categorizing those who share Adorno's concern with imposed unities. He suggests any approach that is sympathetic with Adorno's reservations about systems mistakes the complexity of Adorno's thought for "poetic obscurity."

It is at the very least debatable whether sympathy with Adorno's or post-modernism's distrust of systems can be dismissed as a fetishized mis-perception, i.e., as mistaking "complexity" for "poetic obscurity." And if one interprets Paddison's call for a "systematic . . . reading" of Adorno as a call for rigor and thoroughness, then this goal can be achieved critically—without betrayal and without synthesizing Adorno's writings into a comprehensive system. Unlike Zuidervaart and Paddison, I have ordered my book as a collection of essays whose loose association questions the structural totality of Adorno's thought while seeking out constellations where his writings still have critical force. Though together the essays cover the major issues of Adorno's aesthetics and offer a wide critical survey of his writings, the diversity of their focuses avoids a systematic reduction of Adorno's work.[7]

As far as the cultural dimensions of my audience are concerned, the book cuts across disciplinary lines to partially redress what Russell Berman has called one of the major historical ironies of Adorno's reception in America:

> How historically ironic, indeed wrongheaded a distortion it would be to treat as characteristically German the work of intellectuals forced to leave Germany and to find a home in the United States; for some . . . that American home became permanent; and for Max Horkheimer and Adorno, central texts, like the *Dialectic of Enlightenment* and *Minima Moralia*, are best understood as theoretical accounts of American, not German society.[8]

Berman is not alone in his admonishments against treating Adorno's work as "characteristically German." Peter Hohendahl has also noted the relationship that Adorno's writings from the forties bear to the American social and intellectual climate. In "Adorno's American Years Revisited," Hohendahl meticulously outlines the parallels between *Dialectic of Enlightenment* and *Minima Moralia* and the work of American intellectuals and cultural critics like Sidney Hook, Irving Kristol, Dwight MacDonald, and C. Wright Mill.[9] In their recent work, Berman and Hohendahl point toward promising and largely untapped realms for Adorno scholarship, and inasmuch as my own book attempts a similar path, it seeks new affinities even as it questions the totalizing presumptions in Adorno's thought. By adopting the essay as the form for writing about Adorno and by applying Adorno's theories to works by Samuel Beckett, T. S. Eliot, Ralph Ellison, and Amiri Baraka, the book pushes critical discussion of Adorno into cultural contexts that, while perhaps new for Adorno scholars, are more familiar to scholars whose knowledge of Adorno is perhaps limited. The exploration of such contexts offers, in my opinion, a far more dynamic analysis of Adorno than a mere critical reconstruction of his ideas.

The book has six chapters which fall under three major divisions.

I. Adorno, Dialectics and Aesthetic Theory

The opening section of the book analyzes the unique relation that Adorno's revision of historical dialectics has to the fertile contradictions of his *Aesthetic Theory* (1970). In the first two chapters, I read Adorno's emphasis on the heterogenous against the grain of the latent totalizations in his arguments. I focus specifically on the rhetorical position from which Adorno articulates his aesthetic theory and on the suppositions which precede aesthetic negation. These opening essays on Adorno's aesthetics serve the function of introducing the central theoretical issues of the book while simultaneously providing the rationale for its structure.

1. Historical Dialectics and the Autonomy of Art

In the first of the two essays, I argue that Adorno's conception of the autonomy of art derives from his revision of historical dialectics and in particular from his critical rejection of the notion of dialectical synthesis or *Aufhebung*. I argue that for Adorno the autonomy of art results from an aesthetic work's inability to sublate the socio-historical dimensions that it negates. I then investigate the extent to which Adorno's revision of dialectics, in addition to underlying his theory of aesthetics, produces a theory that is aesthetic as well. Not only does Adorno largely discount the possibility of correlating art and praxis; a close examination of *Aesthetic Theory* reveals that, rhetorically, its arguments are marked by an unbroken refusal to move beyond broad negative allusions to society. In this respect, I argue, Adorno articulates his arguments from the position of art looking back in retrospect on origins whose falsity the work has already negated. Like the critical position of the art it describes, *Aesthetic Theory* assumes a position from which the social whole is always already untrue. Indeed, the presumed lack of truth in the social whole is the one major constant in an aesthetic theory that is structured around an otherwise radical historicization of aesthetic value.

2. Fragmenting the Unities of Aesthetic Negation.

In the second essay on *Aesthetic Theory*, I explore the presumptions underlying Adorno's contention that art resists, exposes, and thus negates the forced reconciliations of its socio-historical context. First, I argue that *Aesthetic Theory* has to be understood as presupposing an historical dialectic, the unity of whose moments and movements is propelled by conceptual exclusions. According to Adorno, art becomes art because it expresses a position that is unaccounted for by the accepted concepts of a socio-historical moment. Expressing the excluded, art thus exposes how conceptual unity is repressive and illusory: it is purchased not through synthesis but by forcibly suppressing the "non-integrable." Secondly, I examine the extent to which art, as conceived in

Aesthetic Theory, succumbs to the very conceptual exclusions that it exposes. I demonstrate how in Adorno's arguments the aesthetic and socio-historical realms comprise a binary opposition whose stability depends upon both realms remaining abstract linguistic categories. I argue that the kind of forced unities that art negates are reflected in the fixed linguistic oppositions that Adorno employs in his theoretical arguments. I show, furthermore, that a work of art can only gain the footing to become non-identical by simultaneously forcing one form of reconciliation so as to unmask another. In short, a work of art can only defend heterogeneity by setting up a unity with which it is at odds.

Although not explicitly argued in the chapters themselves, the relation of the issues in section I to the concerns of the book can be easily summarized. Inasmuch as art sets up conceptual unities even as it exposes the repressiveness of them, and inasmuch as Adorno in *Aesthetic Theory*, rhetorically, never ventures beyond the realms of aesthetic negation, critical assessment of his aesthetics needs to follow two stages. First of all, there is the question of whether Adorno's theoretical arguments, when applied to specific works, actually yield what they claim. The next section of the book examines two modern works whose critical force does in fact affirm Adorno's general claims. By exploring how Samuel Beckett's *Waiting for Godot* and T. S. Eliot's *Four Quartets* position themselves in opposition to dominant conceptual forms, section II develops the critical methodology of Adorno's aesthetics. The second stage of assessing Adorno's aesthetics is more complicated than looking for mere confirmation of his methodology. Thus in section III, critical assessment involves analyses that not only expose the exclusions upon which individual art works rely but that also expose the conceptual exclusions of Adorno's own thought. For this dual critique, I focus on Adorno's controversial discussions of jazz, and in particular examine the representation of jazz in the work of Ralph Ellison and Amiri Baraka. The relation of section II and section III, however, extends beyond a sequential staggering of complexity in analysis. As will be evident momentarily, their themes are inherently related.

II. Adorno, Literature and the Conceptual Forms of Historical Reflection

While considering works of literature philosophically related to the issues addressed in the book's first section, the second section of the book departs from an exclusive focus on *Aesthetic Theory*. Section II begins a series of literary studies that marshal wide discussion of Adorno's writings in analyses of the repressive effects of forced reconciliations in Enlightenment philosophies and in transcendental aesthetic categories. The primary points of reference for this section are *Negative Dialectics* (1966) and *Philosophy of Modern Music* (1949). The first essay addresses the relation of historical reflection to the construction of cultural identity, and the second addresses the relation of music to the crisis in aesthetic value expressed in modern poetic discourse. While initially the two essays may appear randomly situated together, they in fact lay the foundation for a combined focus on cultural identity and music in the final section of the book.

3. Trying to Understand *Godot*: Adorno, Beckett and the Senility of Dialectics

What generally distinguishes this essay from previous discussions of Adorno and Beckett is its focus on *Waiting for Godot* rather than on Adorno's reading of *Endgame*. The essay on *Waiting for Godot* illustrates the connection between Adorno's revision of dialectics and his concern with anti-Semitism and the Holocaust. The essay relates Adorno's considerations on the state of metaphysics after Auschwitz with Beckett's subtle dramatization of the repressiveness of Hegel's master-slave dialectic, a dialectic that is central to both Hegelian and Marxist thought. By demonstrating that *Waiting for Godot* traces the evolution of Hegel's master-slave dialectic back to its original use in a disparaging categorization of a so-called "Jewish mentality," I argue that Beckett characterizes Hegel's conception of the path of enlightened consciousness and historical progress as being paved with obscure but brutal repressions.

4. The Lexicon of Music: Adorno, the Philosophy of Music and Eliot's *Four Quartets*

By examining the conceptual similarities of Adorno's "Music and Language: A Fragment" and Eliot's "The Music of Poetry," I argue in the opening movement of this essay that the production of meaning in music and in language is, at one level, parallel. Both rely on context and historical residue for significance. I demonstrate how this structural parallel between music and language illuminates the implicit theory of language in Adorno's *Philosophy of Modern Music* and how it affects the signification of music in Eliot's *Four Quartets*. I argue that what Adorno calls "constant alteration" in music destabilizes a direct referential signification of music with words. I then show how *Four Quartets*, by using the parallels between music and language as an alternative form of signification, attempts to circumvent music's defiance of direct linguistic signification. The musical-verbal analogies of Eliot's collection of poems, I argue, are thus a structural acknowledgement of the conceptual exclusions perpetuated by words and, simultaneously, an attempt to use structure and form to signify what words cannot.

The decisive critical turn in the essay on Eliot's *Four Quartets* comes when, using Adorno's musicology, I address the ahistorical and monolithic conception of music that Eliot employs in his strategy for circumventing the conceptual exclusions of language. In short, Eliot sets up one conceptual unity in order to combat another. The turn is decisive because the critique of Eliot parallels a larger critique of the monolithic conception of music in Adorno's own writings, particularly with regard to his views on the aesthetic value of popular music and jazz. The critique of Eliot is thus as decisive for the book as it is for the discussions of the representation of music in *Four Quartets*. It prefigures the transition from the final essay of Section II to the first essay of section III.

III. Adorno, Folk Culture, Commodification and National Identity in Literature and Music

In the last of the book's three major divisions, I explore the relation of Adorno's writings on the culture industry to his writings on popular and folk culture. The primary points of reference are Adorno's essays on jazz and the books *Dialectic of Enlightenment* and *In Search of Wagner*. The section is comprised of two essays on jazz and seeks a balance between the rigor of Adorno's cultural criticism and the hidden one-dimensionality of his understanding of oppressed communities. The two essays attempt to understand Adorno's unfavorable assessment of jazz by investigating "the relationship between American culture, in which the recognition of plurality is almost a matter of course, and some very different experiences, intellectual and historical in Germany" (Berman *Cultural Studies* 12). The first essay weighs Adorno's monolithic conception of the cultural community against his assertion that jazz is unable to resist appropriation, and the second essay explores how Adorno's sensitivity to the reductive tendencies of commodification obscures his lack of sensitivity to the differing internal dynamics of repressed cultures.

5. Adorno, Ellison and the Critique of Jazz

In this essay, I maintain that those most critical of Adorno's reservations about jazz examine neither all of his essays on the subject nor the historical context of his arguments, and that those sympathetic to Adorno ignore the vast amount of research on jazz at their disposal. I argue that to understand Adorno's criticisms of jazz requires situating them in a social history that considers the internal tensions within the jazz tradition, a task I achieve by juxtaposing Adorno's criticisms with the representations of jazz in Ralph Ellison's *Invisible Man* (1952). The complexities portrayed by Ellison, I argue, facilitate an evaluation of jazz that adopts the "rigor" of Adorno's arguments while addressing the diversity of cultural contexts which Adorno passes over. Although Ellison's novel exposes Adorno's monolithic conception of society and culture, it nonetheless suggests the method by which to give his cultural theories a critical diversification and flexibility.

6. Cultural Identities, Commodities and Myth: Adorno and Baraka on Wagner and the Flying Dutchman

This essay responds to scholars who, by paralleling Adorno's critiques of Wagner and of jazz, defend Adorno against charges of elitism. Amiri Baraka's play *Dutchman* offers a valuable context for this response because, amid an adaptation of the same myth that Richard Wagner used to assert high German culture in the opera *The Flying Dutchman*, Baraka stages an unapologetic articulation of jazz's sublimated, violent rejection of white American culture. Although in these two pieces Wagner's cultural ideology and a jazz aesthetic intersect, I show how they highlight the incompatibility of Adorno's critiques of Wagner and jazz. Noting, as Wagner himself does, that the myth of the Flying Dutchman derives from the older anti-Semitic legend of the Wandering Jew, I demonstrate that Adorno's conceptualization of the culture industry counters Wagner's attempts to use the Jewish community as a scapegoat for the commodification of culture. Although Adorno discusses both Wagner and jazz in terms of the culture industry, I argue that the function of this concept as a reproof of anti-Semitic stereotypes obscures the different historical forms of oppression experienced by Jews and African-Americans. The parallels between Adorno's critiques of Wagner and jazz are purchased by a naive assumption that African-American experience corresponds to Jewish experience, an assumption that I show Baraka vigorously attacks in *Dutchman.*

This final essay of the book is not only a companion piece to the essay on Ellison, but, in its focus on anti-Semitism and cultural identity, also doubles as a companion piece to the essay on Beckett's *Waiting for Godot*. In this respect, it marks the culmination of the book's considerations of Adorno's emphases on reinscribing the heterogeneous. For it exposes the unities upon which Adorno relies even as he defends the "non-integrable." The essay demonstrates that Adorno's comments on the dangers of dialectics apply equally as well to negative dialectics:

> Dialectical thought is an attempt to break through the coercion of logic by its own means. But since it must use these means, it is at every moment in danger of itself acquiring a coercive character.[10]

I

Adorno, Dialectics, and Aesthetic Theory

1

Historical Dialectics and the Autonomy of Art in Adorno's *Aesthetic Theory*

As Peter Hohendahl has noted, the posthumous publication of Adorno's *Aesthetic Theory* in 1970 disappointed many who expected that it would provide a materialist aesthetic which would cultivate praxis.[1] The Left, who dismissed the work, maintained that, though anti-capitalist, the text advocated an anachronistic cultural elitism.[2] After Hohendahl (re)constructs the historical context in which Adorno's text was so negatively received, he suggests that the time has come (1981; 1991) to reassess the *Aesthetic Theory*. Interestingly, while implying that the apparent flexibility of German society in the 1970s produced an inadequate analysis of Adorno's final work, Hohendahl's reappraisal still embraces the cornerstone of that analysis: like Peter Bürger, he posits the autonomy of art as the central thesis of the *Aesthetic Theory* and then places the work squarely in the historical tradition of German idealism.

The brash rejection of the *Aesthetic Theory* does call for a reassessment, but that reassessment ought not neglect questioning the role the autonomy of art has in the work's overall project. At stake is whether the initial reception cited by Hohendahl centered on a problem of secondary importance to the more subtle and comprehensive analysis occurring in Adorno's text. The dismissal of the *Aesthetic Theory* on the grounds that it advocates an autonomy of art preconceived the meaning of aesthetic autonomy rather than deriving it from the text, i.e., from Adorno's usage. Consequently, the dismissal sidestepped a confrontation with the work's greater concerns: an analysis that explores how historical dialectics are erratic and lack uniformity and stability.[3] As the following arguments will demonstrate, the autonomy of art in the *Aesthetic Theory* is not—as Bürger maintains—merely an historical category describing the detachment of art from practical life. It results from an historic dialectic whose mechanics, Adorno argues, are faltering and unable to enact supersession (*Aufhebung*). In the *Aesthetic Theory*, art is autonomous because of the unique formulation of dialectics posited by Adorno: art manifests itself in dialectical tensions with its own historical moment—in this respect art and life are indelibly intertwined — but these tensions remain unresolved. Although art receives its identity from its negative critical relation with society, it does not have the ability to sublate the social dimensions that it negates. As society inevitably changes, an art work's non-identity becomes increasingly encapsulated—and therein lies the autonomy. For Adorno, the autonomy of art refers to the unresolved dialectical tensions of a work that respond to socio-historical conditions that have subsequently changed. Autonomy denotes the aesthetic tension's lack of resolution, a resolution that only supersession at a specific historical moment could have brought.

When Bürger argues that the autonomy of art is a category that describes art's detachment from practical contexts, he isolates only one aspect of (and thereby impairs) the dynamic at play in Adorno's discussions (Bürger 46). For Adorno, the autonomy of art is double-edged, and although he appears to hold to a philosophy of *l'art pour l'art*, Adorno has a radical theoretical adherence to the relation between art and society. On the one hand, he affirms that socio-historical change makes the separation of art and practical life unavoidable. But on the other, the separation does not denote the irrelevance of art to life. The relevance, however, can only be stated in negative terms. Adorno uses the autonomy of art to sustain art's negative value, i.e., to sustain the integrity of the unresolved negative tensions (the non-identity) a work has with a specific historic moment.

Aesthetic autonomy occurs with the inevitable movement of history, and Adorno uses autonomy to defend art against the reification that results from elevating a work's aesthetic non-identity to a status of validity beyond its historic moment. On its most immediate level, the *Aesthetic Theory* uses the autonomy of art as the foundation for an emphatic plea *not* to turn previous aesthetic *non-identity* into subsequent *positive values*. The plea is the natural heir to Adorno's reservations about supersession. Without supersession, the movement from negation to positive value falters, and a work's non-identity remains intact, i.e., autonomous. The point is this: for Adorno, historicizing a work does not solely relegate its negative (aesthetic) value to the past; historicization revitalizes a work's non-identity in the sense that historicization enacts its own brand of negation.

A criticism that historicizes art in order to counteract reification initiates a negation ancillary to the negation implicit in an art work's original non-identity. Like the art it discusses, the criticism has a negative function: the negation of reification. A criticism that underscores a work's unresolved tensions results in an unresolved tension of its own. Like the art it discusses, the criticism generates an unresolvable tension in the positive value it derives from maintaining what it heralds as essentially negative, art's non-identity. Thus, Adorno revitalizes art in an act of mimicry—a mimicry which his idiosyncratic conception of the autonomy of art to a great extent facilitates. Yet in terms of importance, the autonomy of art is subordinate to the (negating) mimicry that marks the whole of Adorno's *Aesthetic Theory*; both are only possible as by-products of the revision of dialectics that precede them. In the *Aesthetic Theory*, the autonomy of art has to be understood in the context of this revision. This is not to say that the mimicry in Adorno's criticism is without its problems —they will be explored in this work—but it seems to me that an adequate reassessment of Adorno's final work has to look at the dynamic Adorno constructs between his revision of dialectics and his mimicry of art.

The early reception of the *Aesthetic Theory* mistook Adorno's defense of the autonomy of art as an exchange of praxis for an aesthetics of retreat—in fact, the defense of the autonomy of art serves as the premier example for de-reified critical activity. In answer to the calls for an aesthetic that cultivates political praxis, Adorno offered an aesthetic that, by using the autonomy of art as its primary example, challenged the ossified presumptions underlying praxis and that argued "art's critical strength is bought at the price of praxial powerlessness."[4] Not only did Adorno's aesthetic preclude art as a tool for social change, it argued that art exposed the delusory presuppositions of *engagement*.[5] As Lyotard observed in 1974 in his article "Adorno as the Devil": "What can an affirmative politics be, which does not look for support in a representative (a party) of the negative, etc.? That is the question left, abandoned by Adorno."[6] The specific rigor that the *Aesthetic Theory* applies to the concept of art—to proving that as a concept, art itself lacks continuity—is the central strategy of its larger enterprise: that of fostering critical attitudes resilient to reification. More importantly, the critique of aesthetics, the argument that the concept of art lacked continuity, offered a subtle critique of presumed continuity in the goals guiding political activism, certainly during the sixties and seventies if not in general.

The sub-text on history that structures the autonomy of art in the *Aesthetic Theory* employs an historical-materialist dialectic in which neither universals nor particulars are precluded from change.[7] Rather than appealing to immutable, transcendent aesthetic criteria (e.g., Kantian), Adorno posits an autonomy of art bound to society by its non-identity with a specific socio-historical moment.[8] The elements of this dialectic can be seen in the following statement which, interestingly enough, also indicates that Adorno's defense of art's autonomy is not positivist, as Hohendahl suggests Adorno's early reception implies. For Adorno, the autonomy of art makes assumptions about the structure of dialectics, not an assertion that art is independent from practical life or society. He writes:

> Works of art are after-images of the empirically living, inasmuch as they offer to the latter what outside is denied them, and thus liberate from their objective-external experience which shapes them.[9]

The key terms here are "after-images" (*Nachbilder*) and "the empirically living" (*das empirisch Lebendige*), the former not being a mere replica of the latter, but rather a dynamic counter-image to what the "empirically living" denies. Of equal importance to this counter-image is the peculiar formulation, "*das empirisch*

Lebendige," what Adorno also calls "*die empirische Realität*" or simply "*die Empirie*." From the section's sub-heading, "On the Relation Between Art and Society," we can gather that these obscure references to living, to experience, and to the senses make broad allusions to society while trying not to succumb to its reified categories. In other words, Adorno echoes the art works he describes: he employs these peculiar terms to circumvent the denials inherent in the dominant discursive patterns of society. Like art, Adorno's terms "should assist the non-identical, which the coerced identity in reality represses."[10]

Whether the circumvention succeeds is debatable. Adorno's elocutions possess an amazing flexibility which is offset by an equally amazing vagueness. (One need only consider that they accommodate aesthetic discussions as diverse as adultery in *Madame Bovary* and absurdity in Beckett.) But the negative import of the terms "*das Nichtidentische*" and "*Nachbild*" allows Adorno to undercut the fixed criteria normally associated with the autonomy of art—that is, once he supplements the terms with assertions about the ephemeral nature of every work of art. He argues *not* that each work has its place in history but that important works of art "age, go cold and die."[11] Each individual work dies as the conditions of empirical reality change. Rather than contributing to the evolution of a concept, a work's characteristic counter-image or non-identity survives only as long as do the historical conditions from which it emerged. "What was once true in a work of art . . . [was] dismantled in the course of history."[12] This death necessitates a new form of aesthetic criticism, but more importantly, death precludes "*Aufhebung*."

Instead of a movement of negation that resolves itself into subsequent moments (as in Hegel), historical passage is, for Adorno, the steady accumulation of unresolved tensions, repressed beneath the appearance of resolution. By questioning "*Aufhebung*," Adorno can argue that the dialectical tensions between an art work and its origins remain intact and unresolved, buried beneath the passage of time. The autonomy of art is premised upon this lack of resolution, upon temporal movement without a reconciliatory absorption into a greater whole, i.e., upon the persistence of tension between an art work and "*die empirische Realität*" from which it emerges. What Adorno's aesthetics seek, then, is to bring these unresolved tensions back into focus and thereby subvert the appearance of their resolution, the appearance which contributes to their reification.

In the absence of transcendent and inalterable aesthetic criteria, this refocus is, for each work of art, a new project following new criteria—and in the absence of sublation, this refocus is especially in need of persistent revision because the unfolding continuity implied by "*Aufhebung*" obscures and even reifies the tensions upon which the autonomy of art is premised.[13] The disparity and lack of resolution in historical movements, which Adorno posits, allow art to occupy a watershed position within historical passage. Yet the former is inextricably bound to the latter: "Directly as artefacts, however, as products of social work, they [art works] also communicate with the empirical experience that they reject and out of which they draw their content."[14] Art is always in response to the social empirical reality, and the social empirical reality always provides the substance or "origins" from which art emerges. The restructuring of historical dialectics that procures the autonomy of art also binds it: the socio-historical context, "the empirically living," structures art and its autonomy.

The structural relation between the socio-historical and the autonomy of art is most evident in the foundational dynamic Adorno argues exists between the two. The dynamic is itself dialectical. What remains constant in Adorno's aesthetic is that, though neither universal nor particular is exempt from the consequences of historical passage, art always emerges from a negative dialectical or non-identical relation to its corresponding "*Empirie*." But inasmuch as the instability of historic sublation procures the autonomy of art, the negative dialectical movement of art out of its socio-historic context is subject to a corresponding instability. Adorno's contention about the instability of sublation in the socio-historical process, the very instability that allows for the autonomy of art, brings the stability of aesthetic negation into question as well.

While art may in fact owe its existence to a negative dialectical relation with its socio-historical context, art reflects this context foremost in its own inability to prompt sublation with the "origins" or context to which it is bound in antithetical (negative) dialectical opposition; i.e., in its own inability to enact a comprehensive and nonetheless de-reified transformation of the social whole (whether politically oriented or otherwise).[15] The instability of aesthetic negation, its inability to sublate—in the material social environment—the "origins" it negates, procures the autonomy of these same "origins" while confirming art's own. Both the autonomy of art's origins of art itself are contingent upon the instability of sublation. The continued autonomy of an art work's origins, despite their aesthetic negation, is the logical consequence of the law (*Bewegungsgesetz*) creating the autonomy of art itself.[16] What results is not a bifurcation of art and society into separate, autonomous realms, but a bilateral staggering of tensions straining against one another.

While the initial reception of Adorno's study in aesthetics latched on to the prominent position he gives to the autonomy of art, Adorno's questioning of sublation itself, not art's autonomy, is the central focus of the *Aesthetic Theory*. But this clarification would not have been enough to re-ingratiate Adorno with the Left, from whom, in his last years, he was estranged. Using aesthetics as the catalyst for a rigorous inquiry into "*Aufhebung*" did little to meet the Left's demands. While the Left sought an aesthetics for activists, Adorno developed Leftist cultural thought. In this respect, Hohendahl is correct in his assessment: the *Aesthetic Theory* is consistent with Adorno's general resistance to the dogmatic privileging that an emphasis on praxis gives to action (*Reappraisals* 80). If, for Adorno, art and philosophical thought were not the last bastions of critical opposition to society, he at least prescribed them as a seemingly interminable prerequisite to *engagement.*

Hohendahl is cautious not to dismiss the initial reception of Adorno's final work, as the work itself was dismissed. Nor do I want to dismiss this reception. Although my coming remarks argue that to interpret the autonomy of art as the central thesis of the *Aesthetic Theory* is to mistake effect for thesis, the prevalence of this interpretation cannot be explained solely on the basis of the political climate of the 1970s. It is the result of Adorno's rhetorical stance, his articulating his theory from the perspective of art itself, i.e., of his adopting the voice of the aesthetic position he purports to describe.

By positing the autonomy of art as the *Aesthetic Theory*'s central thesis, Hohendahl and the initial reception of Adorno's last work missed a crucial link in the chain of Adorno's reasoning: an argued discontinuity in the concept of art is part of Adorno's project to revise historical dialectics. Once Adorno pinpoints this discontinuity, he can challenge traditional dialectics because, as a system, they provide an insufficient account of art. As his revision unfolds, the autonomy of art comes to signify how art functions in the absence of conceptual continuity. But if the excessive attention Adorno devotes to the autonomy of art while restructuring historical dialectics did not in itself explain why the student and academic Left thought his central thesis was art's autonomy, then Adorno's rhetorical stance gave them what seems to be understandable cause.

In the sections that follow, I argue that Adorno creates the illusion that one can reside (indefinitely) in the autonomy figured by works of art. He does this by rhetorically adopting the voice of art looking in retrospect on what he describes as its negated origins. This rhetorical strategy is arguably an attempt by Adorno to distance himself from the reified social structures negated by art. But in his efforts to avoid succumbing to reification, Adorno side-steps the crucial question of origins itself. He side-steps the socio-historical particularity upon which aesthetic autonomy is based. It seems to me that this strategy displays a preference which obscures a most problematic and unwritten chapter in Adorno's last work. Rhetorically, the *Aesthetic Theory* occupies the same position that Adorno repeatedly asserts must find new and dis-continuous forms in a non-identical relation to specific socio-historical origins.

Articulating the Already Autonomous

Early in the *Aesthetic Theory* Adorno clarifies that the autonomy attributed to art is sustained only in movement, and that this movement, in contrast to immutable criteria, depends not upon what art is, but on art's differentiating itself from what it is not. In other words, art defines itself through a process of negation or a continuous non-identity. Adorno writes:

> It is through its dynamic laws, not through some invariable principle, that art can be understood. It is defined by its relation to what is different from art. This other makes it possible for us to arrive at a substantive understanding of the specifically artistic in art. It is this approach to art that alone meets the criteria of a materialist and dialectical aesthetic, which evolves by segregating itself from its own matrix (Adorno *AT* 4).

In this general statement, Adorno provides the structure, indeed the *modus operandi*, underlying his subsequent claim that art works are "counter-images" to the "empirically living." In these and similar passages in "On the Relation Between Art and Society," Adorno constructs a definition of the autonomy of art based on an ever-changing socio-historical context. Art obtains autonomy in opposition—this is the cornerstone of negation—while its socio-historical context, the object of its opposition, structures (*bestimmt*) both the nature of that opposition and the character of art's autonomy.

When socio-historical context provides the substance "out of which . . . [art draws its] content," and out of which art determines itself in negating recoil, each work of art constitutes a definitive instance of autonomy (Adorno *AT* 6–7). Aesthetic autonomy is indelibly defined by the non-identical tensions it possesses with its historical context. Aesthetic negation, the emergence of the artistic out of its Other, is neither a more accurate articulation nor a progressive unfolding of autonomy. Individual instances of autonomy have only the movement of non-identity in common. Each instance is connected to other instances not in any reciprocal confirmation of having taken different paths to the same destination, nor in having assisted one another in a greater realization of potential autonomy, but in a dynamic, mutually-negating interaction that challenges the universal position of autonomy as a concept. The interaction of heterogeneous autonomies occupied by or articulated through different works of art dispels the reified illusion of autonomy as a realm unto itself. The autonomy of art pivots on the negation of autonomy as a reified ideal. Each work of art is singularly exemplary, its non-identity not being an example of a greater universal, but a singular instance of itself. For Adorno, any conception of the autonomy of art, other than the position a given work occupies in negative relation to its Other, regresses into reification and a repressive positivism.

This last point—which, it seems to me, does much to vindicate Adorno from his critics—is not immediately apparent in Adorno's writing. On the contrary, Adorno gives the appearance of adherence to a fixed conception of autonomy because he attempts to avoid reification by speaking from the general position or perspective of art that is already autonomous, i.e., from the perspective that has already negated its socio-historical context. For example, in the claim that the artistic (*das Kunsthafte*) specifies itself out of its Other (*das

Andere), the movement of aesthetic negation is an event spoken of in retrospect, when the socio-historical is already positioned as an object of hindsight, signified here by the term "the Other." By speaking from the position of art, Adorno eliminates the necessity for exploring the vast complexities underlying the socio-historical, choosing instead to dismiss them as the single collectivity, "the Other." As previously stated, this strategy of adopting the voice of art as a means of avoiding a reified concept of autonomy gave his initial readers the impression that Adorno had traded the goals of political activism for the consolations of aesthetic pleasure.

Yet for Adorno, aesthetic negation could never meet the demands of activists: aesthetic negation is not the direct articulation of criticism nor is it the positing of formulated goals or hypothetical alternatives—all of which sustain prevailing, delimiting discourse by appealing to tolerated and defusing avenues of dissent. Negation would be neutralized if subordinated to protest or if constricted to preconceived reified concepts of autonomy. Aesthetic negation, according to Adorno's argument, occurs when art resists the temptation to oppose the portrayed "unredeemed" state with formulated or implicit ideals. He specifies this in his *Aesthetic Theory*:

> By cathecting the repressed, art internalizes the repressing principle, i.e., the unredeemed condition of the world (*Unheil*), instead of merely airing futile protests against it. Art identifies and expresses that condition, thus anticipating its overcoming. It is this and not the photographic rendition of the unredeemed state or a false sense of beatitude, that defines the position of authentic modern art towards a gloomy objectivity (Adorno *AT* 27-28).

Adorno's distinction between an anticipatory, cathected internalization of the repressing principle (*Lust am Verdrängten*) and mere protests against the principle arguably responds to the demand for an aesthetic that instigates political activism. While politically *engaged* art like Brecht's—which often serves as a point of contrast for Adorno—attempts to adjust the social whole by protesting society's aberration from preconceived guidelines or values, such art fails to recognize that these same values are intrinsically structured by the dominant discourses which they ostensibly oppose.[17] In the place of such limited aesthetic approaches, Adorno suggests the need for art works which incorporate the preconceived notions of autonomy into themselves and thereby expose how the dominant social discourses permeate current ideals. He posits an aesthetic whose autonomy resides in its negative dialectic or non-identity with prevalent conceptions of autonomy.

The futility of protest, its "false sense of beatitude," lies in the mistaken presumption that one can detach him/herself enough from the mediations of repression so as to offer an alternative that does not subscribe to the same repressive forces. Instead of offering protests that attempt to redirect within the status quo, art seeks to deadlock repression and thereby violate its limits. The deadlock generates a crisis in meaning, whereas protest only simulates crisis while still perpetuating prevalent constricting delusions. The crisis occurs through an exposure of stultification and reification in perception, thus exposing the ways accepted interpretations of reality dictate experience. Art is anticipatory in that it upsets or obstructs habitual, unexamined principles of conduct. Adorno argues that "Willfulness and spontaneity—this is the vital element of art," a "willfulness" that facilitates "spontaneity" by negating repression (Adorno *AT* 167). Art demands a willfulness, a courage, which allows new meaning. This meaning is a departure from reification into spontaneity and the unknown.

Art's incorporation of the repressive principle into itself objectifies the dynamic of negation. When an art work objectifies repression, it becomes the progenitor of aesthetic reflection, and its non-identical movement subverts the repression. According to Adorno, objectification alters the social environment of those who come in contact with the work. More than a mere reflection of the social milieu, an art work that objectifies its origins alters the socio-historical context, offering in its "counter-image" to "the empirically living" what the "empirically living" denies (Adorno *AT* 4). The non-identical generates tension between itself and its origins that endures beneath the appearance of resolution. The work becomes a limited part of the social environment, but nonetheless an object to which an individual potentially can respond. Adorno argues:

> Aesthetic expression is objectification of the non-objective. Put more precisely, through its objectification expression becomes a second non-objective substance, one that speaks out of the artefact rather than out of the subject.[18]

The aesthetic voice emerging from the artifact anticipates a new-found autonomy in the contemplation it facilitates. Anticipation would seem the correct term here because aesthetic expression is only potentially autonomous. Negation is not cancellation, i.e., final. It denotes a dynamic impasse in a continuing struggle for dominance. Here we are speaking of two distinct autonomies: one ephemeral and terminal, and the other resulting from historical passage. The former resides in what an art work potentially offers to an individual in the counter-image it provides to a specific socio-historical context. The latter is the autonomy addressed earlier in this paper, the autonomy that results from the unresolved tensions an art work has with a specific historic moment.

The Question of Origins

The autonomy of art depends upon such an elaborate conception of historical dialectics that Adorno's writing from the perspective of the non-identical is arguably a subtle method for talking about the autonomy of art without becoming entangled in the complexities leading to it. But the method also has the tendency to presume that the origins with which an art work is non-identical are non-problematic. Thus Adorno dismisses the question of origins in an early section of the *Aesthetic Theory* entitled "*Gegen Ursprunsfrage*" ("Against Questions of Origin"). The dismissal might not be so problematic were it not for two points. First of all, art owes its non-identical existence to the origins which Adorno dismisses. Immediately after dismissing the question of origins, Adorno specifies that aesthetic negation and the subsequent autonomy of art are meaningless without the origins from which they emerge: "Works of art became what they are by negating their origins" (Adorno *AT* 4). Secondly, Adorno keeps the question open at the margins of his discussions by pushing it into an appendix.[19]

When he finally does return to the question of origins, the reasons for his discomfort quickly become evident: the excursus is a documented explication of his earlier rejection (Adorno *AT* 447–455). The rejection of origins as a topic worthy of consideration is based upon its association with debates concerning the origin of art itself. For Adorno, the origin of art is irrelevant to the origins an art work negates, and he dismisses the question of art's origin because the question presupposes a continuity in art which, according to Adorno, is at odds with art itself. This is ostensibly why in the excursus, he begins with the claim that the endeavor to understand the essence of art by looking to its origins is "necessarily disappointing" (447).

While the distinction between the origin of art and the origins an art work negates is important to the subordination of universals to the influence of historical dialectics, Adorno also overplays the distinction. The excursus rigorously dismantles and obstructs a view of art as a continuous and unfolding concept, but does so at the expense of an adequate explanation of what constitutes the origins an art work negates. Like his structurally binding "autonomy" to socio-historical specifics, his rejection of the "*Ursprungsfrage*" emphasizes historical distinction or particularity over historical evolution or continuity. Adorno's views on the autonomy of art and on the origins negated by art bear the additional similarity that, in both instances, the socio-historical occupies the position of the unarticulated. But the point is that regardless of whether Adorno rejects the term "origin(s)" in its common usage, he still employs a structural conception of it whose explanation he neglects.

Although the excursus refuses to provide an adequate explanation of what is meant by the "origins" an art work negates, the methodology of the excursus lends itself to an inferential construction of the underlying structures governing Adorno's use of the term. Adorno's use of "origins" rests at the center of a dynamic tension between a radical historicization and an equally radical questioning of what comprises historicity. Like the art works whose negative basis they form, the origins to which art works owe their existence are historical (Adorno *AT* 447). But while historicity joins an art work to its origins, one must also understand what constitutes the substance of history to understand origins. Unfortunately, it is not enough to say that the material and the social are the substance of the historical.

The vagueness of the term "origins" hedges between a catch-all phrase and a critical expression that calls into question the material and the social to which it refers. It alludes not only to socio-historical context but also questions the fixity and stability of such a concept. By saying that art negates its origins rather than its socio-historical context, and by adopting the position of art looking in retrospect on the Other it has left behind, Adorno concedes that art responds to social reality, but leaves open the question as to what constitutes that reality.

The scope of the origins to which art responds extends beyond the specifically "material" life men and women lead. As Peter Hohendahl has noted:

> [Adorno] . . . used Hegel's model of history to understand the evolution of literature as representative for the development of social and political history. . . . While he insists on the dialectic of art and society (the art work is also a social fact), he does not, unlike Lukács, conceive of it in terms of reflection (Hohendahl *Reappraisals* 82).

Adorno's opposition to the arguments that art is a reflection of social reality stem from his assumption that consciousness is not merely a reflection of the material. The lives men and women lead respond to a social milieu comprised of ideas as well as materiality. Rather than thought mirroring the material-social environment, art actively contributes to it. The origins negated by an art work denote a socio-historical context that includes art and philosophy—not as reflection but as substance. As Hohendahl notes: "Ultimately, art and society belong to the same stream of history" (Hohendahl *Reappraisals* 82). "Origins" denotes them both.

Once art and philosophy become part of the socio-historical context that a work of art negates, it is not difficult to understand why Adorno is so opposed to studies tracing art back to its prehistoric origins. Such studies presuppose a separate qualitative continuity in art that Adorno claims each work must negate in order to be art at all: "It must turn against that which determines its own concept and thereby becomes uncertain within its deepest fibers."[20] His combining the intellectual with the material in a single milieu subordinates abstractions and concepts—which try to stand "above" or "outside"—to the qualitative substance, i.e., the origins that a work must negate to become art. The consequences of this subordination occur at numerous levels. First of all, it radically alters the notion of "an unfolding concept," by leaving each work of art disjointed and severed from the next. At the same time that Adorno places art amidst specific socio-historical parameters, he expands the width of these parameters by replacing reflection theory with a conception of the socio-historical as an admixture of the intellectual and the material.[21] Combined, these two maneuvers suggest a revision of dialectics that distinguishes Adorno from Hegel. They make up a dynamic that pulls at its own seams: once the historical becomes an admixture of intellectual and material, the elements of history, which include the disjointed concept of art, lose their qualitative continuity.

Adorno's emphatic rejection of a qualitative continuity in the concept of art has implications for the movements of history in general. A discontinuity in concepts implies a corresponding discontinuity in history—especially within the Hegelian model where concepts are traditionally the movers of history itself. Even if the concept of art were a special case—which here it is not, despite other privileges Adorno gives to art—its being an exception among concepts would have ramifications that demand a conceptual restructuring of history. The qualitative discontinuity of the concept of art suggests that, rather than evolving, concepts expire once outside of their socio-historical context. They have a bounded, contextual vitality. This is the essence of their autonomy. Like an individual work of art, concepts in general sustain a dialectical tension which thrives within their socio-historical context, but which reifies once beyond this context.

While reification in place of a dialectical synthesis brings into question the conception of history as a unified process, it has specific consequences for aesthetics as well. Socio-historical change de-stabilizes the referents of the terms and ideals with which previous works of art formulated their non-identity. Historical passage slips these terms into the origins with which later works are qualitatively at odds. Once de-stabilized, previous aesthetic ideals or discourse lend themselves to appropriation and ultimately to the opposite of their earlier non-identical opposition, viz., repression and reification.[22]

With the contextual, qualitative specificity of the concept of art, an additional element vies for position within the dynamic tension of its negated origins: Adorno's radical historicization is not only offset by a rigorous questioning of what comprises history but by a questioning of supersession as well. Art's non-identical origins are a socio-historical context in which the content of the social and the historical are brought into question, and in which reification prevails beneath the appearance of supersession.

The "origins" of Adorno's *Aesthetic Theory* presuppose a model of history in which even the basic oppositions of Hegelian dialectics are brought into question, a model in distinct contrast to Hohendahl's Hegelian reading of Adorno and to the reading of Eugene Lunn, who defends a similar position. Lunn notes Adorno's frequent juxtaposition of "seeming opposites . . . so as to mediate them by developing each of the apparent antinomies out of the other in mutual critique." This strategy is, according to Lunn, "a dialectic procedure which . . . [Adorno] owed to Hegel."[23] With origins, however, the mediation quickly extends beyond the mutual critique of antinomies. Adorno's dialectical model escalates instead into a constellation of mediations that radically challenges binary oppositions: at one level, there is the socio-historical that brings its own substance into question, and at the same time this socio-historical is in dynamic tension with a rigorous inquiry into the presumptions underlying supersession (the continuity thought to gauge temporal passage). While one can single out specific elements—as, for example, the apparent antinomy that the continuity of a concept becomes a litmus test for its reification—the question of socio-historical substance is no less a mediating factor to a concept (*ein Begriff*, in the Hegelian sense) than is the question of its continuity. The complex mediation within "origins," indeed, mediation in general, occurs at a level where the antinomies are never quite clear because opposites are themselves never stable enough to polarize and ossify into the Hegelian categories of thesis and antithesis. For Adorno, aesthetic non-identity and the particularity it embodies is seen, as Peter Dews has noted, "as standing in a pattern of relations to other particular, a historically sedimented 'constellation' which defines its identity."[24]

The diverse and dynamic mediation occurring beneath Adorno's own use of the term "origins" helps to pinpoint the referent in the sentence with which he opens "*Gegen Ursprungsfrage*": "Art has its concept in the historically changing constellation of moments."[25] The weight of this sentence rests on the definite article, on the specificity that it connotes. The constellation to which he refers is the "origins" that he says an art work must negate. But the concept of art is not that which is changing or evolving, at least not evolving beyond the constellation itself, within which it continues to unfold because its dialectical tensions remain unresolved. It is the constellation of moments that changes and the constellation from which art receives its concept, each new constellation necessitating a new non-identical concept of art and of autonomy. The dialectic evolution continues within the constellation itself, but the concept has no continuity outside of the contextual origins structuring it.

While Adorno's polemic against the so-called origin of art does emphasize a discontinuity that is presupposed in the autonomous, non-identical movement of aesthetic negation, and while the description of origins as a constellation or dynamic of tensions does much to highlight the presumptions functioning beneath Adorno's own application of the term "origins," these characterizations still describe the consequences of aesthetic negation and not really origins *per se*. The characterizations are part of Adorno's rhetorical stance. They still come from the perspective of art looking in retrospect on the origins or the Other it has negated. Aesthetic negation uncovers the discontinuity of concepts—i.e., the breakdown in sublation—and it illuminates the unresolved, thriving dialectical tensions obscured beneath the appearance of supersession.

To say that art has its concept in the historically changing constellation of moments is to describe origins in their negated relation to an art work, to describe origins after the appearance of continuity and stability has given way to an aesthetic force capable of reinscribing the constellation which appearance obscures. But it makes sense, at least according to the dictates of Adorno's argument, that the origins as Adorno presents them must already be in their negated state: if the origins were already obviously discontinuous and unresolved, an artwork could not find the stable basis—however illusory that basis proves to be—against which to build its non-identical relation without positing continuity so as later to dispel it.

The origins negated by art remain unarticulated in Adorno's theories, more so than the non-identity of art itself. One might think that this is as it should be, given that the *Aesthetic Theory* is after all a work on aesthetics, and given that the theory itself emphasizes the socio-historical specificity of origins, a specificity articulation might dilute. Yet for all its non-identity, art presupposes a corresponding specificity as well, the structure and not merely the details of which Adorno neglects by addressing the consequences of negation instead of clarifying his own use of the term "origins." As a result, both the non-identity of art and its negated origins remain cryptic and formulaic. Crucial structural aspects of the dynamics between art and society persist in the form of mostly unexplored terms—e.g., "non-identity," "what it is not," "the Other" and above all "origins"—although their exploration would foster a clarity rather than dilution. In part, this lacuna results from and is even obscured by Adorno's having selected the concept of art to illustrate the discontinuity of concepts in general, the discontinuity that aesthetic negation exposes. This unexplored territory results, in part, from Adorno's mesmerizing account of the consequences of negation—an account that is in itself suspect because, by articulating the consequences of negation rather than the structural conditions leading to it, the account comes dangerously close to the formulation of immutable criteria which artifacts must meet in order to be art. At the very least, the account of the consequences of negation cultivates registers with which a critic/reader can search for that which appears to correspond to preconceived results. It borders on begging the question. While these last possibilities are at odds with more dominant tendencies in Adorno's text, their emergence in the theory's central dynamic raises questions that cannot be ignored. For the present, suffice it to say that, though the terms may remain unexplored, their function is to provide the means with which to discuss the aesthetic exposure of the heterogeneity which society obscures.

Heterogeneity and the Crisis in Dialectics

Rainer Nägele argues that "if Hegel's dialectic is the attempt to master the heterogeneous in philosophical concepts, negative dialectics is the attempt to reinscribe the heterogeneous as heterogeneous also in thought."[26] In Adorno's *Aesthetic Theory*, art's non-identity is this reinscription. This means that the non-identity of art, because it re-inscribes heterogeneity, presupposes the homogeneity, i.e., a continuity in concepts, which negation dispels. More than a mere reversal of Hegel, reinscribing the heterogeneous articulates a crisis in the basic mechanics of Hegelian dialectics. Without continuity in concepts, sublation comes to a standstill—in this respect there is a brilliance in Adorno's having focused on the discontinuity or disunity of the concept of art.[27] Art's own heterogeneity gives it the conceptual basis from which to question and negate the appearance of continuity in concepts; its heterogeneity is its non-identity with its origins; and it is at the *avant-garde* of the heterogeneity it uncovers.

Adorno's rejection of theories on "the origin of art" and this rejection's connection with his reworking of historical dialectics are but two aspects within a larger critical constellation. While the discontinuity of art suggests that sublation forces or creates the illusion of unity "where none in fact exist[s]," Adorno's rejection of continuity also initiates a reworking of the idea of reification—which here signifies the glossing over or repression of heterogeneities beneath the appearance of unity.[28] The appearance of a resolution (*Aufhebung*) that leads from one historical constellation into another robs art of the dialectical vitality it has within its specific socio-historical context.

In contrast to the continuity of origins implied by supersession, Adorno posits layers of constellations whose essential tensions have not resolved, but are buried beneath a reified rhetorically-imposed supersession which accompanies temporal passage. This same lack of resolution is, for example, what allows Adorno to make the claim with which he opens *Negative Dialectics*: "Philosophy, which once seemed obsolete, lives on because the moment to realize it was missed" (Adorno *ND* 3). Philosophy is not a floating potential waiting for realization—its moment has passed. It is rather the premier example of unresolved tension surviving within its specific moment or constellation and providing a point of focus from which to scrutinize fabricated resolution. In the unity and stability presupposed by the origins art negates, Adorno finds a false and reified history—just as the question of the origin of art is a false question based upon a reified concept of art. While origins presuppose historical continuity, negation reinscribes historical heterogeneity. Art's negation of its origins is two-fold: it uncovers unresolved dialectical tensions that the apparent unity within origins obscures; and its non-identity with these origins generates a dialectical tension that also knows no resolution.

In *Negative Dialectics*, Adorno argues that unity was fraudulently posited at the expense of plurality, and that whatever the initial source of this fraudulence might have been, the end result was that as "unity" gained in prominence, it also gained the power to repress those resisting it (Adorno *ND* 315). He argues:

> The universal by which every individual is determined at all, as one of his particular kind, that universal is borrowed from what is extraneous and therefore as heteronomous to the individual as anything once said to have been ordained for him by demons (315).

Adorno's resort to the image of demons in his description is not gratuitous. The image forms a negative contrast to the Hegelian Spirit, specifically a contrast to the continuity so central to the movements of Hegelian dialectics: a contrast between the singularity of an all-superseding and unifying Spirit and the diverse plurality of demons reinscribing heterogeneity. The image of demons admonishes against concepts of unity because these concepts erase the history they purport to trace. Art negates these posited origins with the reinscription of particularity, the cornerstone of heterogeneity. The contrast in imagery extends even into the structural morphology of Adorno's descriptions: while origins project retrospectively an evolution through sublation, art recalls "an objectivity removed [enthoben] from categorical frameworks."[29] The contrast between the subsuming supersession of Spirit and the heterogeneous reinscriptions of demons resides in the distinction between an "*auf-*" and "*ent-*" "*(ge)hobene Objektivität*." The polarities of demons and Spirit, the "*Enthobene*" and the "*Aufgehobene*," are the opposing elements in art's non-identity with its origins. The reinscription of heterogeneity is the recovery of the "*Enthobene*" vis-á-vis the overwhelming appearance of the "*Aufgehobene*."

Yet despite the forcefulness of this contrast, it still remains within descriptions of consequences at the expense of an explanation of the structural conditions leading to it. By articulating the discussion from the perspective of art looking in retrospect on the origins or the Other it has negated, Adorno posits his (art's) oppositions rather than allowing art to formulate them on its own. In this case, the necessary opposite is Hegel whose dialectics foster the appearances with which art is non-identical, but which persist in each instance of art's non-identity to them. Inasmuch as art persists in the lack of resolution of its dialectical tensions, so too do the counter-elements of these tensions. Though Adorno attempts to circumvent Hegel by arguing that art recalls a reality before the Hegelian system, "*eine dem kategorialen Gefüge enthobene Objektivität*," his having built aesthetic negation in opposition to Hegel reflects Adorno's own irresolute and unresolved tension with his origins.

2

Aesthetic Theory and Fragmenting the Unities of Negation

In Adorno's aesthetic theory, the work of art becomes the focal point for a two-fold materialist critique of the dialectical notion of *Aufhebung*, which, depending on the context, has been variously translated as sublation, synthesis, reconciliation, or occasionally even as unity. Since *Aufhebung* refers to a synthesis within individual moments and also to the movement of history, Adorno, in his explorations of art, develops two distinct facets of negative dialectics. His critique alternates between examinations of art's negative relation to the posited unity of given historical *moments*, and examinations of art's negative relation to the posited *movements* of synthesis in historical dialectics. Adorno's argument that the autonomy of art derives from the discontinuity of the concept of art coincides with an assertion that the particularity embodied in a work originates from its disunity or non-identity with the dominant conceptual modes that mediate any given historical moment. For Adorno, the non-identity of art expresses what concepts in dialectics preclude. A work gives voice to the cost of conceptual unity and synthesis. Within the context of its historical moment, art emerges as a force of irreconcilable dialectical opposition to the posited unity of the concept. Art thus challenges the stability of historical dialectics with a crisis in the very unity of the concepts upon which the subsequent temporal movements of synthesis in historical dialectics depend. Yet because Adorno nonetheless adheres to a materialist aesthetic, this crisis in the momentary unity of the concept does not preclude works of art from historical determination.

For Adorno, the crisis in the unity of the concept restructures the conceptual movement of history and forces a radical historicization of art. This historicization results in art's autonomy and is premised upon a breakdown of sublation, not only in historical moments and movements but in art as well. While the non-identity of art discloses the fictitious unity of concepts, art achieves such disclosures only within an aesthetic realm, an illusory realm. In empirical reality, art is unable to sublate or overturn the momentum of the fictitious unity it discloses. Since the conceptual modes with which art is non-identical are nonetheless subject to historical change, the dialectical tensions of individual works of art are left unresolved, shielded beneath layers of subsequent historical constellations, each of which is comprised of unresolved dialectical tensions. The unresolved dialectical tensions which give art its (non-)identity also confine individual works to their historic moment. Art thus resists not only the momentary unity of the concept but also the sublated continuity of the concept in the movement from one historical moment to the next. With regard to the concept as such, art is the expression of disunity and discontinuity.

Adorno's use of art as the basis of a restructuring of dialectics is not, however, without its problems, and in *Aesthetic Theory* Adorno attempts to deal with these problems by framing them as contradictions inherent to art. The first of these contradictions involves aesthetic negation. On the one hand, aesthetic negation counters the repressive unities of historical dialectics. But, on the other, aesthetic negation also incorporates "the repressive principle" (*das Unheil*) into itself: whereas art negates to dispel false unities, in historical dialectics negation results in repressive unities and synthesis (Adorno *AT* 27). Adorno's attempt to contend with this contradictory dimension of negation is a driving force in *Aesthetic Theory*. Briefly, the non-identity of art presupposes a dialectical opposition within the very structure of negation. *Aesthetic Theory* consequently posits the existence of two incongruous but intertwined dialectics: a negative dialectic of art that (re)inscribes heterogeneity; and an historical dialectic that forcefully inscribes unity. From a theoretical perspective, the argued coexistence of these disparate dialectics asserts the heterogeneity that art reinstates; by locating contradictory tendencies in negation, Adorno polarizes the very conceptual mechanism through which historical dialectics achieves its repressive unities and syntheses.

What remains questionable in Adorno's aesthetics is whether the theoretical formulation of an incongruous negative dialectic of art actually circumvents the repressive tendencies that Adorno recognizes in the negations of historical dialectics. In order to answer this question, it is necessary first of all to separately explore the two dimensions of the negative dialectic of art that Adorno formulates: the dialectics of an individual moment; and the dialectics of historical movement. A critical scrutiny of these two dimensions will provide the basis for an immanent critique of Adorno's aesthetic theory, in which I will argue that, rather than opposing "the repressive principle," art, in Adorno's aesthetics, merely appropriates it under a negative veil.

Dialectics in a Moment: Synthesis, Unity and Disunity.

Within the isolated conceptual structures of its historic moment, the central function of art, according to Adorno, is "the summoning to appearance of an essence that is otherwise hidden in empirical reality" (Adorno *AT* 154). Art fulfills this function in what Adorno specifically acknowledges as an aesthetic synthesis that negates the false unities that dominate society and paradoxically reinscribes heterogeneity:

> Art is true to the extent to which it is discordant and antagonistic in its language and in its whole essence, provided that it synthesizes those diremptions, thus making them determinate in their irreconcilability. Its paradoxical task is to attest to the lack of concord while at the same time working to abolish discordance (241).

Albrecht Wellmer has argued that for Adorno this truth of "discordance" and "antagonism" in art functions in opposition to the unacknowledged violence in "the unity of the traditional work of art and in the unity of the bourgeois subject." Art discloses that the traditional unities have only been possible "at the price of suppression and ostracism of things disparate, non-integrable and repressed."[1] Modern aesthetic "discordance" and "antagonism" respond to the preclusions of traditional sublation. Wellmer reads Adorno's conception of aesthetic "discordance" and "antagonism" as a challenge to the Hegelian triad of the subject, object, and concept (Wellmer "Truth, Semblance, Reconciliation" 91).

Following this same reading, one can argue that art—by reinscribing what traditional dialectics suppress and ostracize, viz., "things disparate"—opens otherwise inaccessible avenues of dialectical mediation between subject and object. In this function, the syntheses of art are fundamentally different from the syntheses of dialectics:

> Implied . . . [in art's function] is the idea that every work of art spontaneously aims at being identical with itself, just as in the world outside a fake identity is everywhere forcibly imposed on objects by the insatiable subject. Aesthetic identity is different, however, in one important respect: it is meant to assist the non-identical in its struggle against the repressive identification compulsion that rules the outside world (Adorno *AT* 6).

While the function of art in this explanation is "to assist" in the "struggle against the repressive identification compulsion that rules the outside world," the struggle itself is nothing new in Adorno's thought. The challenge to the Hegelian triad, which Wellmer cites, is traceable as far back as the *Dialectic of Enlightenment*, where Adorno and Horkheimer argue, for example, that "bourgeois society is ruled by equivalence" and that it "makes the dissimilar comparable by reducing it to abstract quantities."[2] As a tool of the Enlightenment, abstraction "liquidates" its objects beneath concepts (Horkheimer and Adorno *DE* 13). By reinstating the "dissimilar," art's negative dialectic opposes "equivalence" with a reassertion of the sacrificed elements that determine particularity.

With regard to the dialectical structures of individual moments, it can be argued that Adorno posits the aesthetic syntheses of art so as to rescue—albeit to an obscure realm—the dialectic which he has diagnosed as irreparably faltering. According to this view, art serves a redemptive function, giving voice to "things disparate" and achieving in the sphere of aesthetic illusion the non-repressive syntheses that are beyond the posited unity of historical dialectics. On one level, art does perform an act of synthesis which the socio-historical context of a work of art does not otherwise permit, and thus counteracts the reductiveness through which "the active spirit" of dialectics maintains forceful domination:

> Aesthetic illusion seeks to redeem what the active spirit, which brought about the artefacts or vehicles of illusion, has reduced to materials dominated by itself (Adorno *AT* 157).

But to leave Adorno's argument in this form would be to suggest that art formulates a parallel or shadow dialectic, a kind of sliding supplement that completes the syntheses lost in the inevitable and reductive preclusions of dialectics itself.

Insofar as art opposes "traditional unities" with "discordance" and the "non-integrable," it questions dialectics as a conceptual whole. Consequently, Adorno speaks of art's "paradoxical task . . . to attest to the lack of concord while at the same time working to abolish discordance," a task which he also denotes as "impossible" and as indicative of "the paradox of aesthetics as a whole" (Adorno *AT* 241; 157). Adorno does not attempt to (re)solve the paradox, but rather argues that it has to be conceived in terms of the difference between aesthetic "content" and "illusion" (157). Art emerges from a synthesis of illusion, which, as a product of art, announces itself as illusion, and which, as Adorno argues, "is the vestige of injury that art seeks to undo" (157). Art posits illusory unity in order to dispel the exclusory illusion of unity of empirical reality; the fictitious syntheses of art disclose parallel tendencies in society, which in their repressiveness are dialectically opposite to those of art. Since art has no other content than that "given to it by illusion"—and in this case "illusion" can be understood as the illusory syntheses of empirical reality—it offers a "redemption of illusion" (157). Just as aesthetic negation counteracts the repressive negations of historical dialectics, the truth content of art results from its use of illusion in order to expose illusion. Aesthetic illusion redeems illusion from empirical reality, and the two illusions are dialectically opposed.

The paradoxical nature of this "redemption of illusion" lies in the fact that art must work from within dialectics in order to redeem illusion from it. In that art opposes dialectical synthesis with "discordance" and the "non-integrable," it establishes, as Lambert Zuidervaart has noted, a unity of irreconcilable opposites:

> Adorno's arguments are dialectical in the sense that they highlight unavoidable tensions between polar opposites whose opposition constitutes their unity and generates historical change. The dialectic is negative in the sense that it refuses to affirm any underlying identity or final synthesis of polar opposites (Zuidervaart *Adorno's Aesthetic Theory* 49).

Working from within dialectics, art polarizes its concepts, and art's refusal "to affirm any . . . final synthesis" of opposites results in a shattering of the initial binary opposition between aesthetic negation and the negations of historical dialectics. Whereas the dialectical moment of historical dialectics presupposes a negation that resolves tensions in an emerging conceptual unity, aesthetic negation brings this presupposition into question by revealing the steady accumulation of unresolved tensions within the conceptual structure of dialectics. Rather than moving towards a greater whole, the negations of art have the opposite effect: they particularize into ever unravelling diversity. Art's negative dialectic programmatically undoes the systemic unity upon which historical dialectics is based.

Zuidervaart interprets this reassertion of heterogeneity in dialectics as "an expression of suffering and an appearance of society's essential antagonisms." He argues that the dialectic within an art work "can play a political role" by disclosing "society's dialectic" and by pointing "beyond this dialectic" (Zuidervaart *Adorno's Aesthetic Theory* 130). But while these expressions "of suffering" uncover the preclusions in apparent unity, i.e. uncover the "antagonisms" which are suppressed when "the dissimilar [is made] comparable by reducing it to abstract quantities," the expressions are also aesthetic negation's greatest limitation. As Adorno argues, "aesthetic autonomy as the image of suffering remains fundamentally uninvolved in suffering" and "autonomous art is not just an echo of suffering, it also tends to diminish the scope of suffering" (Adorno *AT* 57). This lack of involvement is what "on the part of works of art increases their burden of guilt" (57). Art uncovers what it fundamentally cannot change without becoming a part of what it desires to change. Art works are impotent beyond the forced unities of their socio-historical context. Indeed, Adorno specifically states that art's "redemption through illusion is itself illusory and powerless, and therefore apt to compound the art work's illusory quality" (157). Zuidervaart acknowledges that "by themselves, artworks cannot actually transform society," but he underplays the ephemeral quality of an art work's dialectic (Zuidervaart *Adorno's Aesthetic Theory* 130). With aesthetic negation, works of art may well posit an illusory synthesis so as to unravel the appearance of unity that "the repressive principle" creates and that is the source of suffering, but this unravelling cannot initiate a moment of sublation in historic movement; it cannot lead to the secondary "political role" that Zuidervaart attributes to art. To extend a work's negative dialectic beyond its context is to render it susceptible to all the repressive (and reified) tendencies of a dialectic that achieves domination via the illusory unity and the continuity of the concept.

Dialectics in Movement: The Historical Concept, Particularity, and Discontinuity

What finally affirms the irreconcilability of historical dialectics with the dialectics of art and what finally refutes the notion that art forms a parallel or shadow dialectic to historical dialectics are the opposing views of the two dialectics, particularly with regard to the concept (*Begriff*) and its historical continuity. For it is in the presumption of the continuity of the concept, what in German would be *ihre historische Aufhebung*, that the historical particularity which art reinscribes is repressed. The non-identity of art constitutes a qualitative alteration, a rupture in the temporal continuity of the concept, a rupture that confines the concept of art to an unfolding of increasing particularity within its specific socio-historical constellation. Aesthetic negation expands the depth and vitality of the temporal plane by reinscribing heterogeneous tensions obscured by the appearance of continuity. Art thus liberates the particulars of history from the conceptual (dialectical) structure through which ostensibly they are understood but in reality are repressively reduced to "equivalences." In that art liberates historical particulars from the illusory syntheses of historical dialectics, it announces its own discontinuity and ultimate decay; it announces its historical specificity. In short, aesthetic negation achieves what one might call a burgeoning, vertical negative dialectic on a horizontal historical continuum. What art negates on a vertical plane does not affect movement on the horizontal plane. The momentary disclosures of art succumb to the movements of history. As Adorno argues: "In the final instance, the unfolding of art works is the same as their decomposition" (Adorno *AT* 256). What this "decomposition" means then is that each work of art constitutes a new and discontinuous dialectic which is confined to its own socio-historical context and which cannot be extended beyond this context without perpetuating the continuity and unity of the concept with which art is non-identical.

With regard to temporal passage, the relation of an art work to the movements of historical dialectics also falls into dialectical polarization without resolution. Bound to its historical moment, aesthetic negation resists the sublating movements of historical dialectics. In this respect, the negative dialectic of art in fact expresses the suffering of "the non-integrable." Art expresses the impossibility of an integration either in or beyond its socio-historical moment. Temporal movement in historical dialectics presupposes the unities with which a given work within a given historical moment is dialectically at odds, and integration would further compromise the integrity of "the non-integrable" that art struggles to articulate. Furthermore, the historical particularity of an art work's non-identity is unsublatable in the movements of historical dialectics because each successive historical moment adds new preclusions in its conceptual structures. The added forced unities of subsequent historical moments condemn the validity of previous aesthetic non-identity to the past.

Art's re-inscription of "the non-integrable" thus constitutes an unsublatable articulation that is both non-identical with its socio-historical moment and with the dialectical movements of history. Being non-identical with its socio-historical moment excludes aesthetic expression from the dialectical movements of history from one moment to the next. In temporal passage, art suffers the same displacement of its critical force that, Zuidervaart argues, plagues the goals of political *engagement*: "Just as the irrationality of labor and politics under current conditions make them forget their transformative purpose, so the rationality of art relative to labor and politics makes it unable to carry out the transformation needed" (Zuidervaart *Adorno's Aesthetic Theory* 137). Yet in its inability "to carry out the transformation needed," art reflects the breakdown in sublation that it exposes. A work's "decomposition" exposes the falsity of the continuities upon which the dialectical movements of history rely.

In binding the non-identity of art to its socio-historical moment, Adorno further polarizes the concept of negation. Initially, the polarization focused on the moment-as-such and was manifested in the contradictory tendencies of the negations of traditional dialectics and the aesthetic negations of art. Whereas in historical dialectics negation resulted in repressive unities, in art aesthetic negation dispelled the false unities of its socio-historical moment. With regard to temporal passage, the polarization is manifested in the contradictory tendencies of historical dialectical movement. In historical dialectics, temporal negation results in a conceptual *historische Aufhebung* or a conceptual unity in continuity. In art, on the other hand, aesthetic negation dispels the false conceptual continuities of the movements of historical dialectics. This polarization of negation also results in a polarization of the concept of synthesis. In the movements of historical dialectics the integrity of the particular is preserved in its conceptual synthesis. In art, on the other hand, the integrity of the particular is preserved by fixating "the non-integrable" in opposition to the "equivalences" necessary for the conceptual syntheses upon which the movements of historical dialectics rely.

Just as the non-identity of art emerges as a moment of disunity, it also emerges as discontinuity in temporal movement—the former resulting in the latter. Yet in its negation of synthesis (both at the level of the historical moment and at the level of historical movement) art's non-identity nonetheless perpetuates, indeed incorporates, "the repressive principle" that it opposes. While "the non-integrable" expressed in art undercuts the moments and movements of historical dialectics, these same moments and movements structure art's own (non-)identity. As Adorno argues: "Even the most purely aesthetic category, i.e., appearance, is mediated with reality as its determinate negation" (Adorno *AT*

152). In its negation of the illusory syntheses of "reality," art takes form not as a separate and distinct entity but as a locus of opposition. As a "determinate negation" of forced unity, the very concept of aesthetic non-identity is an impress of unity. For it only finds expression in negation.

Specifically as the expression of the suffering of "the non-integrable," art preserves the reductive "equivalences" and unities that it negates. Adorno expresses a similar point in less theoretical terms in "Theses Upon Art and Religion Today," where he argues that art "always was, and is, a force of protest of the humane against the pressure of domineering institutions . . . no less than it reflects their substance."[3] Although art may be "a force of protest of the humane," it incorporates "the substance" of "domineering institutions" because these "institutions" reduce "the humane" into the form of protest. Likewise as the expression of suffering of "the non-integrable," art incorporates reductive "equivalences" and unities because they reduce its expressions to the form of suffering. The continued domination of "the repressing principle" in aesthetic expression represents what I will call a resurgence of art's negated origins.

While I will argue that this resurgence gives rise to a hidden negative dialectic working within and against Adorno's aesthetic theory, a few observations must preface its full discussion. If, as Adorno claims, the non-identity of art can only unravel apparent continuity within a specific socio-historical context, if "what was once true in a work of art afterwards became false in the course of historical time," it is at first unclear how a work remains accessible at all (Adorno *AT* 60). Once the historical constellations change, the work would seem to have little value beyond that of a relic or an example for the more general argument that diversity or heterogeneity prevails beneath the repressive appearances to the contrary—an argument that on one level Adorno is in fact making. Adorno circumvents this problem by suggesting first of all that a work "can reveal its truth a second time when the conditions which undermined its truth in the first place are changed" (60). Adorno does not have much faith in this first possibility, however, because he adds that "past art must be not abstractly negated, but consciously criticized from the vantage point of the present" (60). From "the vantage point of the present," a work's contextual dialectical tensions, which survive beneath their apparent resolution, assume a secondary function as a position of reference for detecting critical concepts that have gained reified prevalence (i.e., the appearance of historically sublated continuity) beyond their particular constellation. These are not so much the continued prevalence of the concepts whose unity a work shatters—although this certainly is a possibility—but rather the specific critical validity the work itself represents as a "concept in the historically changing constellation of moments."[4]

Not only does the work become art by dispelling the appearance of unity of its own socio-historical context, but the work's failure to resolve the preclusions of its negated origins also gains it a reverse notoriety. Within its socio-historical context, an art work challenges the tyranny of the Hegelian concept, i.e., its illusory momentary unity and historical continuity, yet at the same time each work risks the propagation of new concepts in the challenge that it issues. The work gains a reverse or negative notoriety as a critical expression which when extended beyond its context vitiates and becomes rigid and oppressive. Like the "critique of social problems" mentioned by Adorno and Horkheimer in the introduction to *Dialectic of Enlightenment* which change "no less than the ideology to which they referred," previous works of art also change:

> They suffer what triumphant thought has always suffered. If it willingly emerges from its critical element to become a mere means at the disposal of an existing order, then despite itself it tends to concert the positive it elected to defend into something negative and destructive" (Horkheimer and Adorno *DE* xii).

Taken from "its critical element," an art work succumbs to the "existing order" with which it initially was non-identical and becomes an appropriable "means" for maintaining that order. This does not mean that a work loses all relevance once its socio-historical context has passed. Rather an art work's critical relevance survives in a dialectical reversal of its original import. An art work maintains continued relevance as a tool for tracing repressive ideas, concepts and tendencies back to originally liberating contexts. Like the foundations of critical thought, works of art are subject to an inevitable and alarming decay:

> When public opinion has reached a state in which thought inevitably becomes a commodity, and language the means of promoting that commodity, then the attempt to trace the course of such depravation has to deny any allegiance to current linguistic and conceptual conventions, lest their world-historical consequences thwart it entirely (Horkheimer and Adorno *DE* xii).

With regard to previous works of art, the denial of "any allegiance to current linguistic and conceptual conventions" is tantamount to a denial of allegiance to any current conceptual acceptance of a previous work's originally critical position; it is tantamount to a rejection of the work in defense of the work itself; it is tantamount, in short, to a historicization of the work that rejects the possibility of its conceptual continuity. This negative dynamic, in many respects, explains what, for David Roberts, is the contradiction in Adorno's aesthetic: that modern art "whose legitimation can be given only by progress, *lies at the end of progress*" and that "the new can be defined only by the paradox that it marks the endpoint of progress."[5] In its specific constellation the work's critical vitality is a liberating force. But when that constellation has past and one considers the work in retrospect, the originally critical vitality becomes reified and repressive unless the work is seen as the context and articulation of critical perspectives no longer valid. The work becomes the voice against the extension (and thus vitiation) of its own critical import.

The Momentary Weakness of Aesthetic Oneness

The defense of a work vis-á-vis the denial of a conceptual continuity in its critical import is significant above all because it demands an immanent critique of Adorno's own theory. Indeed, the need to critically examine the persistence of dialectical synthesis (*Aufhebung*) in Adorno's theory exists not only on the level of the illusory continuity of concepts but also on the level of the exclusions inherent in momentary synthesis as well. There are pressing questions as to whether Adorno's awareness of the exclusions inherent in momentary synthesis and his awareness of the illusory continuity of concepts are exempt from the "liquidations" to which the rest of empirical reality appears to be susceptible: one must ask whether and where conceptual unities and conceptual continuity emerge in the argued collapse of them. As Adorno notes, similar questions confront the position of art: "While no work of art is a total unity, every work of art pretends that it is and thus comes into conflict with itself" (Adorno *AT* 154). Art's heterogeneous non-identity is, according to Adorno, contingent upon an antithetical tailoring to and an unmasking of identifiable, apparently unified origins. But if constellations of accumulated and unresolved tensions are the latent empirical structures which art reinscribes—and the structures that Adorno the critic already presupposes when gauging the repressive domination of abstract "equivalences"—a work of art can only gain the footing to become non-identical by simultaneously succumbing to or perpetuating one form of illusory unity so as to unmask another: In art, "a certain residue of illusion remains and it is borne with embarrassment" (152). This residue means that art posits unity in order to dispel it and that "art's 'path of progressive negativity' also contains the opposite moment" (Wellmer "Truth, Semblance, Reconciliation" 104).

While art emerges in a moment of opposition to the enforced unities of empirical experience, the opposite is also true: the forced unities of empirical experience emerge in art in a moment of opposition to it, or rather what is posited as the forced unities of empirical experience emerge. Art employs meaning, "the agent that generates oneness," in order to press the restrictions of meaning and in order to express the ineffable (Adorno *AT* 154). In an acknowledgement of the embarrassing resurgence of forced unities in art's use of "the agent that generates oneness," Adorno argues: "Every profound analysis of an art work will invariably uncover weakness in the aesthetic oneness" (Adorno *AT* 154). The type of analysis to which Adorno refers moves beyond the initial argument that the fictitious unities of art disclose parallel strategies which in society are repressive.

Rather it is in the immanent excavation of "weakness in the aesthetic oneness" that "profound analysis" uncovers the aesthetic in art. In "the weakness of aesthetic oneness" lies art's strength, its non-identical moment, and its discordance. The "weakness" denotes a failure of aesthetic reconciliation, and this failure gives space to "the non-integrable" which art inadvertently voices in opposition to its own "oneness." In that each work of art posits an "aesthetic oneness" that falters, art becomes aesthetic in spite of itself. But in the emergence of "the non-integrable" out of the "weakness of aesthetic oneness," a central question emerges regarding art's representations of socio-empirical reality. Does the "oneness" reflect the forced unities of society, or have the aesthetic representations of socio-empirical reality been "pre-selected with an eye to oneness" which art then opposes (Adorno *AT* 154). In other words, does art force a unity upon the socio-empirical that is otherwise too diverse for art to contend with?

During the twenty years that separate *Aesthetic Theory* and the *Dialectic of Enlightenment* Adorno did not forget the need "to deny any allegiance to current linguistic and conceptual conventions," whether this non-allegiance occurs in the disunities of art or in formulation of his own critical positions. Adorno's *Aesthetic Theory* evinces an acute awareness of how susceptible his own position, like that of art itself, is to "an eye to oneness." As Jameson has noted, Adorno does much to avoid an ossified position by means of the dynamics contained within his own writing (Jameson *Late Marxism* 68). The dynamics of Adorno's sentence structure incorporate the dialectical structures of art which they analyze. Just as there is "weakness" and disunity in "aesthetic oneness," so too is there a disunity structured into Adorno's writing, sentence elements being at such odds with one another that they initiate an unresolvable dialectic of their own that repeatedly destabilizes unified meaning, "the agent that generates oneness." Peter Osborne has criticized Jameson's "attempt at an exposition of the 'mimetic component' of Adorno's sentence structure" by arguing that throughout *Late Marxism* Jameson breaks "off the internal investigation of Adorno's thought at precisely those points at which it approaches the fundamental philosophical issues at stake." At these breaks, Osborne argues, Jameson displaces immanent critique "with 'translations' into other generally more recent, critical idioms deriving from quite different philosophical traditions."[6] These "translations" are indeed a troubling dimension of Jameson's book because they cloud the central a role that rhetorical analysis of structure has in Adorno's own arguments on disunity and meaning.

While the "mimetic component" of Adorno's writing attempts a meaningful disunity, it is subject to criticism on two levels. First of all, insofar as Adorno's sentences evince a mimetic structure of the art they analyze, they also demand an analysis that leads from structural examinations to referential specifics. The attempt to convey the dialectical tensions of art through the structural tensions in sentences courts the possibility of turning aesthetic disunities into "abstract [linguistic] quantities" (Horkheimer and Adorno *DE* 7). Furthermore, the "mimetic component" of Adorno's writing opens it to the problems of the dialectics it describes. As the coming arguments will show, Adorno's aesthetic theory is also open to his criticism that the conceptual disunity of art derives from a "preselected" unity which is forced upon a diversity in empirical origins. To see how these two problems emerge, it is, first of all, worth returning to the passage where Adorno argues art's non-identical relation to "its other," where he argues that art is understandable only through its "law of motion" (*Bewegungsgesetz*) and not "through some invariable principle" (Adorno *AT* 4).

In this early passage of the *Aesthetic Theory*, Adorno addresses the historical movement of art while simultaneously imitating its momentary disunities. Art's momentary disunity with "its other" becomes most clear in the linguistic contradictory play between "the law of motion" and an "invariable principle." Only Adorno's assertion separates the "law" he embraces from the "invariable principles" he denounces. More importantly, by juxtaposing the "law" of art with a renunciation of "invariable principles," Adorno blurs the clarity between the two distinct dimensions of synthesis (*Aufhebung*) which are at the center of his aesthetic critique of dialectics. While he describes art's movement, Adorno writes himself into the dialectical disunity that he argues results from "the weakness of aesthetic oneness." Insofar as the statement "Art is meaningful only in its law of motion and not through some invariable principle" collapses under the weight of its own demands, the collapse simulates the discordance that Adorno attributes to art. His argument gives voice to "the non-integrable" by precluding the invariability of its own "law." The passage generates an irreconcilable crisis in its own foundation that is parallel to the more complex crises that Adorno claims are inherent in the momentary unities of the dialectical concept, and by way of implication, in aesthetic negation as well.

Adorno's dialectical sentence does not, however, collapse beneath the weight of something more profound that emerges in its place. Nor does the sentence leave its antithetical tensions behind. Indeed, the lack of resolution in Adorno's sentence coincides with what Hohendahl has called "the poststructuralist insistence on Adorno's refusal to support the grand design of historical synthesis and teleology—his refusal, in other words, to read the Marxist tradition through the lenses of Hegel."[7] The charge of "invariant" beleaguers Adorno's "law" with a perpetual state of crisis. While not voiding Adorno's claim, neither does the charge reconcile itself to the force of the passage's greater argument, save for the fact that its antithetical tensions illustrate the irreconcilability which, according to Adorno, (re)emerges with art's non-identity. The "invariables" negated in Adorno's sentence constantly reassert themselves, as even the contrary pull between "*Bewegung*" and "*Gesetz*" demonstrates. Rather than a resolution, the relation between negation and "invariables" is one of persistent instability. Like the sublation, whose faltering gives art its autonomy, the negation upon which art builds this autonomy is itself not secure. Negation is not erasure.

As Adorno's dialectical "*Bewegungs [-] gesetz*" illustrates, the crisis in art extends beyond the struggle for the often sought but seldom achieved expression of the suffering of "the non-integrable." Whatever the non-identical movement of art, its origins continue to vie for dominance over their negation. The negation of origins in aesthetic theories or in art itself by no means ensures that origins have been left behind or have been exhausted. Even as the charge of "invariant" shadows Adorno's "*Bewegungsgesetz*," so too the charge of resolution beleaguers art's negation of the appearance of resolution and haunts its non-identity. Negation and the resurgence of the negated, in both Adorno's "*Bewegungsgesetz*" and art's non-identity, splinter into discordant irreconcilable tensions. More importantly, their lack of resolution indicates how vast and diverse the origins are with which an art work is non-identical. Adorno's dialectical sentence is but a simple and specific imitation of a subtler, and more complex, negative aesthetic movement.

While the antithetical tensions between "*Bewegung*" and "*Gesetz*" do much to reveal the irreconcilable dialectical tension between art and its origins, Adorno's sentence only has to contend with the shadow of its own invariability, a shadow of logic. In this passage, the resurgence of negated origins occurs within a linguistic opposition, a contradiction whose stability is maintained by the obscurity of its referents. The play between these tensions may reflect a central momentary aesthetic dynamic, but it relies on abstractions like the phrases "origin," "the other" and "what art is not," and these abstractions arguably have stability only insofar as they build linguistic and logical tensions (Adorno *AT* 22). They are stabilized by the passage's simplicity, whereas with art the negations are not merely a question of logic and linguistics. What separates the dialectical dynamics of Adorno's sentence from the actual aesthetic instances to which these descriptive terms refer is that as the terms move from Adorno's abstract generalities to specifics, the play of opposition loses stability because it loses the antithetical clarity upon which it depends. Adorno's terms foster an opposition that is linguistically "pre-selected" and that when given specificity quickly disperses into disunity.

Critics have attempted to come to terms with Adorno's pre-selections by locating the specific source of his opposition in the philosophical traditions that Osborne argues are ignored by Jameson. Shierry Weber Nicholsen argues, for example, that the relative absence of concrete elements in *Aesthetic Theory* results from a focus on previous aesthetic theories and not cultural artifacts: "The stuff of *Aesthetic Theory* is concepts . . . from other theories, Kant and Hegel's chief among them."[8] As far as locating the philosophical underpinnings of Adorno's aesthetics is concerned, Nicholsen is correct, but at the same time "the stuff" of *Aesthetic Theory* forms the basis for an extension of a modified Hegelian-Marxist critique of the cultural industry under capitalism. For Adorno, the culture industry is the dominant social force that "makes the dissimilar comparable by reducing it to abstract quantities" (Horkheimer and Adorno *DE* 7). Adorno is concerned with concepts in general because it is through the specific dominance of the concept of market or exchange value that consciousness regresses into a state of reification and is unable to assess cultural value in other terms.

Adorno sees the regression as insurmountable and as leading to a closed system. As Wellmer has noted, Adorno and Horkheimer agreed with Weber—against Marx—that the *immanent* logic of capitalism pointed to "a closed system of instrumental and administrative rationality, rooted not at last in the reified consciousness of individuals who were increasingly subsumed under the capitalist production process."[9] In his efforts to combat this reified closure, Adorno circumvents its delineation, reducing its complexity to the unified concepts of "origins" and "the other." One might argue that this strategy is a necessary reversal of the tendencies that Adorno seeks to counteract, but, in a work that is so concerned with the repressive consequences of a reliance on concepts, the reduction constitutes an interference in the implications of the dialectic that Adorno has set in motion.

Obviously, Adorno's arguments are not limited to the contradictory disunity between a "law of motion" and a simultaneous denouncement of "invariables." But when Adorno moves toward referential specifics, the structural polarization in this early passage remains intact. His explanation of art's social idea, for example, adopts the same dialectical structure that is observable in his assertion of art's law of motion:

> Were the atomistic structure of society changed, art would not have its social idea: to offer to the social universal, how a particular is at all possible: as long as the particular and the universal diverge, there is no freedom. Rather this would grant the particular that right which aesthetically today presents itself nowhere else than in the idiosyncratic coercions that the artists have to obey.[10]

What earlier was posited as a structural opposition between a "law of motion" and "invariable principles," here becomes an irreconcilable empirical opposition between the particularity that art "offers to the social universal" and the "freedom" that the "social universal" denies "the particular." The denial in turn distorts particularity into idiosyncracies, which, like the "protest of the humane" or the expression of suffering, is the only possible expression of particularity that is left (Adorno "Theses Upon Art and Religion Today" 678). In that particularity is coerced into idiosyncratic expressions, it perpetuates "the social universal" that mediates its distorted form, even as art expresses opposition to the un-freedom forced upon it. At the same moment, however, art's "idiosyncratic" expressions manifest disunity with the universal forced upon it.

With the double use of the colon, which traditionally indicates "equivalence," Adorno emphasizes the unresolvable social tensions that form the basis of art's non-identity. His argument can be read as an assertion that art's social idea is equal to the presence of two mutually exclusive phenomena. Art's social idea equals a stable but irreconcilable tension between the particularity which, on the one hand, an art work offers up (sacrifices) to the universal, and the universal, on the other, whose subordination of the particular to itself precludes undistorted particularity. The irreconcilability of these two phenomena is in itself an assertion of "the non-integrable" quality of aesthetic particularity and of the illusory quality of the universal. It asserts that the universal is "a limiting principle," because the irreconcilability defies the movement of resolution upon which a genuine universal depends. Art's social idea is thus a mediated opposition to the coerciveness of the universal whose unity is gained only through force. In that Adorno's discussion of the coerciveness of the universal occurs in an explanation of art's social idea, the universal signifies the social totality, a totality whose essential characteristic, for Adorno, is its "limiting principle":

> Were it [society] to become a totality which no longer contained within itself a limiting principle, it would also be rid of the duress which subjects all its members to such a principle; it would no longer be a totality: no forced unity.[11]

Just as art's "law of motion" opposes any "invariable principle," so too does art's social idea oppose the "limiting principle" or "forced unity" that defines the social totality. This conception of the social totality remains fixed and insurmountable in Adorno's aesthetics, and the fixity of this definition is what constitutes Adorno's most radical departure from Marxist theories of art.

Materialist Aesthetics and the Limits of Dialectical Materialism

Once art's "non-integrable" sacrifice to an insurmountable "forced unity" is placed within the movement of history, one can see how the social idea of art, as it is conceived in the *Aesthetic Theory*, distinguishes the competing positions of Marxist aesthetics of Lukács and the aesthetics of Adorno. For Lukács, the repressiveness of social totality does not preclude its malleability, and art thus functions as a provocateur which assists in a struggle toward the eventual possibility of culture, culture only emerging once freedom has been achieved. For Adorno, on the other hand, art expresses how the social universal always compromises the particular, regardless of the form that the social universal adopts. In this respect, even Lukács's cultural vision, if it were realized, would not escape the repressiveness to which art, according to Adorno, responds.

In the temporal dialectic between the aesthetic particular and the social universal, "the limiting principle" of the universal is its tendency to dilute and absorb particularity, to forcefully integrate particularity into a greater movement of synthesis by compromising its integrity. For Adorno, the social universal can only be understood in terms of "the limiting principle" that art momentarily discloses, and, with the passage of time, art's disclosures inevitably succumb to the social universal's diluting pull. The gradual dilution precludes a positive continuity in aesthetic expression beyond its historical moment and thus precludes the progressive function which Lukács assigns to art. As an expression of the "non-integrable," art necessarily reconstitutes its non-identity again and again, opposing even previous aesthetic expressions of particularity because they too are not exempt from a subsequent and inevitable vitiating appropriation.

Despite its temporal limitations, the non-identity of art is, according to Adorno, the one place of continued struggle and opposition that does not succumb to the coerciveness which haunts even the most "enlightened" *telos* for the social whole. As Albrecht Wellmer has noted: "For Adorno . . . the work of art . . . becomes the last residue of reason in a rationalized world" (Wellmer "Reason, Utopia, and the Dialectic of Enlightenment" 93). Art incorporates resistance without attempting to impose a universal order on those who do not want to come along. In one respect, it is easy to understand the privileged social position which Adorno grants to art. The social idea, which is embodied in works of art, argues on behalf of a non-repressive society, exemplifying the path toward it in a moment of particularity which is based in opposition to repression and totality. But this aspect of art comprises only half of the dialectical tensions that make up its social idea. The particularity that art offers up as a sacrifice to society is locked in an irreconcilable tension with the oppressive consequences of a society in which particularity and the universal diverge. For all its claims to opposition, an art whose resistance to the social totality resides in its momentary idiosyncratic assertion of its own particularity is open to accusations of complicity. It is open to charges of sustaining the order which it purports to oppose because it is not actively *engaged*, indeed according to Adorno, cannot be *engaged*, in transforming that order on a grand or universal scale, choosing instead to embody the momentary particularity which the tendencies of the social order threaten. From the perspective of historical change, art is beset by the question of whether aesthetic particularity is really particularity or rather conformity.

The defense of art in Adorno's aesthetics derives from the implicit argument that the evolution of the social totality has eliminated the possibility of positive social change. Art serves as a "*medium* . . . rather than a *model* of reconciliation itself," giving space to the particularity that the social totality precludes (Wellmer "Reason, Utopia and the Dialectic of Enlightenment" 94). As a "medium," the work of art functions as a meeting ground for individuals; it serves as an orchestrated transitory position of resistance to the unstoppable forceful integrations of the social universal. In its individual manifestations, art affirms the hope that the evolution of the social totality has not eclipsed the possibility of particularity altogether.

The question of conformity raised by Adorno's argument strikes at the very core of his conception of particularity itself. The momentary achievement of aesthetic particularity argues on behalf of particularity not as a future goal or universal but rather from its embattled determinate manifestation. To posit particularity as a subsequent historical goal too easily succumbs to idealism and in turn to appropriation in a diluted form—in short, it too easily succumbs to an ideology for subsequent repressions. To avoid an idealism of the particular, Adorno embraces particularity while simultaneously calling attention to its culpability.[12] He circumvents the charge of art's conformity by arguing that, given the dynamic of the social universal, aesthetic particularity is powerless against its diluting tendencies, at least insofar as opposition is presumed to have a transformative power on the social universal. This powerlessness is part of the dialectic which comprises art's social idea. The non-identity of art is achieved in the aesthetic exposure of the irreconcilable tension between an opposition to "the limiting principle" of the social universal and a socio-historical impotence. Both sides of this dialectic make up art's social idea. Art is at once neither and both. Its particularity lies in a resistance to the "forced unity" which reduction to either interpretation would impose. By explicating both sides of this dialectic, Adorno attributes to art a position of non-identity with the dialectical tensions which he describes. But the position is itself not articulated, only implied, an implication that preserves irreconcilable tensions that direct explanation would falsely resolve: "In fact, the true language of art is speechlessness" (Adorno *AT* 164).

Hidden Invariables in Art's "Law of Movement"

The social idea of art, which emerges in the dialectical play between unresolvable tensions, presupposes that the irreconcilability is not merely an instance of ambiguity, but that the ambiguity is indicative of the conceptual constraints of discourse, that the ambiguity exposes how conceptual meaning "is the vehicle of illusion" (Adorno *AT* 154). This argued aesthetic exposure finds its parallel in the antithetical tendencies of Adorno's own sentence structure. Both testify to the existence of social elements which are repressed and left unaccounted for in the discursive structures which mediate and govern experience. Insofar as Adorno's own written delineation of aesthetics attacks the semantic structures of conventional discourse, his aesthetic theory is primarily concerned with dismantling the unity of concepts, concepts as semantic unities. But in his definition of art as a resistance to "the limiting principle" of the social totality, Adorno seeks a direct conceptual correspondence, indeed a conceptual unity, between the social constraints of discourse and the delimiting consequences of a capital-driven culture industry that subsumes cultural artifacts beneath a unifying concept of commodity or exchange value. As Andreas Huyssen has noted, for Adorno, the "culture industry leaves no meaning, no signification unscathed"; it forcefully integrates them all.[13]

Just as conceptual "meaning" compromises the integrity of the particular, the culture industry, according to Adorno, contaminates the integrity of art by reducing it to its abstract exchange value. By attempting thus to maintain a conceptual unity between the abstract "limiting principle" of the universal and the "scathing" influence of the culture industry, Adorno reduces all aspects of the culture industry to an "equivalence." He reduces to a concept what he considers to be the source of reified concepts and thus denies the culture industry the diverse particularity or heterogeneity which he sets out to defend. On this point, Huyssen is absolutely correct when he challenges Adorno's presumption "that function and use are totally determined by corporate intentions, that exchange value has totally supplanted use value" (Huyssen 22). The presumption is "pre-selected with an eye to oneness" that is based in a discursive concept. This is not to suggest that the whole of Adorno's theory collapses because of his attempt to sustain a conceptual continuity between an abstract limiting universal and the organizing principle in capitalistic societies. Nonetheless, Adorno can equate the "limiting principle" of the universal with the influence of the culture industry only by a reductive forceful integration. Like the repressive unities of society, this equivalence is shadowed by a "non-integrable." Insofar as Adorno's aesthetic theory succumbs to the "pre-selected" construction of "oneness," it too demands the same type of "profound analysis" which "uncover[s] weakness in the aesthetic oneness" and thereby discloses "the non-integrable" in illusory unity (Adorno *AT* 154).

With increased specificity, the origins negated by art also increase in sophistication, complexity, and heterogeneity, as do the art works bound to them in non-identical relation. This fact is obscured in the lopsidedness of Adorno's dialectic. He grants art a "law of movement," a disunity, and a particularity, while attributing an "invariable" unified stagnancy to empirical reality, which he reduces to the abstract concept of the social universal. Hohendahl has observed that as Adorno refined his aesthetic theories during the 50s and 60s, "his concept of the advanced capitalist society as a totally administered society froze and did not take in later development" (Hohendahl *Reappraisals* 213). It is not enough to posit a symmetrical correspondence between the structure of Adorno's dialectical sentences and art's non-identical relation to its origins. Though the dialectical tension between art's non-identity and its origins remains an unreconciled struggle between negation and resurgence and thus affirms the unresolvable tensions exposed by art, the de-sublating tendency of art vies against a constellation of opposition and discord—a constellation that Adorno obscures beneath the conceptual reductiveness of his own dialectic. What this discordance means is that the resurgence of negated origins occurs at numerous levels. This resurgence is arguably the undeveloped negative shadow of Adorno's aesthetics.

A non-identity of art that provokes an endless uncovering of heterogeneity within a particular historic constellation presupposes a questionable appearance of resolution of equally endless proportions. Without a grand illusory appearance of unity, there is, in Adorno's theory, no need for art to reinscribe heterogeneity. In this respect, Adorno's aesthetic theory appears to maintain its proportional relation with the discursive oppositions that he builds into his sentences, the reinscription of heterogeneity in each work of art responding to a preexisting, and repressive, apparent unity. The staggering accumulation of unresolvable dialectical tensions is offset by an equally staggering appearance of uniformity, the two forming a vast irreconcilable dynamic. But the relation quickly becomes disproportional. As art's non-identical origins become more specific, they test the limits of art's ability to incorporate "the limiting principle" into itself: they call into question whether art is capable of being as vastly non-identical as its origins are capable of increasing in complexity. The uncovering of disparity within origins is not a single act of disclosure, not a grand rupture of apparent continuity with a single blow. The illusory unities of the socio-empirical cover so many dimensions of experience that no work of art can contend with them all, even within its limited specific socio-historical constellation. With each reinscription of heterogeneity there is not only a corresponding appearance of unity; each new reinscription is a potential point of departure for subsequent appropriation by the origins with which it was initially non-identical. In addition to matching the non-identity of art, the forced social unities have the momentum of history as their motor, which is a gravity pulling everything into itself.

Whereas the dialectical tensions of Adorno's "law of motion" need only contend with the shadow of their own invariability, the diversity of reflexes which origins have against the non-identity of art indicates their unacknowledged diversity in Adorno's aesthetics. The resurgence of negated origins is not limited to appropriating the non-identity of art, i.e. not limited to diluting its negative opposition into an altered, subservient role. At a second level, the resurgence of negated origins results from the initial, dominant position of origins. While impotence of art may inadvertently offer countless avenues to its negated origins for re-establishing the unity and continuity that art disrupts, the articulation of non-identity always falls to art itself. The origins negated by art need not be assertive to maintain themselves. They are the status quo. In a manner of speaking, the unity of socio-empirical reality can afford to be indifferent to art's non-identity until art obtains enough force to offer a substantial challenge, a challenge that is by its nature ephemeral. The autonomy of art is not always the result of its non-integrable status: the movement of history may simply circumvent art's assertion of its non-identity, altering the form of the origins that the art work opposes without ever having taken into consideration the instances of aesthetic non-identity it left behind. The origins to which the non-identity of art is bound are not bound to art in return.

Whether vitiated, appropriated, or bypassed, the non-identity of art competes with the resilience and complexity of its origins, especially with respect to the position art itself has in the continuity with which it is non-identical. Art is small in proportion to its negated origins, despite any antithetical balance the term "non-identity" or the reference to origins as "the other" might imply. The aesthetic heterogeneous tensions that Adorno privileges are hopelessly outnumbered by the overwhelming diversity of socio-empirical reality which subsumes them. In terms of its consequences, the movement from the generality of Adorno's term "origins" to the diverse specifics of this referent means that art's negation of unity and continuity in one dimension is quickly subsumed by another. It also means that art's non-identity presupposes marginalizations of its own, the repression of some origins in favor of others. This marginalization may be the result of art's own limitations, but it is already evident in Adorno's avoidance of a full exploration of art's non-identical origins. The avoidance privileges art and represses origins. Against the unacknowledged diversity of its negated origins, art's negativity succumbs to the same synthetic ideology of history that, according to Adorno, it seeks to disclose.

Inasmuch as the origins, which an art work negatively objectifies, refer to a posited uniformity in a work's socio-historical context, the resurgence of negated origins indicates that art works cannot objectify the entirety of the origins they negate. Art must suffice with what Wellmer calls a desire for "knowledge in its entirety" that can "only grasp complementary fragmented forms of truth" (Wellmer "Truth, Semblance, Reconciliation" 92). The resurgence of negated origins, the acknowledgement of what negation does not delete, eradicate or abolish, perhaps best indicates the complex, multifarious dialectic that the term "origins" so insufficiently signifies. This resurgence is both the affirmation and reification of an art work's non-identical movement out of "its other." That art works are not monolithic in their objectifications evinces the heterogeneity aesthetic negation reinscribes, but it also means that art's non-identity obscures the heterogeneity that it sets out to uncover. Art paradoxically encourages the endurance of apparent unity and continuity.

The negation of origins in Adorno's aesthetic theory is founded upon unavoidable marginalizing presuppositions about successive moments in the historical process. The aesthetic negation of origins presupposes the heterogeneity that it reinstates; it implodes because the term "origins" already denotes a heterogeneous miscellany reasserting itself within its own dialectic of negation and resurgence, and unity and disunity. It is, however, with these presupposition that Adorno's term "origins" writes its own history, that it asserts its particularity through the obscured heterogeneity which it would reinscribe. Since art works cannot be monolithic in their objectifications, they are actively involved in positing or constructing the socio-historical context to which they respond, a positing that determines the character of the autonomy they anticipate.

Thus Adorno's rhetorical stance as the voice of art looking in retrospect on its "negated origins" is perhaps the best indication of the tendencies he argues that art disrupts. By dwelling on the posited consequences of art's negative force rather than exploring the conditions leading to that force, Adorno sacrifices a vast heterogeneous complexity for a single term, "origins," whose exploration he dismisses as "necessarily disappointing." His is a sacrifice in preference for a cultural phenomenon, which, he argues, in each of its individual instances has the ephemeral critical force to expose the marginalizations inherent in such sacrifices. But Adorno's sacrifice of heterogeneity is arguably the moment in which his theory reflects the "weakness of aesthetic oneness" out of which the aesthetic in art emerges. His *Aesthetic Theory* is fraught with implications, whose strongest imports, like those of art, often emerge in spite of Adorno's preferences.

II

Adorno, Literature, and the Conceptual Forms of Historical Reflection

3

Trying to Understand *Godot*: Adorno, Beckett, and the Senility of Dialectics

Since Theodor W. Adorno's death in 1969, Anglo-American Scholarship has used his general critical esteem for Samuel Beckett to situate Adorno within a constellation of arguments on politics and modernity by Adorno, Lukács, Bloch, Benjamin, and Brecht.[1] More specific studies of Adorno and Beckett gravitate toward the drama *Endgame*, largely as a result of Adorno's classic essay "Trying to Understand *Endgame*" (1961).[2] Yet numerous digressions on *Waiting for Godot* intersperse Adorno's seminal analysis of *Endgame*. These and similar digressions on *Waiting for Godot* in Adorno's later philosophical and aesthetic work remain largely undeveloped in criticism of Adorno and even in Adorno's own writings. To examine these digressions offers new insight into Beckett's play. It also leads critical discussion of Adorno and Beckett into an area not already overburdened with the twentieth-century controversies of Marxist aesthetics.

Jack Zipes argues that Adorno uses Beckett to assert his belief "that artists had to devise new means for projecting the consequences which German fascism, Auschwitz, the Holocaust, and the atomic bomb have had for reality." As accurate as Zipes's assessment is, his argument only generally explores the extent to which Adorno's embrace of Beckett coincides with Adorno's own gradual theoretical formulation of "new means" for "projecting the consequences" of the Second World War.[3] In Adorno's work on Beckett, the "new means" to which Zipes refers begin in the form of a question: what is the post-war status of the methodology of historical dialectics?

Exploring the status of historical dialectics in *Waiting for Godot* first necessitates a consideration of the status of "waiting" itself. It is the one constant throughout the play which can briefly be summarized as follows. When the curtain rises, Didi and Gogo await the arrival of Godot who may or may not have promised to come and who may or may not exist. While Didi and Gogo wait, two additional characters, Lucky and Pozzo, appear on the stage. Lucky carries baggage and has a rope around his neck that is held by Pozzo who consequently has control over Lucky. After a few short exchanges between Pozzo and Didi and

Gogo, Lucky is forced to think aloud, and when he will not stop, all subdue him forcibly. Lucky and Pozzo leave. Didi and Gogo continue to wait for Godot. In the second act, Lucky and Pozzo return, but in a noticeably decrepit state. Another scuffle ensues, this time Pozzo is attacked. Lucky and Pozzo leave. Didi and Gogo continue to wait.

Since *Waiting for Godot* begins and ends with "waiting," it easily generates the appearance of being a phenomenal absolute or an ahistorical condition.[4] Yet waiting is not an isolated phenomenon in the play. The comings and goings of Lucky and Pozzo mediate the status of Didi and Gogo and their waiting—just as the constant expectation of Didi and Gogo accentuates the decay of Lucky and Pozzo. Unfulfilled expectation stands in dynamic tension with a deteriorating, aimless and memory-less movement. The two comprise a single temporal constellation, overlapped in unspoken likeness. Didi and Gogo are temporally related to Lucky and Pozzo because both pairs are variations of the same dialectic: that of "lordship and bondage." Waiting cannot be an ahistorical condition in the play because as a dialectical paradigm it is the historical precursor to the full blown master-slave relationship which is manifested in Lucky and Pozzo. The relation which Didi and Gogo have to Godot corresponds with the unresolvable subservience which the Jews, according to Hegel, had to their law.[5] Yet Hegel's subsequent version of the master-slave dialectic by no means constitutes an advance or progress within the play. In that Beckett presents both versions of "lordship and bondage" and stages a decay of the latter, waiting assumes a peculiar historical status in the play. It falls further and further into the past as the play progresses—even though the play progresses without synthesis and even though the master-slave dialectic of Lucky and Pozzo is incapable of superseding itself.

Despite being left-overs of an earlier dialectic, Didi and Gogo are in a better condition than their subsequent counterparts who hypothetically signify an advance in Hegel's dialectic. Insofar as the physical deterioration of Lucky and Pozzo suggests a temporal disfigurement of the central analytical paradigm of historical dialectics, "lordship and bondage," so too does their decline imply that history is disfiguring the conceptual methodology used to understand it. In other words, the decline of Lucky and Pozzo demands a revision of the very discourse which uses them as a methodological paradigm to account for change. Indeed, conceptual restructuring is necessary in order to understand the historical implications of Didi's and Gogo's qualitatively better condition than the dialectic of Lucky and Pozzo, which presumably has negated and superseded them. Only a concomitant restructuring of dialectics can historicize the "waiting" of *Waiting for Godot.*

Thus, what follows in this essay is an historicization of *Waiting for Godot* that will consider Beckett's drama vis-á-vis three movements of revised dialectics. Each movement combines Adorno's own restructuring of dialectics with his comments on Beckett, and together the three seek to (re)construct the philosophico-historical configuration in Beckett's play. The first examines the deterioration of "lordship and bondage" represented in Lucky and Pozzo. The second examines the structure of the Jewish version of the same dialectic represented in Didi's and Gogo's relation to Godot. The third examines the crisis in dialectics that results from simultaneously staging these two dialectical paradigms.

Adorno and Beckett and Dialectics in Decline

In *Waiting for Godot*, the separation of the two versions of "lordship and bondage" juxtaposes moments which, according to traditional dialectics, are cumulative or overlapped. Although their aesthetic separation subjects the mechanisms of historical dialectics to critical scrutiny, the separation itself is as much a consequence of history as it is an aesthetic maneuver. Juxtaposing Lucky and Pozzo with Didi and Gogo depicts dialectics in disrepair, because dialectics cannot account for the simultaneous presence of both pairs. Adorno sees in this juxtaposition an historical eclipse of dialectics, a staging of Hegel's master-slave dialectic which depicts it as senile, demented and, because of the aging that is implicit in senility, as anachronistic:

> *Waiting for Godot* revolves around the theme of lordship-and-bondage grown senile and demented in an era when exploitation of human labour persists although it could well be abolished. This motif, truly one of the essential characteristics of present-day society, is taken up again in Endgame. In both instances Beckett's technique pushes this Hegelian theme to the periphery: lordship and bondage are reduced to an anecdote in terms of both dramatic function and social criticism (Adorno *AT* 354).

Although Adorno talks about the potential abolition of the exploitation of human labor, his reference to the senility of "lordship and bondage" dismisses the traditionally accepted mechanism for the abolition. A dialectic grown senile cannot resolve or supersede itself; it lacks the mental faculties, the necessary consciousness, to do so.[6] Senility renders supersession inconceivable. By focusing on the Hegelian theme which Beckett pushes "to the periphery," Adorno turns the "push" into a full-scale critique, not only of Hegel but also of the Hegelian-Marxist tradition which appropriated Hegel's paradigmatic dialectic. Through Beckett, Adorno reaffirms his skepticism regarding the potential revolutionary consciousness of the proletarian class—a skepticism which, as Susan Buck-Morss has noted, marks the fissure between Adorno and Lukács.[7]

In one respect, Adorno accepts the senility of dialectics as a given, and the whole of his philosophical inquiry can be described as a search for its sources. As

Jean-François Lyotard was also later to do, Adorno discredits the master-slave dialectic so crucial to the entire project of Hegelian-Marxism.[8] Whereas Lyotard discounts the "itinerary of Spirit" in German idealism, calling it narrative, Adorno discounts it as "anecdote." Lyotard maintains that the master-narratives hinder awareness of history, i.e., remembrance: loss of memory is a symptom of the senility which Adorno identifies in Beckett's drama. In *Waiting for Godot* this senility manifests itself in at least three forms: Lucky's baggage, his senseless soliloquy and finally Pozzo's lack of memory.

Referring to Günter Anders's analysis of *Waiting for Godot*, Adorno singles out the slave, who as a result of history is no longer in a position to grasp and abolish the reins of domination.[9] Lucky's hands, after all, are already full of unnecessary baggage. Anders, who was among the first to discuss Beckett's use of "lordship and bondage," argued that this dialectic was significant because, in western thought, it had supplanted the paradigmatic image of Prometheus (228). Adorno's critique concurs with Anders' recognition that paradigms expire and necessarily shift, but the incapacitation of the slave bespeaks the already expired validity of "lordship and bondage" as an adequate conceptual structure for analysis.[10]

These shifts are not unlike what Peter Hohendahl, citing the relationship of Hans Jauss to Thomas Kuhn, describes as the parallels in shifts of literary and scientific paradigms.[11] For Adorno, however, the shift in historical paradigms derives not—as Kuhn argues is the case in "normative science"—from "the successive transition from one paradigm to another via revolution"[12] but rather from an historic rupture, an unsupersedable historic moment that has its horrific apotheosis in the form of Auschwitz. Insofar as Adorno uses the incapacitation of the slave as the basis for his argument, he relies on a double referent for this single critical term. The slave refers both to the subject who succumbs to and even perpetuates his/her own domination in the dialectic of Enlightenment and, as the coming arguments will demonstrate, to the Jewish subject before and after Auschwitz.

In *Dialectic of Enlightenment*, Adorno and Max Horkheimer maintain that the progressive mastery of the forces of nature—which ought to have a liberating effect for humanity—inadvertently subordinates humanity to domination. Because humans are part of nature, harnessing it means harnessing them as well, and this means that freedom is gained only at the expense of generating new and rarely comprehensible oppressions.[13] Foremost among these oppressions is a fractionalization of society that perpetuates itself, a fractionalization dramatized in the divergent preoccupations of Lucky and Pozzo and Didi and Gogo.

To focus more specifically on the slave and thus on Lucky: the subjugated perpetuate domination in the reified pursuit of an unavoidable path of labor, which, necessary for their own survival, produces their own subordination (Horkheimer and Adorno *DE* 22). Whatever the hypothetical knowledge that

Lucky attempts to convey when commanded to think, it is too specialized for anyone to comprehend. Its "profundity" fosters isolation and hostility rather than a shared enlightenment or a reciprocally unfolding self-consciousness. For Adorno, the Hegelian integrity of the subject is no longer tenable in a society where technological knowledge is a prerequisite for labor. Technological knowledge obstructs the unfolding of Spirit (*Geist*) because it blights the dialectical interaction between growing self-consciousnesses. The mind is simply not beyond the processes in which it finds itself (Adorno *ND* 200). The integrity of the subject cannot be presumed, but rather must be attained, and the technical demands of labor on consciousness keep the subject subjugated.

Adorno accounts for the abstract quality of Beckett's drama by arguing that Beckett's abstractions are only "as abstract as the real relations among men" (Adorno *AT* 46). Systemic repression remains because technical demands preclude the development of a consciousness which is capable of superseding the dialectical impasse; repressive uniformity emerges by default since there is no longer space for critical opposition.[14] Beckett's work thus embodies "historical experience," assimilating itself to an historical situation in which "realism and symbolism have been completely invalidated." The lack of meaning in Beckett—and this lack is also reflected in Lucky's soliloquy—articulates a "film negative" of a specific historical moment, the negativity of which simultaneously depicts and resists the historical sway that has led to "a crucial emaciation of subject and reality" (Adorno *AT* 46). Insofar as Beckett's dramas are without meaning, they give voice to a "poverty and fragmentation" in the lives of men and women which "in its immediate non-artistic form" precludes the foundation for its expression.

Like the Enlightenment philosophers, Adorno and Horkheimer regard reason as a servant, but, unlike their philosophical predecessors, they see it as the servant that "the master cannot check as he wishes" (Horkheimer and Adorno *DE* 37). The gist of Adorno's argument acknowledges that as a civilization we have as yet to create a discourse, doctrine, creed, or philosophical methodology that does not lend itself to appropriation, that resists manipulation for repression or for barbarous inhumanity.[15]

Adorno and Horkheimer argue that once the philosophy of history attempted to conceive of humane ideas as active and triumphant forces in history, they lost their innocence. In other words, humane ideas regressed into ideology which justified the triumph of the forces that appropriated them (Horkheimer and Adorno *DE* 224).[16] This loss of innocence suggests that the history of "humane ideas," like the history of Lucky and Pozzo, follows a path of degeneration. Lucky's eventual muteness, like Pozzo's blindness, evinces historical dialectical movement without an enduring and expressible goal or vision. Adorno's claim, which assumes the sincere and positive intent of most political agendas, focuses on the inescapable regressive shadow of these agendas, a shadow which, at least, has structured the course of material history if not wholly comprised its substance.[17] The dark side of the Enlightenment, the negative shadow which follows its every step, is that advances and progress, whether technical or discursive, tend to lend themselves to appropriation for repressive ends.[18]

How and why Adorno's argument becomes a defense of Beckett can only be understood by first placing the claim within the context of how, according to Adorno, Enlightenment philosophies and their accompanying political ideals have tended to manifest themselves in history. In perhaps his most laconic statement on the course of history, Adorno notes that "no universal history leads from savagery to humanitarianism, but there is one leading from the slingshot to the megaton bomb" (Adorno *ND* 320). The unspoken subtext to this claim is that the path from slingshot to megaton bomb is paved with humanitarian rhetoric. The polemic quality of the statement underscores Adorno's conviction that theory and praxis have a highly mediated relationship at best, if not being completely non-identical from one another.

According to Adorno, Beckett's avoidance of meaning, his not meaning anything, is his only hope for making "an uncompromising reprint of [a] reality" whose contamination he seeks to avoid (Adorno *AT* 28).[19] It is his only chance to avoid appropriation for repressive ends and his only hope to illuminate meaning's susceptibility to such appropriation (Adorno TUE 137).[20] Abstractly stated, Beckett's uncompromising stance evinces an irreconcilability with an historic moment whose promise of freedom produces a viciously circular domination and whose even genuine advances carry in their shadows an irresistible capacity for abuse and a regressive predisposition.[21] This stance shifts focus to the inevitable subject of domination and abuse: the other or the contrary—in other words, those who are different or dissonant with the dominant course of history. Adorno is drawn to Beckett's uncompromising side because it gives expression to dissonance within the movement of history: a dissonance which, in its repressed form, is neither resolved nor ultimately resolvable; a dissonance confined to a specific historic moment which the dissonance cannot supersede except in the most hollow and appropriable rhetorical form.[22]

Beckett's refusal to mean anything places each instance of dissonance within a specific historical configuration. It acknowledges the ephemerality of dissonance. It is no coincidence that, in his handling of Beckett, Adorno suspends him between "poetic euphemism" and "discursive barbarity" (Adorno *AT* 47). The former warns against the negative shadow of discourses on liberation, against their susceptibility to appropriation, and the latter against their tendency to gain gradual historical ascendancy only at the expense of regressing into barbarism. Not only is the movement of history marked by repression; the continual change in historical configurations robs dissonance of the substantive basis upon which to redress its oppression. The extremity of Beckett's "meaningless" abstractions evinces the historical eclipse of the discursive foundations of critical opposition.

Irreconcilable Servitude

In *Waiting for Godot*, the dialectic which is unable to supersede itself because of senility is offset by a dialectic whose very historical structure is based upon an irreconcilable tension. The deterioration of Lucky and Pozzo is offset by the unfulfilled tragi-comic expectations of Didi and Gogo in their relation to Godot. In his discussion of "lordship and bondage," Hyppolite notes two irreconcilable forms of the master-slave dialectic—which we will see parallel Didi's and Gogo's relation to Godot—whose limitations Hegel, in the *Phenomenology*, tried to supersede by revising the dialectic of master and slave: the first form is that embodied in the Jewish people who, according to Hegel, remained enslaved to their law; and the second is that fostered in Kant's philosophy (Hyppolite *Genesis* 172). Hegel depicts the irreconcilability of the Jewish master-slave dialectic as a "slavish" and "mechanistic" devotion to a set of laws which, like Kantian ethics, prescribe and dictate behavior rather than cultivate a self-conscious understanding which would compel autonomous ethical behavior (Hegel *ETW* 68–69).23

In the *Early Theological Writings*, Hegel caustically denounces the limitations of Jewish faith as "ignoble," "lifeless," "unnatural," "horrifying," and "unholy" (Hegel *ETW* 68–69, 205). One might be tempted to dismiss Hegel's comments as anti-Semitic religious dogma, but Hyppolite and other critics have warned against doing this too quickly:

> It should not be overlooked that, from his earliest reflections . . . [Hegel] considered religion as a representation of human life, individual life, but above all of collective life, a sort of projection on the symbolic level of concrete human problems. Hegel's occasionally mystical language should not obscure his early positive preoccupation and concern with political, social, and even economic problems.[24]

The young Hegelians recognized quickly the argument which Hyppolite formulates here. Indeed, Marx, in a rather infamous essay "On the Jewish Question," equates Jews with commerce and implicitly argues that, to get rid of commerce, Jews must also be got rid of, both of which his essay posits as desirable.[25] The conflation of religious and social stereotypes in Hegel and post-Hegelian traditions carries over into the subtleties of Adorno's own historicizing of the master-slave dialectic in *Waiting for Godot*.

Within the Judaic religion the master-slave dialectic, rather than superseding itself, remains suspended in a negative tradition of allowing "no word that would alleviate the despair of all that is mortal"—much in the same manner that Godot's broken appointments with Didi and Gogo allow for no alleviation of their despair (Horkheimer and Adorno *DE* 23). The Jewish tradition places hope only within a fervent negative dialectic which is sustained by the denunciation of illusion, a rejection of attempts to invoke the infinite with the finite.[26] Adorno employs this negative tradition in combination with the philosophical implications of *Shoah.* He uses the un-superseded antinomy of the Jewish master-slave dialectic to reveal a demented synthesis in Hegel's logic and to suggest by implication that Hegel's fabricated resolution of Jewish antinomy leads to the attitudes that programmatically set out to negate the "negative" Jewish social element. Insofar as Adorno returns to a previous version of lordship and bondage in order to undermine its present form, his strategy coincides with the claim that "there is no other way to break out of history than regression" (Adorno *ND* 106).

Adorno's interpretation of Beckett's significance as a poet "after Auschwitz" is based in part upon the presence of the Jewish version of "lordship and bondage" in *Waiting for Godot.* Within this Jewish structure, Didi and Gogo cannot leave because they are emblematic of an unresolvable dialectic. Their departure would mean resolution. But this is not the only reason that their attempts to leave are unsuccessful. The presence of Lucky and Pozzo, a subsequent historical version of "lordship and bondage," encapsulates Didi and Gogo in the past. As a dialectical paradigm, Lucky and Pozzo ostensibly have superseded and progressed beyond Didi and Gogo. For the latter to leave would be equivalent to an irretrievable past walking into the present. The injustice of Didi's and Gogo's irretrievable state is arguably the motivation behind their attack on Lucky, whose act of reason is an incomprehensible account of some sort of death; it is also the motivation behind their later kicking Pozzo in the crotch when he returns after he has claimed that since "the tears of the world are a constant quantity," we should not "speak ill of our generation."[27]

In *Waiting for Godot,* these physical assaults are an aesthetic construct which pulls the unresolvable Jewish dialectic out of the distant past in order to address recent atrocities. This act is in itself a disruption of the syntheses upon which historical dialectics traditionally have been based. It is, furthermore, consistent with the general tenor of the play. When Didi exclaims, "To all mankind they were addressed, those cries for help still ringing in our ears," he indicts an entire subsequent generation who allowed the extermination of the people whose religious sentiment he and Gogo embody (Beckett *WG* 51). He is the necessary spokesperson in the play because Lucky and Pozzo are based upon a paradigm which, to follow Hegel, presumes itself to be an advance beyond the limitations of Jewishness and which, again to follow Hegel, presumes that the dialectical movement of history—even the atrocities of Auschwitz—is one of progress.

Although, as Adorno claims, Beckett seems "deliberately to have provoked" a charge of repetition, by juxtaposing the incessant waiting of Didi and Gogo with the gradual decay of Lucky and Pozzo he brings the very notion of progress and reconciliation under critical scrutiny (Adorno *AT* 45). In its most immediate sense, Beckettian repetition undermines dramatic *a priori,* but in terms of its philosophico-historical significance, the repetition undermines the presumed dialectical advance of civilization. In this respect Beckett's drama coincides with Adorno's own revision of dialectics:

> Dialectics is not only an advancing process but a retrograde one at the same time. To this extent, the picture of the circle describes it correctly. The concept's unfoldment is also a reaching back, and synthesis is the definition of the difference that perished, "vanished," in the concept. . . . Only in the accomplished synthesis, in the union of contradictory moments, will their difference be manifested (Adorno *ND* 157).

Adorno's reference to the retrograde inherent to dialectics provides a philosophical account which explains the presence of Didi and Gogo in *Waiting for Godot.* Insofar as they embody a rejection of attempts to invoke the infinite with the finite, so too do they embody a rejection of the Universal or Absolute which Hegel defends when he blames Jewish sufferings on the Jews because they lack "the spirit of beauty" and because they will not "appease" their fate "by reconciliation" (Hegel *ETW* 200).

While the crimes of Nazi Germany annihilate any basis for a belief in positive history (and thus preclude synthesis), these same crimes precipitate a retrogression in the structure of dialectics, a return to the original structure of the master-slave dialectic as it appeared in Hegel's *Early Theological Writings.* This retrogression in turn challenges the historical manifestations of synthesis which caused difference to "perish" rather than creating a union that accommodated contraries. And it is in this challenge to synthesis that the contrast between Didi's and Gogo's relation to Godot, and Lucky's and Pozzo's relation to each other attains perhaps its most ironic turn against Hegel: When Hegel blames the Jews for their own suffering because they will not "appease" their fate "by reconciliation," the reconciliation which he is talking about is an assimilation to the community at large—something he considers to be a positive advance over Jewish identity and belief. Yet when one considers the respective qualitative states of Didi and Gogo and then Lucky and Pozzo, it quickly becomes evident that, in their unresolved relationship to Godot, Didi and Gogo lay the foundation for the only instances of personal interaction (their interaction with one another) that even remotely resemble a sense of community. In other words, Didi and Gogo have a community that results from rather than being obstructed by their dialectical impasse, i.e., their unresolvable relation to Godot.

The dialectical retrogression, furthermore, unlocks the world of Beckett's comedy. As Anders has noted, the humor of clowns derives in part from a metaphysical ahistoricism which allows them to treat the existent as non-existent and vice-versa (Anders 217–18). Beckett employs this strategy with tragi-comic effects. The retrieval of Didi and Gogo from the past exposes the present conceptual structures of history to be a bad and vicious joke, to be a means of treating the existent as non-existent. Indeed, Adorno argues the identical point in the opening pages of *Negative Dialectics* where, in order to denote the pernicious silliness of Hegel's Absolute knowledge, he adopts a Kantian line (which, coincidentally, is implicated in Hegel's rejection of Jewish law). He argues that though every "un-naive thinker knows how far he remains from the object of his thinking," the necessity to "talk as if he had it entirely . . . . brings him to the point of clowning" (Adorno *ND* 14).

A graphic illustration of Adorno's concerns regarding the lethal implications of such philosophical "clowning" emerges in the source to which he attributes the clowns in Beckettian drama. Adorno notes that Beckett's clowns were often modelled on the "the slapstick comedy of the early cinema" (Adorno *AT* 121). Just as traditional, non-experimental cinema often uses splicing and editing in order to construct the illusion of a social universal from a single situation, so too do the demands of philosophy necessitate that thinkers construct "an entirety." The dangers of philosophical constructions are the dangers Adorno observes in cinematic illusions. Witness his comments on Chaplin's films: "*The Great Dictator* loses all satirical force and becomes obscene when a Jewish girl can hit a line of storm-troopers on the head with a pan without being torn to pieces. For the sake of political commitment, political reality is trivialized: which then reduces the political effect."[28] The critique of Chaplin's film—especially with its allusion to the dismemberment of a young Jewish woman—coincides with Adorno's arguments on the barbarism seething beneath the pretense of Absolute knowledge.[29] Adorno maintains that the laughter initiated by Beckett's clownish characters ought to suffocate laughter because it emerges in a situation which no longer has "any place for reconciliation," i.e., no place for synthesis or universality. (This may explain why Beckett calls his play a "tragi-comedy.") It is the clowning itself that serves as a unifying principle for Didi and Gogo and Lucky and Pozzo—clowning in the sense that juxtaposing these two forms of the master-slave dialectic can only be achieved, as Anders indirectly notes, with the help of a metaphysical ahistoricism. Beneath the clowning irreconcilability remains.[30]

The clowning is offset by the play's lack of closure. The fact that Beckett's work begins all over again rather than closing (Adorno *AT* 212) reflects an historical situation that harks back to the master-slave dialectic in its first form in Hegel, in the form of the Jewish believer and his/her relation to God. Thus in the aftermath of death camps and *Shoah*, the historical regresses both in terms of dialectical method and in terms of evolution beyond barbarity. Dialectics regresses back to an un-superseded negation, Jewish resistance to assimilation. Barbarity resides in the presumption of a progressive resolution, a positive history no longer tenable after World War II. Barbarity also resides in the presumption that the "Jewish" version of the master-slave dialectic was superseded in the first place.

Irreconcilable Configurations

In *Minima Moralia* Adorno argues that historicism needs to address the "waste products and blind spots that have escaped . . . [historical] dialectics" (Adorno *MM* 151). This call, which is in response to Benjamin's claim that history needed to be rewritten from the standpoint of the vanquished, is in one respect a history of the demise of both critical opposition and dissonance.[31] A history of waste and blindness inverts the subordination of the particular to the universal so as to expose the regressive tyranny of posited universals. Such a history records how the universal serves as a crippling restriction on the particular or the dissonant. In that dialectics has never derived its universals from the entirety of the particulars, waste and blindness are unavoidable.[32] The wasted are unsalvageable, and the blind deprived of vision. Both are ravaged, and their history is, like the subtitle to *Minima Moralia*, a reflection on "a damaged life." The "waste products and blind spots" of history are historically dissonant or negative elements within an order that eventually triumphed over them.

For Adorno, vanquished dissonance is most apparent in the history of the Jews. Their history underscores "the dual relationship of progress to cruelty and liberation" (Horkheimer and Adorno *DE* 169). Jewish history underlies Adorno's belief that rather than respecting the integrity of the particulars, universal history negates it. In terms of the Enlightenment, dissonance manifests itself in the incompatibility of Jewishness with the demands of assimilation. This incompatibility is two-sided: it results first of all from a denial of the vast diversity within the Jewish community, from the stereotype in Enlightenment philosophy and Nazi ideology that all Jews are alike. Secondly, it results from the inflexible adherence of the Jews to their own divergent forms of life. Adorno defends this inflexibility. It is also affirmed in Beckett's uncompromising resistance to a closure in *Waiting for Godot* and in the tension that exists between the dialectics represented by Lucky and Pozzo and by Didi's and Gogo's relation to Godot. The former are emblematic of the dialectic of Enlightenment which was so brutal to the latter. The Jews are the painful reminders of the shadows of "cruelty" that accompanied the Enlightenment because the assimilation demanded of the Jews neutralized (rather than tolerated) Jewishness. Rather than assimilating their values to those of the dominant order, the Jews expected an order which would accommodate them.[33] These expectations proved be disastrous because the Jews were not "in command."[34]

Adorno's embrace of Beckett's uncompromising negation presumes that "the seriousness of unswerving negation" lies in its implicit criticism of the way things are (Adorno *ND* 159–60). As Martin Jay argues: "The Jews . . . by their very refusal to be assimilated, represent an obstacle to the total integration of the 'administered world' or 'one-dimensional society', as Marcuse was to call it" (Jay *Permanent Exiles* 99–100). Beckett shares this notion of implied criticism with the position that the Jews had in relation to Enlightenment philosophies. Neither can initiate a positive synthesis, and both constitute an unresolved opposition, a dissonance, within an order that forcibly subsumes them. In short, the implied negation is negated.

In Beckett's case, the stakes are clearly different: the inability of aesthetic negation to initiate a positive sublation is by no means as catastrophic as negating (exterminating) the existence of a people whose identity and lives implicitly refuse to sanction "things as they are" (Adorno *ND* 159).[35] But Beckett does articulate that catastrophe. In fact, his ineffectiveness in initiating a positive synthesis is the direct result of the historic attempt to negate (exterminate) European Jewry.[36] The logic of this argument is that the negation of negation is an appropriation that incapacitates negation as a positive critical force.[37] Dissonance in Beckett cannot overcome the vanquished dissonance of the Jews.[38]

On the one hand, Beckett's drama is comparable to the revolutionary implications of Schoenberg's atonality (Adorno *AT* 29). A conceptual parallel joins atonality and dissonance. The fate of musical keys which were once fresh and untrodden is also the fate of words. Beckett is irresistible because, as Adorno writes, he abandons himself "to the process of disillusionment that has devoured the traditional concept of the poetic" (24). He circumvents trodden discourse. On the other hand, dissonance too has suffered irreparable decline.[39] One can speak of parallels between atonality and dissonance, between legitimate Jewish inflexibility and Beckett's "unswerving negation." However, history has so disjointed these parallels that even as a history of the vanquished, to follow Benjamin, they cannot serve as a rallying cry.[40] After Auschwitz, the individual's claim of dissonance or autonomy has become incredible (Adorno TUE 127). It is no longer possible for Jewish identity to remain what it once was. In one respect, this incredibility coincides with Hegel's own interpretation of the "struggle unto death," which precedes the master-slave dialectic. While death is certainly a possibility in the struggle, those who survive have "put an end to their consciousness in its alien setting of natural existence, that is to say, they put an end to themselves and are done away with as *extremes* wanting to be *for themselves*, or to have an existence of their own."[41] Unfortunately, the twentieth-century elimination of "*extremes*" has tended to occur in the darkest shadows of Hegelian idealistic discourse. The events of history not only involved a brutal systematic attempt to "do away with" Judaism, but, in the aftermath of this attempt, Jewishness can no longer "have an existence of . . . [its] own"; it has been robbed forever of an identity that is autonomous from the attempt to destroy it. No positive reconciliation exists between the death of Jewish "unswerving negation" and the risk of life, which Hegel argues is prerequisite to "recognition as an independent self-consciousness" (Hegel *PHS* 114).

Jewishness is now defined not by its resistance to assimilation, but by the systemic attempt to annihilate, i.e., negate, Jewry. In short, the position of Jewish identity after Auschwitz is like a photographic negative to the conception of identity which Butler has recently expressed in positive Hegelian terms: "we come to see how the 'difference' between consciousness and its object becomes the ground for a new identity" (Butler *Subjects* 44). For Hegel, this new identity is an essential step on the road to "Self-Certainty" and ultimately to "Absolute Knowledge."[42] For Adorno and the survivors of the Holocaust, for whom Auschwitz is an unavoidable object of consciousness, this identity is enmeshed in the question "whether after Auschwitz you can go on living—[and] especially whether one who escaped by accident, one who by rights should have been killed, may go on living" (Adorno *ND* 363). In that Adorno claims that Beckett has formulated the only fitting response to the concentration camps (380), the only possible answer to this essentially unanswerable question is: "I can't go on, I'll go on."[43]

To write a history of waste and blindness controverts any claim that after the defeat of dissonance, i.e., its negation, positive synthesis is possible. Stated theoretically, the dominant order's response to "unswerving negation" is the provocation leading to the formation of negative dialectics, which, like a history of waste and blindness, is a method for exposing cheated, irretrievable possibility (Adorno *ND* 52-53). Historically, the events of the Second World War demand a reassessment of the basic logic of dialectics: the negation of negation can no longer be considered a positive. Interestingly enough, Adorno second-guesses his critics and acknowledges that his rejection of the positivity of the "negation of negation" violates "the vital nerve of Hegel's logic," a violation which according to that logic would bring dialectics to a standstill. He acknowledges that without the positivity of negating negation, the Hegelian "system would unquestionably fall" (160–61). But the empirical substance of dialectics exposes the positivity of the Hegelian double negative to be anachronistic, regressive. "After Auschwitz," Adorno argues, "our feelings resist any claim of the positivity of existence as sanctimonious, as wronging the victims" (361). Hegelian logic would somehow have to place Auschwitz within a moment of the positive movement of history. There is no such positive moment, and, for Adorno, the avoidance of meaning in Beckett circumvents the barbarity of suggesting that there is.

This same avoidance of meaning circumvents a euphemistic protest against the events of *Shoah*. If such a protest were to be "genuine," it would need, as Adorno says, a knowledge of "what is incommensurate with all experience," a knowledge that in its Absolute and unappropriated form is tantamount to death (Adorno TUE 123; *ND* 362). Adorno argues that Beckett achieves his circumventions through "the ritual of clowns, whose babbling becomes nonsensical by presenting itself as sense" (Adorno TUE 138). In this self-negating ritual, silence emerges, a silence which acknowledges "the violence of the unspeakable," and which locates itself as an "incomprehensibility" of the Holocaust (123).

When, following Adorno, Lüdke paraphrases the general structure of *Waiting for Godot*, he argues that Lucky and Pozzo are the "carriers" of the dialectic who in their "senile" and "demented" form stray past two (Didi and Gogo), who specifically have fallen out of history in order to show what history was and what it has become (Lüdke 146). Although Lüdke's argument is problematic because it does not recognize that Didi and Gogo are also "carriers" of the dialectic, on a more subtle and perhaps coincidental level the argument makes a major contribution toward understanding the affinity between Beckett and Adorno: the spacio-temporal relations which Lüdke observes in *Waiting for Godot* raise questions concerning the position of Beckett and Adorno once the master-slave dialectic comes unraveled. In that Didi's and Gogo's relation to Godot is both the catalyst of this unraveling and a prototype of the dialectic they undercut, *Waiting for Godot* ends on an awkward historical note. It appears to undercut the historical validity of dialectical methodology by reinstating an even older form of the dialectic, by reinstating a dialectical tension whose moment of realization, like philosophy itself, has passed (Adorno *ND* 3).

Didi and Gogo represent the previously un-superseded, the wasted and presently unsublatable, the unresolvable dialectical tensions forcibly and irretrievably subsumed by the passage of time. They are historically eclipsed and encapsulated, and they cannot leave their historical moment because it did not facilitate their realization. What finally distinguishes their position from the historical present represented in *Waiting for Godot* is the status of that signified by Godot. In Hegelian fashion, the play dislodges the non-transmutability of the Jewish Law and Lord and supplants it with unsublatability of barbarism and the Holocaust. Although Adorno argues that "art works signal the possibility of the non-existent," these signals are not so much guiding beacons as they are indicators of past possibilities that are condemned to remain "unreal" (Adorno *AT* 192). If freedom is "to come to pass at all," Adorno says, it lies somewhere in the un-plotted and unfamiliar realms beyond "lordship and bondage" and in the recognition not of the dialectics' resolution but of its expiration.

4

The Lexicon of Music: Adorno, the Philosophy of Music, and Eliot's *Four Quartets*

The year after having published the last two poems of the collection that would shortly appear as *Four Quartets*, T.S. Eliot delivered a thematically related lecture at Glasgow University entitled "The Music of Poetry" (1942).[1] As the title suggests, the lecture explored the musical dimensions of poetry or how poetry is like music. Roughly fifteen years after Eliot's lecture, Theodor Adorno, in a related essay entitled "Music and Language: A Fragment" (1956), explored the converse of this relation, viz., the linguistic dimensions of music or how music is like language.[2] The two essays are related by the conceptual parallels in the initial attributes that Eliot and Adorno assign to the contrary targets of their comparisons: the attributes which Eliot assigns to music Adorno assigns to language. Close examination of the complementary aspects of these two essays offers valuable theoretical insight into the aesthetic tensions between poetry and music in *Four Quartets*.[3]

In an effort to explain the historical relation that poetry or music has to convention and tradition, both Eliot and Adorno liken their respective objects of inquiry (language and music) to the dynamics of the other art form (music and language). From their contrary positions, both Adorno and Eliot assert that significance (in either language or music) derives from a compound of temporal sequence and historical residue. In the published version of Eliot's lecture, Eliot argues that, because the "musical pattern of sound" and "the secondary meanings of the words" which comprise a poem "are indissoluble and one," the primary function of "the music of poetry" is to circumvent the "allusiveness" of words and to facilitate a use of them that enables words to "insinuate the whole history of a language and a civilization" (Eliot "Music of Poetry" 26). Language is like music because its "musical pattern of sound," the sequence and repetition of sounds, effects meaning and insinuates previous meanings. Such insinuations, Eliot maintains, are historically determined by "the period in which" the poet finds him or herself. The musical component of poetry, he argues, resides "with the *changing* language of common intercourse" [my emphasis] and emerges in response to the stagnancy of "established conventions" (21; 28).

Whereas Eliot likens poetry to music in its response to "established conventions," Adorno argues that the relation of a musical composition to "established conventions" is that which makes music like language. In language, "established conventions" appear in the form of linguistic concepts, and music composition imitates language by responding to the "primitive concepts" which have emerged in "cadential progressions" or "stock melodic figures" (Adorno "Music and Language" 2). According to Adorno, music resembles the intentionality of language in its sequential internal structure and in the historically determined nature of an individual work's responses: "Everything becomes what it is in memory and in expectation through its physical contiguity with its neighbor and its mental connection with what is distant from it" (Adorno "Music and Language" 5). Music thus resembles language because the significance of chords in a musical composition parallels the significance of individual words in the context of works like poetry: both chords and words are mediated by the formal context in which they occur.[4] Furthermore, both the chords of a musical composition and the words of a work of poetry carry residues of previous usages that influence meaning and significance. With the references to "physical contiguity" and "mental connections," Adorno posits the individual moments of a work of music as aesthetic intersections of internal temporal sequence and historical response.

While Adorno argues that "physical contiguity" and "mental connections" in music make music like language, Eliot argues the converse and, by speaking of the "music of a word," asserts that language is like music:

> The music of a word is, so to speak, at a point of intersection: it arises from its relation first to the words immediately preceding and following it, and indefinitely to the rest of its context; and from another relation, that of its immediate meaning in that context to all the other meanings which it has had in other contexts, to its greater or less wealth of association (Eliot "Music of Poetry" 25).

Although in this passage Eliot focuses on the temporal sequence of a "word" in its poetic "context" and on the word's relation to historical or residual meanings from previous contexts, the implicit suggestion of Eliot's analysis is that the sequential and historical influences on the meaning of words are what makes language like music: these influences are "the music of a word." From Eliot's perspective, then, *Four Quartets* is aptly titled because—as the coming arguments will show—its poetic structure specifically calls attention to "the music" of its words, i.e., to the semantic tension between their sequential and historical meanings. Even from Adorno's perspective, *Four Quartets* is aptly titled: the tension between sequential and historical meaning, highlights that dimension of music which is like language.

Despite the complementary arguments of Adorno and Eliot, the parallels between music and language are, according to Eliot, merely structural. He cites a hypothetical situation in which one is "deeply stirred by hearing the recitation of a poem in a language" which we not only do not understand but which turns out to be "gibberish and has no meaning." Confronted with the absence of meaning, one would be forced to concede, Eliot argues, that "this was no poem, it was merely an imitation of instrumental music" (Eliot "Music and Poetry" 22). Thus for all the parallels between music and language, the demarcation between the two in Eliot's essay gives meaning to language and ultimately withholds it from music. One might expect that Adorno would have trouble with so clear a distinction. Yet Adorno's essay culminates precisely in the implications of this distinction.

Although the presence of temporal sequence and historical residue in music leads Adorno to claim that music is like language because it may "be said to create lexical items" or what he calls "primitive concepts," the difference between music and language, Adorno concedes, is that "the identity of . . . musical concepts lay in their own nature and not in a signified outside them" (Adorno "Music and Language" 2). Music is largely a self-referential system, whereas language, Adorno argues, is structured around "intentionality," i.e., the attempt to represent phenomenal reality. In this respect, "Music and Language: A Fragment" echoes Eliot's claim that language has meaning and music does not. For Adorno, however, the absence in music of gestures toward a "signified outside" are not "gibberish" but a central aesthetic characteristic of modern music. Consider the arguments of *Philosophy of Modern Music* (1949), where Adorno praises Ernst Krenek's early compositions because his "music reveals itself in the antipode of verbal language." Based on this same praise, Adorno asserts that "the emancipation of music today is tantamount to its emancipation from verbal language."[5] While Adorno's conception of music is similar to Eliot's conception in "The Music of Poetry," his conception of language, on the other hand, problematizes language's "meaning" in a way obscured by the opposition that Eliot posits between language and music.

Though language intends a signified outside itself, music ironically likens itself to language, Adorno maintains, through its own disparity with it. Indeed, Adorno ends his short essay with the statement: "It is by distancing itself from language that . . . [music's] resemblance to language finds its fulfillment" (Adorno "Music and Language" 6). The fulfillment of music's "resemblance to language" in "distancing itself from language," like the "emancipation of music" from "verbal language," follows a specific logical pattern. First, the "distancing" is music's movement toward self-referentiality and away from intentionality or reference outside itself. Music, Adorno argues, "aspires to be a language without intention" (2). Secondly, the "emancipation of music" from "verbal language" denotes at one level a "distancing" of signified (the phenomenon of music) from signifier (verbal language). For Adorno, the "distancing" or slippage of the signified (music) away from its signifier (language) occurs as an historical evolution of music and ruptures the parity between music and its verbal signification. In its movement away from intentionality, music ironically likens itself to—as it simultaneously exposes—the referential shortcomings of language. As Peter Dews has observed: "Adorno sees language as directly dissecting and deforming reality, rather than as being the means whereby subjects communicate to each other about a reality which is nevertheless preserved in its non-identity."[6] With regard to music, the "deforming" occurs because the temporal evolution of language and music are not in sync.

For all the temporal structural parallels between music and language as systems, music and language are by no means synchronous in their historical evolution: the "constant alteration" of music and "the changing language of common intercourse" are discordant in their historical movements (Adorno *PMM* 56; Eliot "Poetry of Music" 21). The rupture between music and its verbal signification fulfills music's resemblance to language because it illuminates language's own predisposition for self-referentiality. Regardless, therefore, of whether one adopts Adorno's line that music is like language or Eliot's that language is like music, the final assertion of Adorno's essay establishes music and language as two parallel systems, while (logically) giving them no a point of intersection. Historical movement constantly collapses the bridge connecting signified (music) and signifier (language) into ruins.

One can summarize Adorno's conclusion as an inversion of his study of music's likeness to language. The final assertion of "Music and Language: A Fragment" implies that language is like music because language cannot signify music. The magnitude of this implication in terms of the addition it makes to the arguments that Eliot formulates in "The Music of Poetry" should not be underestimated. Although Eliot cites the need of poetry to maintain "its contact with the changing language of common intercourse," this contact never interferes with the stagnancy of the conception of music in Eliot's essay, a conception that he himself acknowledges is without "much technical knowledge of musical form" (Eliot "Music of Poetry" 32). Nor does the contact interfere with the conception of music in the poetry that Eliot completed shortly before giving his lecture at Glasgow, viz., in *Four Quartets*.

Adorno's conclusion illuminates an insurmountable contradiction in the aesthetic composition of *Four Quartets*: the same "musical-verbal analogies" in "The Music of Poetry" and *Four Quartets* which, according to R.W. Flint, do not bring us "appreciably nearer enjoyment of the poems than if we had never heard of the string quartet," are, in their implications, radically at odds with the verbal allusions to or significations of music within the poems themselves.[7] While constituting a structural parallel with the historicity of language—an historicity explored not only in "The Music of Poetry" but also in *Four Quartets*—the influence of temporal sequence and historical residue as sources of "constant alteration" in music negates a stable, meaningful signification of music in words. Indeed, it is through the formal parallels with the structure of music that *Four Quartets* attempts to circumvent the "allusiveness" of music from its verbal signification. The "musical-verbal" analogies are thus a structural acknowledgement of the inadequacy of words and simultaneously an attempt to use structure and form to signify what words cannot.

The contradictory gesture at signification through the acknowledgement of its failure is, for Adorno, a signature of modern works of art and what connects them to the outside world. "The threshold of modern art," he argues, "grasps its own contradictions with such depth that they can no longer be arbitrated." Yet this modern perceptiveness is not only a source of resistance to arbitration; it is also the work's "evidence of the contradictions in the world in which it dwells" (Adorno *PMM* 125). On this point, Adorno and Eliot concur. "The Music of Poetry" argues that the structural parallel of language to music has two functions in poetry. It can "insinuate the whole history of a language *and a civilization*" [emphasis added] (Eliot "Music of Poetry" 26). Just as the influence of temporal sequence and historical residue disrupt, through "constant alteration," a stable, meaningful signification of music in words, so too do historical events and context disrupt the stability of accepted notions of progressive or teleological achievements of civilization.

With the assertion that the music of poetry insinuates both the "history of a language" and also of "a civilization," Eliot provides what in general terms is the poetic agenda of *Four Quartets*. While most directly concerned with the inability to represent music linguistically, the gesture at structural signification through the acknowledgement of linguistic failure evolves into an exploration of how the influence of historical events—namely the advent of World War II—negates the position of music as a meaningful and stable signifier of civilization and culture. Indeed, his assertion that the music of poetry "insinuate[s] the whole history of a language and a civilization" provides a rough outline of the development followed by the poems of *Four Quartets*: whereas in their contradictory gesture at signification (the reliance on form as a compensation for the inadequacies of language) the first two poems, "Burnt Norton" and "East Coker," represent language as being subject to historical decay and exhaustion, the contradictions of the outside world surface most forcefully in the last two poems. "The Dry Salvages" and "Little Gidding" challenge the historical stability of the form that the first poems resort to in an effort to circumvent the "allusiveness" of words. The two pairs of poems are thus in dialectical tension with one another: the latter accepting the conclusions of the first regarding language but questioning the solutions they offer, and the former challenging the latter two in their inability to escape from the language that they accept as inadequate.[8]

Musical Terminology, Self-Referentiality, and Form in "Burnt Norton"

"Burnt Norton" is marked by a growing skepticism regarding the stability of language's intention to signify an "outside world." The skepticism is particularly evident in the poem's references to music. The poem's aesthetic force emerges in a tension between its attempt to signify music and its increasing similarity to the self-referential lexicality of music that Adorno mentions in his essay. What is significant about this tension is that "Burnt Norton" exploits its self-referentiality in an implied imitation of the quartet form, which, as Keith Alldritt has argued, develops in a dialogue between four distinct voices.[9] Although the relation of the poem's form to the content of its poetic exploration does not become clear until the fifth movement of the poem, the sense in which this form carries a redemptive gesture is foreshadowed in the initial semantic positioning of music within the poem itself. The imitation of the quartet form occurs against the background of a poetic exploration that, through a focus on absence, non-realization, and negation, seeks redemption from the decaying influence of temporal passage. Music is at the center of this redemption. The poem positions the redemption within the discursive categories of absence and non-realization established in the poem's first movements. The imitation of the quartet form emerges thus as a consistent effort to circumvent the poem's own contradictions: the very words it uses in its association of absence and non-realization with redemption from time prove in fact to be subject to the same temporal decay from which the poem seeks release.

The first movement of "Burnt Norton" asserts conditions for redemption which presuppose that time is potentially both absent and present. Eliot posits the absence of time as the necessary condition for redemption when he formulates the syllogism: "If all time is eternally present / All time is unredeemable" (Eliot BN 5–6).[10] The logic of this syllogism implies that if some time is not "eternally present" and is absent, then some time may be redeemable. Though the syllogism does not logically demand more than a time that is occasionally absent, semantically the notion of redemption demands something more permanent. Consequently, Eliot emphasizes a hypothetical past, a "What might have been." This "What might have been" is the only time that is "eternally" absent and thus eligible as an enduring redemptive force against temporal passage.

When the initial temporal reflections give way to a new voice of a "thrush" who evokes a fanciful flight into the redemptive realms of the unrealized or the "What might have been," the significance that the poem's reflection on time has with regard to its appeals to music emerges on two levels. On one level the shift in voice is indicative, as Alldritt has noted, of the poem's imitation of the quartet form and introduces the second of "the four verbal roles which we hear" in each of the poems of *Four Quartets* (Alldritt 39). Secondly, the flight into the unrealized realms of "What might have been," which is signalled by a call to follow "the passage which we did not take / Towards the door we never opened / Into the rose-garden," includes the poems' first direct reference to music (BN 12–14). In that "Burnt Norton" associates "the rose-garden" with "What might have been" and "what might have been" with redeemable time, the presence of "unheard music in the shrubbery" of the "rose-garden" links music with the categories of absence, non-realization and redemption from time (27). In its explicit form, the link, as the coming arguments will show, ultimately proves incompatible with the logic of the poem itself, and in this respect the poem's inexplicit imitation of the quartet form serves as a default signifier for the inadequacies of the poem's explicit attempt to signify music through direct referential means.

While the semantic association of music with redemption may be more obvious than the actual imitation of the quartet form—which the poem initiates through the introduction of a new voice—the justification for the imitation follows from the consequences of the explicit (albeit fanciful) trek into the "rose-garden." The "thrush" who challenges us to follow the echoes of "what might have been" into a place where "unheard music [lingers] in the shrubbery" and who makes present the absent, never realized past, suddenly changes his initial invitation to "find them, them find" ("other echoes" in the garden) into a plea to "Go, go, go" because "human kind / Cannot bear very much reality" (BN 19; 42–43). In its reference to bearing "reality," the plea to depart emphasizes that if that which "might have been" becomes present, i.e., at hand, it too suffers the fate of that which actually "has been": it suffers, to borrow a phrase from Hugh Kenner, from "the impurities of personal presence."[11] The allusion to music in the "rose-garden" suffers these "impurities" because of the explicit signified presence it receives in the conjured image of the "rose-garden" experience. The presence subjects music to temporal passage and is at odds with the poem's association of redemption with absence.[12]

The "impurities of personal presence" of the "unheard music in the shrubbery" stand in contrast to the implied imitation of the quartet form. This implied imitation sustains its redemptive status precisely because as poetry it cannot explicitly become present as music; it remains always "What might have been." The relation between the poem's explicit allusion to music and the poem's unrealizable imitation of music is thus that of a "what has been" to a "What might have been," and this relation, which is based on a dialectic between content and form, offers an alternative to the explicit description of the "rose-garden" experience and its unredeemable descent from "What might have been" into "what has been" (BN 45). Yet the formal alternative occurs amid continued explicit efforts to achieve what "East Coker" later calls getting "the better of words" (Eliot EC 176).

Unlike the conjured image of the "rose-garden" experience in which the allusions to music refer to the determinant substance of the experience itself, the opening passage of the second movement employs musical terms as metaphorical constructs for the representation of a dialectic of movement and arrest—movement being associated with the unrealized and indeterminant (the "What might have been") and arrest with the realized and determinant (the "what has been").[13] Here in the second movement of the poem music is associated with a movement that contrasts with the experiential determinacy or fixity of the music in the "rose-garden." By speaking through musical terms rather than specifically referring to music, the second movement alludes to music without making music present. The second movement thus attempts to preserve the redemptive integrity of musical form from the corrupting influence of time. It not only links direct experience with determinacy but determinacy with stagnation and even death. Movement and music's association with it initially functions as a redemptive alternative to the temporal fixities of experience. The poem situates both movement and music in atemporal realms.

The strategy of associating music with a redemptive movement is reflected in the opposing tensions of the statement: "The trilling wire in the blood / Sings below inveterate scars" (BN 49–50). The allusion to "Sing[ing]" reinforces the sense in which "trilling" refers to the technical repetition of a musical note. But at the same time "trilling," as an adjective, is diametrically opposed to the term "inveterate." The former denotes that which flows and the latter that which is firmly established or habitual. The connection between musical technique and a state of flux recurs in the image of "the dance along the artery," "dance" serving as a metaphor for circulation (52). "Trilling," "Sing[ing]," "dance"—music in general—are thus associated with fluidity, life-blood and circulation. They are the negation of determinant experience and its association with habituation, stagnation, and a choking coagulation. The flowing implied by the "trilling" which "Sings" and also by "the dance along the artery" emerges as a dialectical contrast to "inveterate scars," which are fixed, visible reminders of what the poem posits as the corrupting effects of determinant experience.

In this metaphorical use of musical terminology, the second movement of "Burnt Norton" partially overlaps with what Adorno calls modern music's validity "as an eruptive revelation of negative experience" (Adorno PMM 37). The overlap is perhaps most readily evident in Adorno's coincidental repetition of Eliot's constructed opposition between music and coagulation. For Eliot and for Adorno—who argues that modern music embodies a challenge to the "mechanical" adherence to "congealed formulae"—the metaphorical opposition posits music as a negative phenomenon with the redeeming properties of a solvent (Adorno "Music and Language" 2). For both writers, this negative conception of music opposes fixed previous conceptions of history. As Ferenc Feher has commented: for Adorno, "the 'attitude' of music (music being a primarily temporal art) to the process of time is the most significant criterion in terms of its relationship to the concept of progress."[14] For Adorno, the attitude of music "to the process of time" paradoxically initiates progress in music by historicizing the criteria by which historical progress in music has been measured. Modern music thereby serves a redemptive function by dissolving the "congealed formulae" or reified categories through which music has previously been perceived. A comparable attitude is visible in the rhetorical strategies governing the second movement of "Burnt Norton."

The second movement of the poem positions music beyond the "congealed formulae" which it initially portrays in the peculiar opening "Garlic and sapphires in the mud / Clot the bedded axle-tree" (BN 47–48). The poem attempts to circumvent the "clot[ting]" from a vantage point that rhetorically occupies a position comparable to that which Adorno assigns modern music in its relation to the "congealed formulae" of music material. After building the opposition between "trilling" and "inveterate," the poem claims to position us "above the moving tree," from which position it is also "above" the contraries of "trilling" and "inveterate" (56). Indeed, from this vantage point the poem not only supersedes the "clot[ting of] the bedded axle-tree," it attempts to withdraw music altogether from its dialectical relationship with the "inveterate scars." The stakes here are nothing less than procuring a space for music that is entirely free from the mediations of determinant experience, mediations that in fact govern how music is perceived.

These stakes are most evident in the poem's transition from an image of a "dance along the artery"—which contrasts with "clot[ting]," coagulation, or arrest—to a dance "At the still point of the turning world" (BN 52; 62). This new "dance" is unlike "the dance along the artery" in that its locus is specifically described as "neither arrest nor movement" (64). Conceptually, the negation of "arrest" and "movement" doubles as a negation of the closely related antinomies of "inveterate" and "trilling." Since the "dance along the artery" is associated with the movement of "trilling," the poem's transition to "the dance" "at the still point of the turning world" signals an attempt to pull music out of previously conceived temporal spheres. The attempt is openly acknowledged. Whereas "the unheard music in the shrubbery" of the "rose-garden" arises as part of an experiential alternative to "what has been," "the dance" in the poem's second movement preserves the integrity of the "what might have been" because the poet is unwilling to qualify it with a "where," a "how long" or a placement "in time" (68–69).[15]

Though not explicitly assigned to a temporal or spacial position, what links "the dance" of the second movement to the "unheard music in the shrubbery" of the first movement of "Burnt Norton" is the presumption that the presence of spacial and temporal particulars places music within an experiential, phenomenal realm that is the domain of temporal passage. The poet's unwillingness to qualify "the dance" with a "where" or a "how long" assumes an absolute and separate realm of music that precedes temporal experience. In this respect, neither the first nor the second movement of "Burnt Norton" conceptualizes music itself as historical substance when explicitly referring to it. Both presume that music will remain structurally intact even if separated from temporal and spacial particulars. Furthermore, both also presume that language itself signifies music in a state before temporal experience. They presume that their own discourse refers to a stable, unchanging and ideal order toward which our experiences aspire but always fail to attain. This failure is why the concept of the "Here" in the third movement of the poem is described as "a place of disaffection," and the "*there*" of "the dance" is described as a "release from action and suffering" (90; 72).[16] With these two presumptions, the representation of music in "Burnt Norton" finds a tenuous resemblance to music even as the overlap with modern music's validity "as an eruptive revelation of negative experience" begins to break down (Adorno *PMM* 37).

For Adorno, the habituated or "inveterate" presumptions that modern music negates are those which presume music to be comprised of an ahistorical or natural relation of sounds—in other words, those which like "Burnt Norton" presume a structural and absolute existence of music prior to its placement in time. Modern music's negations occur in a self-acknowledged historicity, in a critical rejection of any conception that does not inseparably ground the material of music in historical substance. By admitting that its own structure is historical and by foreshadowing its own inevitable decline into "congealed formulae," modern music feels "the shattering effects of that very process of enlightenment in which it participates and upon which its own progress depends" and strikes at the previously conceived course of the progress of music itself (Adorno *PMM* 13). "Herald[ing] its own demise," modern music signals an end to the reified, illusory history of music (10). To follow Adorno's arguments, modern music is thus the negation of the referential conception of music explicitly perpetuated in "Burnt Norton."

With regard to music, the language of the second movement of "Burnt Norton" intends "a signified outside" itself, but inasmuch as this intent seeks "a signified" that precedes and remains unaffected by experience, signifier and signified diverge (Adorno "Music and Language" 2). Music is no absolute. Severed from their "signified outside," the musical terms "Trilling," "sing[ing]" and "dance" take a self-referential turn. Their "identity," like the rudimentary concepts of music itself, lies in what Adorno calls "their own nature," a nature that is determined by the lexical system in which they appear (2). They do not signify musical forms but rather a more general notion of a redemptive universal that is masqueraded in referential particulars. To follow the arguments of Ronald Bush, they attempt "to get '*beyond* music'," and are consequently "constantly in danger of reifying."[17] Beyond the explicit musical signifiers resides an absent, implied absolute (a "what might have been"). Yet while the chasm between the poem's musical terms and their "signified outside" radically undercuts the explicit referential content of the poem, it simultaneously strengthens the poem's structural relation to the quartet form.

Keith Alldritt has argued that in the second movement of the "Burnt Norton," the poem continues a structural imitation of the quartet form by introducing the last two of the poem's four voices. He identities them according to tone, labeling the first a "seer" and the second a "conversationalist" (Alldritt 42). Whether the dialogues of such voices are enough to support a structural analogy between poetic and musical forms is certainly debatable. But the self-referentiality of the musical terminology in "Burnt Norton" lends credence to Alldritt's claims. It is indicative of language's similarity to music. As Adorno has noted, music's self-referentiality, while initially distancing music from language, ultimately fulfills music's "resemblance to language" (Adorno "Music and Language" 6). Conversely, "Burnt Norton's" self-referentiality builds its resemblance to music. But the resemblance contrasts vividly with the absolute conception of music and of signification posited in the poem's content. By using language as the medium and substance for an imitation of music, the poem calls attention to the fact that music constructs itself out of "lexical items" whose substance derives from a combination of (historical) references to previous usage and of the items' contextual (temporal) sequence in the system where they appear (2). Rather than being fixed or absolute, music material thus emerges essentially as historical substance—not only "in time" but comprised of time. Indeed, the image of music that is suggested by the poem's form undercuts the poem's referential content. It reinforces the chasm between signified music and the poem's signifiers of music while simultaneously offering an alternative representation of music. This alternative not only contrasts with the poem's explicit references to music, but inasmuch as it rejects an absolute conception of music, it also rejects the poem's conception of a stable and absolute realm of signification. The use of language as the substance of its imitation of music challenges the "congealed formula" of the poem's references to music.

When in the fifth movement of "Burnt Norton," the poem refers to music for the final time, the reference makes a last ditch effort at redeeming the stable and absolute realm of signification that the implied imitation of the quartet form disrupts. Rather than placing music within a conjured experience or metaphorically using musical terminology, the poem now explicitly acknowledges *in content* the parallels between language and music that the imitation of the quartet implicitly makes *in form.* This acknowledgement is evident in the parallelism of the phrase "Words move, music moves." But the parallelism is followed by an emphatic reassertion of the structural relation of "words" and "music" prior to the mediation of temporal and spacial particulars. The movement of "words" and "music" occurs, according to the poem, "Only in time" (Eliot BN 137–38). In effect, the explicit reassertion of an absolute realm preceding temporality polarizes the poem's content and form, the former positing music and its signification as ahistorical absolutes and the latter positing music and signification as historical substance.

When the poem subsequently claims that "Only by the form, the pattern, / Can words or music reach / The stillness," the agenda of the polarization of content and form becomes clear (BN 140–42). The "form" or "pattern" of "Burnt Norton" imitates the structure of a quartet and, using language, thereby reveals the historicity of musical material. As a more adequate representation of the temporal structure of music, the poem's formal imitation of the quartet debunks the presumptions governing the poem's explicit references to music. But in doing so, it sets these presumptions within the category that the poem values most, that of the "what might have been." Inasmuch as the poem's explicit references to music presuppose characteristics in music that the poem's form negates, the negation also redeems the content from the "impurities of personal experience."[18] For the music signified in content is a music that "might have" but has never "been" and a music that resides in an ideal, indeed unrealizable, realm. This imaginary music maintains the unrealized potential which is signified by the poem's idiosyncratic usage of the term "stillness" and by the "Chinese jar['s]" allusion to Keats (Eliot BN 143). As George Wright has noted, the music in "Burnt Norton," like "the pipers on Keat's Grecian urn," lacks "pitch, volume, timbre, and accent," but "such melodies, Keats tells us, are 'sweeter' than the ones we actually hear, because it is 'to the spirit' that they 'Pipe . . . ditties of no tone'."[19]

Even the poem's closing explicit acknowledgement of the frailty of words figures into the uncorrupted image of music associated with the redemptive realms of "what might have been." The claims that "Words strain, / Crack and sometimes break" and that they "slip, slide, perish, / Decay with imprecision" are the necessary prerequisites for the music signified in the poem's content (BN 149–52). If words did not "strain," "break" or "decay with imprecision," the redemption from time which the poem seeks in its explicit allusions to music would not be possible. For it is in the "slip[ping] and "slid[ing]" that the signifiers of music diverge from the historical object of reference (music) and assume new significations, significations such as those that "Burnt Norton" assigns to the words ostensibly referring to music. In the failure of the poem's language to signify the specifics of the world outside of itself, it actually becomes more and more like music. Just as Adorno claims that "It is by distancing itself from language that . . . [music's] resemblance to language finds its fulfillment," so too does "Burnt Norton" come closer to resembling music the more its intended signification of an "outside" fails and the more its self-referentiality increases (Adorno "Music and Language" 6).

The Aging of Musical Material in "East Coker"

As is the case with each of the *Four Quartets*, the signification of music in "East Coker" emerges in a play between content and form: between the poem's direct allusions to music and the poem's implied formal status as one of four quartets. The "music / Of the weak pipe and the little drum" which accompanies "dancing" is offset by the volume's title (*Four Quartets*) which, as Robert Schweik has noted, refers to "a form to which the work . . . [is] in some way structurally related" albeit in a problematic and ambiguous manner (Eliot EC 25–27).[20] Schweik observes that, while implying "some kind of correlation between the structure" of the poems and the quartet form, the function of Eliot's titular reference as a guide to interpreting the individual poems is at the very least uncertain (Schweik 44). Amid the uncertainties of these correlations, "East Coker" serves an inverted function. The internal dynamics of its content serve as a guide to interpreting the historical status of Eliot's titular reference to the quartet form. Indeed, as the coming arguments will show, when "East Coker" suddenly modulates from the term "dancing" to the old English "daunsinge," it accentuates the historicity of the musical material in *Four Quartets* and exposes the temporal and historical limitations of the quartet form (EC 27; 29).

This accentuation of the historicity of musical material distinguishes "East Coker" from "Burnt Norton." While "Burnt Norton" situates music in the unrealized realms of "what might have been" or forgoes temporal placement altogether, "East Coker" equates music with aging substance (Eliot BN 6). In "Burnt Norton," "music" and "dance" signify an absolute beyond temporal experience. There is the "unheard music hidden in the shrubbery" of the "rose-garden" or the "dance" "at the still point of the turning world" (27; 62–63). In "East Coker," "music" and "dance" converge in a single image that, while reinvoking the attempt in "Burnt Norton" to associate music with the absolute, announces an overlooked historicity.[21] Subtly challenging the association of music with the absolute, "music" and "dance" in "East Coker" supplant what was mistakenly perceived to be an "open field" (EC 24). The "open field" is not empty at all but filled with traces of music and dancers from bygone days—which the poet tells us "if you do not come too close, / on a summer midnight, you can hear" (25–26).

Inasmuch as the "music / Of the weak pipe and the little drum" announces the unnoticed historical layers of the "open field," it functions like the image of the "early owl" whose appearance at dusk when "the sultry light / Is absorbed, not refracted, by grey stone" denotes a fleeting moment of clarity (EC 20–23). Like the owl whose appearance marks the exposure of a "Shuttered," preexisting "deep lane" that "insists on the direction" of that which "passes," the "music / Of the weak pipe and the little drum" seeks a redemption from time that does not appeal to absolutes but rather is contingent upon a revelation of the unnoticed "insist[ing]" influences of the past which determine the present (15–23).[22] The agenda of the "music" and "dance" on "that open field" is thus primarily negative: by making explicit the residues of the past, "the dancing around the bonfire" seeks to subvert the influence that the residues have so long as they remain unobserved (28).

While the imitation of the quartet form in "Burnt Norton" occurs against the background of a poetic exploration that seeks redemption from its own temporal decay, "East Coker" critically responds to this exploration by refocusing attention onto the unnoticed but continued presence of the past in the present. Whereas "Burnt Norton" attends to the tension between "what has been" and "what might have been," "East Coker" explores the tension between "what has been" and what will, can, or might be. This shift in focus emphasizes that, although subject to the altering forces of time, previous experiences (and words) affect and shape the present. What "Burnt Norton" laments as temporal decay and loss, "East Coker" posits as the substance of what will and will not be. What "Burnt Norton" would redeem from the decaying passage of time, "East Coker" argues, is always already comprised with the residues of the past.

Nowhere is the "insist[ing]" effect and the need for an excavation of the residues of the past better illustrated than in the "Lifting heavy feet in clumsy shoes, / Earth feet, loam feet" of the dancers (EC 36–37). The image of "the dance," whose integrity "Burnt Norton" attempted to preserve by never qualifying it with a "where," a "how long," or a placement "in time," appears in "East Coker" constricted by ground that clings to the dancers' feet (BN 68–69).[23] As is the case with the dance itself, the "loam feet" recall the temporal arguments of the previous poem. "Loam" is a more aged and solidified version of the "mud" and "sodden floor" which in "Burnt Norton" signified the very temporal process which "the dance" is supposedly positioned "above." In "East Coker" not only does the "loam," like "the sodden floor" in "Burnt Norton," signify a gradual aging and solidification, but, by attaching the loam to the shoes of the dancers, "East Coker" emphasizes how previous decay "insists" on the direction and nature of the dance whether "here / Or there or elsewhere" (EC 49–50). The image of the dancers with their "loam feet" thus contests the presumption in "Burnt Norton" that redemption from time can be obtained by an elimination of temporal particulars.

In *Aesthetic Theory*, Adorno argues: "If an artist were to root out all the time-related facets of his work, retaining only what he thinks is timeless, he could not thereby hope to achieve duration because he would be sacrificing the ground on which duration is constituted (Adorno *AT* 41)."[24] The "loam feet" of "East Coker" exemplify a glaring figurative attempt to reinstate the temporal "ground on which duration is constituted." Yet these "clumsy shoes," because they are figurative, do not possess the "time-related facets" that the image theoretically and metaphorically defends. They merely allude to a temporal stratification that first emerges in the poem's sudden shift to archaic forms of English: "daunsinge," "matrimonie," "necessarye coniunction," "eche," and "Whiche betokeneth concorde" (EC 38; 29–33). The presence of this antiquated language in the construction of the rustic celebration of music and dance highlights the "time-related facets" of language itself and counters the separation of language from the changing historical events and experiences that it signifies.[25]

The use of old English in "East Coker" calls attention to how the aging of language within its own system parallels music's attempt "to deal with the antinomies of . . . handed-down musical material."[26] No longer merely referring to different periods, the language of "East Coker" becomes self-referential and reveals its own temporal stages. This self-historicization is especially evident in the juxtaposition of the two terms "dancing" and "daunsinge." The modulation to old English sets the obscured historicity of the term "dancing" into critical relief.

Although the juxtaposition of the related terms implies that, like its historical precursor, "dancing" too will succumb to decay and obsolescence, the shift from "dancing" to "daunsinge" indicates more importantly that the term "dancing" is as incapable of replacing "daunsinge" as the term "daunsinge" is of replacing "dancing." On the one hand, the term "daunsinge" refers to historical conditions that its being replaced by "dancing" acknowledges are now archaic. On the other hand, as much as "dancing" signifies some intended musical form, it also unavoidably signifies the exhaustion, decay and ruin of the term "daunsinge." In a manner of speaking, the shift from the earlier to the latter term does not recall a mere succession or "rise and fall" (EC 2). Rather, "daunsinge" clings to "dancing" like "loam" to the feet of rustic dancers, "insist[ing]" on the direction of its signification. The term "dancing" is predicated upon the decay of its etymological predecessor and always already signifies "daunsinge's" exhaustion and ruin. Consequently, it cannot signify what "daunsinge" once did because it always first signifies the historical decline of "daunsinge" as a category of perception. Temporally, "dancing" is broader in scope and thus cannot reduce its significations to the limitations that, in superseding "daunsinge," it intends to overcome. Like "the deep lane [that] insists on the direction / Into the village," "dancing's" intended supersession of "daunsinge" "insists" upon a path of signification that steers it perpetually away from unqualified reference to the conditions signified by the old English form.

This then is the moment of clarity in the conjured image on "that open field" in "East Coker," the moment when the previously "shuttered" and "insist[ing]" influences of the past are revealed: the inability of "dancing" to circumvent the signification of the ruin of its etymological predecessor impedes its own adequacy as a signifier or category of perception for anything except the passing away of things in time. As a signifier, "dancing" has in this respect much in common with what Adorno calls music's self-referential "lexical" characteristics, effectively only signifying temporal passage within its own etymological system, but failing—in its gesture toward an "outside"—to signify a unified concept of dance or music that is not placed "in time" (Adorno "Music and Language: A Fragment" 2).[27]

Although its full implications have not been developed, critics have already forged the link between "East Coker's" explicit but problematic references to music and the poem's implicit relation to the quartet. Both Gardner and Alldritt have noted that the poems of *Four Quartets* rely on a structure patterned after the sonata which, as Alldritt explains, "is the original and principal feature" of the quartet form (Gardner 120; Alldritt 27–28). In its use of the sonata structure, "East Coker" builds a direct parallel between its etymological self-reflections on dance and the historical relation of dance to the quartet. Not only does the sonata provide the structure for the quartet as a musical form, but, as Adorno has noted, the sonata is historically related to dance and emerged as a negation of its temporal implications. Just as the ruin of "daunsinge" is always already implied in "dancing," the ruin of dance as a musical form is always already implied in the quartet.

In *Philosophy of Modern Music*, Adorno notes that the sonata "came to replace" dance because as "an art of static time, a turning in a circle, [and] movement without progress" dance "contains an anachronistic element" (Adorno *PMM* 196).[28] This description, which responds to a conception of dance that is almost identical to "Burnt Norton's" placement of it "at the still point of the turning world," posits a linear evolution in music from dance to the quartet via the sonata form.[29] Seen from Adorno's historical musicology, the quartet is thus predicated upon the decay of its musical forerunner, the dance. Like the relation of the term "dancing" to its etymological predecessor, the quartet as a musical form always already signifies dancing's exhaustion, decay, and ruin. For Adorno, such significations are the very core of musical material, the substance of music's "lexical items" being inseparable from historical mediations.

For "East Coker," the signification of dancing's exhaustion constitutes a moment of reconciliation between the poem's content and form. But it is a reconciliation that is built upon numerous negations—not the least of which is the negation of the absolute status that "Burnt Norton" attributes to dance by placing it at the atemporal "still point of the turning world." While the archaism of "daunsinge" implied that "dancing" too would succumb to the ravages of time, the quartet is simultaneously the signification of that negative implication's fulfillment and a diagnosis of the quartet's own decline. Indeed, at the time of Eliot's poem, the quartet as a musical form had long since lost the vitality that it possessed in the hands of composers like Haydn, Mozart, or Beethoven. In *The Classical Style*, Charles Rosen notes: "After Schubert, music generally seeks to avoid the kind of linear definition implied by the string quartet, and it becomes an archaic and an academic form—a proof of mastery, and a nostalgic recall of the great classicists."[30]

The historical connection between dance and the quartet form, like the etymological connection between "daunsinge" and "dancing," denotes a temporal passage in music that is devoid of real progress. The movement from dance to quartet is not one of progressive succession or *Aufhebung* but one of an incessant and insurmountable signification of decline and exhaustion. Music in "East Coker" has, in this respect, much in common with what for Adorno were the most significant aesthetic trends in modern musical forms like the dodecaphonic system. As Edward Said has noted: for Adorno, the advent of modern music marks "an elimination of transcendence" and the coming "to a paralyzed standstill" of characteristic musical concepts like "creativity, composition, [and] variation."[31] In "East Coker," the "elimination of transcendence" is most readily visible in the two-fold historicization of the dance which "Burnt Norton" represented in absolute terms. "East Coker" severs dance from transcendence through etymological and musicological devices. And inasmuch as these devices excavate the obscured historicity of dance as a linguistic or musical form, they do so not by superseding the historicity that they expose but by acquiescing to it as well. In signifying the historicity of their predecessors, both the linguistic term "dance" and the quartet form preclude their own transcendence.

In this acquiescence, music in "East Coker" coincides with the paradoxical contribution that, according to Adorno, modern music attempted by forcing "a paralyzed standstill" in the assumptions of progress that previously governed musical history. The historicization of dance acknowledges that "what once was true . . . afterwards became false in the course of historical time." Yet like modern music, the poem's acquiescence to this inevitable course subtly acknowledges that "nothing is to be dumped . . . just because it has waned" (Adorno *AT* 60). For "East Coker" the "waning" of dance and the quartet form is a devolution in function, a transformation of the past from mere ruin and exhaustion into a force whose decay serves as a beacon for that which is to be avoided.

The aesthetic tension between the dancers "lifting heavy feet in clumsy shoes" and the poem's relation to the quartet form stresses to the potential "receipt for deceit" bequeathed by "elders" who, given the poem's emphasis on music, not coincidentally are "quiet voiced" (EC 35; 76–77). The representation of music in "East Coker" pivots on an aesthetic strategy that does not dismiss the remnants of the past but neither does it succumb to an "arbitrary preservation of the antiquated," a preservation that Adorno contends "endangers that which it wishes to maintain" (Adorno *PMM* 7). Rather, "East Coker" negatively reinvigorates the critical power of dancing and the quartet form. Like the "early owl" whose appearance highlights the unnoticed "deep lane [that] insists on the direction," the historicizing tensions that are part of the formal structure of "East Coker" attempt to expose and thus to counteract the "deep lane[s that] insist on the direction" of music's signification.

The tension between dance and the quartet impedes any "attempt to deny . . . [the] irretrievable historical constitution" of "past musical phenomena" (Roberts *Art and Enlightenment* 36). But it turns this admittance into a source of redemption. The negative aesthetic that transforms the past from mere ruin and exhaustion into a force whose decay serves as a beacon for that which is to be avoided peaks in the fourth movement of "East Coker." While the images of the "wounded surgeon" and "the bleeding hands . . . of the healer's art" reaffirm the decay which accompanies "the wisdom of the age" and "the quiet-voiced elders," it also gives the decay a sacrificial and redemptive quality (EC 147; 149–50). As John Booty notes: "In a sense the lyric [of the fourth movement] is a Good Friday meditation on the Lord, who by the Incarnation accepts a personal death and becomes the wounded one as well as the one who comes to heal."[32] In this religious image, it is, of course, the wound that does the healing—just as in "East Coker" temporal decay generally becomes a guiding, negative source of redemption. The poem transposes this same "Good Friday mediation" of a healing wound into the "fever [that] sings" (EC 163). Its final representation of music is thus an assertion of the redemptive quality of its historicity and ruin (166).

Music, Language, and the Sinking Communicative Universal in "The Dry Salvages"

The imagery of "The Dry Salvages" draws heavily but critically on the inverted aesthetic significance that "East Coker" recognizes in the gradual decay of words and music. "The Dry Salvages" are, as the parenthetical preface to the poem explains, "a small group of rocks, with a beacon, off the N.E. coast of Cape Ann, Massachusetts." They are a source of redemption because they announce themselves as danger and indicate a safe course by exposing what it is not: "The ragged rock in the restless waters . . . In navigable weather it is always a seamark / To lay a course by" (Eliot DS 118–122). On one level, "The Dry Salvages" thus transposes "East Coker's" aesthetic strategy of "sacrificial decay" into an illustrative nautical metaphor where music "whistl[es]" from a "buoy" and "Clangs a bell"—neither of which signals an absolute ideal but rather illuminates peril and threat (DS 47–48). Moving beyond "East Coker's" specific focus on the internal historicity of musical material, however, "The Dry Salvages" examines the position of art and music in relation to external historical contexts. Initially, the admonishments of the "whistle" and "bell" dialectically oppose art and the presumed advances of civilization. Musical form counterbalances illusory social progress and critically illuminates the onslaught of reification. Yet as the force of this opposition falters and leaves music in an autonomous, indeed impotent, state, "The Dry Salvages" considers the extent to which "the objects of our cultural heritage, including our most cherished works of art [like music], are wholly independent and innocent of unjust material and social conditions and untainted by the ideologies promoting those conditions."[33]

After the poem's prefatory clarifications, the opposition of art and society first appears in the "rhythm" of the river whose unpredictable force has been reduced to a solvable problem for specialists in instrumental reason: that is, for "the builder[s] of bridges" or, more disparagingly put, for the "worshippers of the machine" (DS 11; 5; 10). In their initial association with the "Unhonoured" and "unpropitiated" river, music and art retain their critical potency, having in the image of the river's "rhythm" the potential to be a "destroyer" of the restrictive categorical structures through which civilization is organized (8–9). The utilitarian categories of "commerce," engineering, and mechanization are depicted as propagating a blinding reification that the seasonal "rages" of the river's "rhythm" are capable of exposing (4; 8). In this respect, the initial representation of music in "The Dry Salvages" coincides with what Rose Subotnik has called the moral impetus of Adorno's music criticism which, she argues, is "motivated above all by the exposure of reason in modern Western history as a construct incapable of governing the universe or of rendering the human species humane."[34] As is the case with the role that Adorno assigns to art in general, the river's "rhythm" challenges the conceptual exclusions that govern the presumed progress wrought by instrumental reason; it serves as a reminder "of what men choose to forget" (9). The "rhythm" of the river thus illuminates how civilization advances only by fostering a spurious and reified conception of time. Even "the tolling bell" on the high seas opposes this spuriousness and "Measures time not our time" (55). Like the opposition of the "rhythm" of the river to instrumental reason, the time of the "tolling bell" and the whistling "groaner" contrast with "time counted," with "calculating the future" and with trying to "piece together the past and future . . . when the past is all deception" (39–43).

Within this nautical metaphor, the most rudimentary forms of music (e.g., "rhythm," "whistl[ing]", or a clanging "bell") have the aesthetic wherewithal to subvert the conceptual exclusions of instrumental reason. Initially, then, "The Dry Salvages" explores whether language, given its parallels with music, can transcend its own cultural specificity. The incentive for the exploration is two-fold. Written at a time of growing international divisions, "The Dry Salvages" first seeks in music a kind of communicative universal that can counteract the divisiveness of national specificity and also the concomitant self-destructiveness of modern civilization. In this respect, the poem initially shares Adorno's own view that to attribute national specificity to music "is but an ideology."[35] Drawing on the parallels of music and language, the poem looks to the communicative universal of music for a parallel for its own poetic discourse.[36] And inasmuch as the poem associates music with the defiant force of the "rhythm" of the river, it seeks through the parallel to empower its own poetic endeavor with a potent cultural universality.

Framing this image of music within a nautical metaphor is not as inapplicable as it might at first seem. In fact, it is precisely such a metaphor that underlies Adorno's *Philosophy of Modern Music*. When in the preface to *Modern Music* Adorno says that the "book should be regarded as an extended appendix" to *Dialectic of Enlightenment*, his interpretative guideline also elucidates a contradictory allusion to classical literature in "The Dry Salvages" (Adorno *PMM* xiii). In its association with music, the nautical imagery from "The Dry Salvages" invokes a classical motif from Homeric narrative that Adorno and Horkheimer discuss at length—namely, Odysseus's voyage past the sirens whose song lures passing sailors into the rocks. This classical allusion coincides with the poem's problematic (re)presentation of music as a communicative universal and accentuates Eliot's search, on the one hand, for a potent shared tradition among Western European cultures, and his subsequent concession, on the other, that the seemingly unstoppable destruction taking place at sea while he wrote "The Dry Salvages" subverts the cultural universal that the poem tries to maintain both in its allusions to music and to classical literature. For "The Dry Salvages," the potential of music as a source of resistance increasingly resembles the sirens' luring music against which Odysseus shrewdly guards himself. As the resemblance becomes more pronounced, music in "The Dry Salvages" reverses its function and, rather than being a source of unity, becomes an aesthetic force that illuminates its own potential destructiveness.

Although the classical allusion in the nautical imagery propounds a common cultural heritage, it also emphasizes the disparities between European nations, in particular between Britain and Germany. Eliot published "The Dry Salvages" when "the war at sea was at its height" (Gardner 128). As was the case in the previous poems, the tensions of "The Dry Salvages," thus, surface in a dialectic between form and content. On the one hand, the poem is structurally related to a musical form whose "prestige comes entirely from its pre-eminence in the classical period" when Haydn, before being enthusiastically invited to London, appropriated relics from the Baroque dance suite and "established the string quartet as the supreme form of chamber music" (Rosen 137). On the other hand, the nautical imagery of poem's content—especially images like the prayers "for those who were in ships, and / Ended their voyage on the sand"—coincides with a national effort to keep the Germans out of England (DS 179–80). The former common cultural unity proves to be incapable of deterring later irreconcilable altercations. Ironically, as the war at sea subverts Eliot's hope to assert a unifying cultural heritage through classical allusion, the subversion reproduces the dynamics of the Homeric narrative.

According to Adorno's analysis of Odysseus's journey, the sirens' song lures one into "losing oneself in the past" (Horkheimer and Adorno DE 32).[37] Knowing of the irresistible lure of the sirens' song, Odysseus has himself chained to the ship's mast. He hears without peril and contemplates the song according to the implications that its historicity has for the present. In the absence of peril, the song "becomes art" for Odysseus, and he reverses its lure: instead of succumbing to the destructive temptation to abandon the present for the past—in other words, the temptation to jump ship and swim into the reefs—Odysseus uses the song to differentiate the present from the past and to undercut any illusions he might have about the progress his ship is making (34). In one respect, the music heard by Odysseus, combined with the relation to it that his unique position affords him, transforms a threatening lure into "a seamark / To lay a course by" (DS 121–22). Odysseus's position allows him to understand the historicity of the song's musical material while not being lured into its repetition. David Roberts argues that "the resistance of Odysseus, chained to the mast, to the siren song of nature, is [for Adorno] the moment of the birth of music" (Roberts 57).[38] The implied "birth of music" in Adorno's analysis issues from music's ability to expose and thus foster resistance to the insisting, luring currents of the past. Inasmuch as this ability marks "the birth of music," it also indicates the function that music finally serves in the first movement of "The Dry Salvages." Indeed, the "bell" that "clangs" and the "whistling buoy" announce that the ossified substance at their base is treacherous.

The implications of this announcement are perhaps best seen in the poem's quick handling of the "rose-garden" experience from "Burnt Norton," which is reintroduced via a "briar rose" with "salt" on it (DS 25; 33). Inasmuch as the "rose-garden" is associated with and contains music—e.g., the "unheard music in the shrubbery"—coating the "briar rose" with "salt" encapsulates and forces the music of the first movement of "The Dry Salvages" to ring from within a crystallized form (BN 27; EC 26). In effect, "The salt . . . on the briar rose" will cause the rose to wither, and the music from within the "rose-garden," taking the form of a "heaving groaner" and a "tolling bell," identifies not an idealized realm of "What might have been" but rather the dangers of a retrospective idealization of it (DS 25; 32; 35). "The salt . . . on the briar rose" equates crystallization and withering with an unrealized past, the embrace of which is as hazardous as "granite teeth" or an unseen "Ground swell" at sea "under the oppression of the silent fog" (DS 30–37). The musical groaning of the "rose-garden's" expiration, like the "Groaner" described in the poem's preface, signals warning and directs passers-by away from the dangerous ossified forms of "what has" and "What might have been."

Just as "The salt . . . on the briar rose" and "The tolling bell" suggest a "birth of music" within a dynamic that parallels Odysseus's relation to the sirens, they also demand that the poem adopt an historical attitude regarding its parallel with the classical narrative. In "The Dry Salvages" this attitude emerges in the second movement of the poem, the tone of which comes across as a kind of dirge on the unforeseeable end to "The silent withering of autumn flowers," and "drifting wreckage" (DS 50–52). Initially, the second movement distances itself from the earlier classical motif, lamenting that "There is no end, but addition" and "Years of living among the breakage / Of what was believed in as the most reliable— / And therefore the fittest for renunciation" (58–60). More importantly, the second movement turns the recognition that "There is no end, but addition" into a moment of aesthetic and historical self-reflection, which mourns the ineffectiveness of music: the "Clamour of the bell of the last annunciation" is heard within "a drifting boat with a slow leakage" (66; 64). The representation of music that dominates the poem hereafter is caught between two conceptions of history. As an aesthetic form, it is capable of a critical and illuminating "annunciation" of its own reified status. Ironically, however, the self-reflective "annunciation" gives its warning to a "boat with a slow leakage" that is destined for ruin even if it does avoid the reefs. In this respect, the "annunciation" is not unlike Odysseus's experience of the sirens' song: as Joel Whitebook has noted, the Odysseus of *Dialectic of Enlightenment* renounces "the unfettered ecstacy of the Sirens' song," "his bondage to the mast, i.e., the constraints of civilized life," degrading the quality of "his musical experience" for his own survival.[39]

In contrast to the music in "East Coker," music's sacrificial decay in "The Dry Salvages" amounts to critical impotence. While this impotence might seem a repetition of the idea that the decaying effect of time cannot be halted, the historical context of "The Dry Salvages," i.e., the war raging at sea, transforms the abstract temporal considerations of the previous poems into a lament about the impotence of music and culture as historical forces. This lament is reinforced by the fact that "The Dry Salvages" reduces the representation of music to a single sound, e.g., the clang of "a bell," and thus places emphasis not on the relation of one sound to another but rather on the relation of the music to its socio-historical context. Placed in direct historical terms, whatever appeals that "The Dry Salvages" may make to the communicative universality of music or the common heritage of western cultures, the carnage at sea continues.

Just as Adorno "argues that Schoenberg and Stravinsky both end up repressing the individual with the universal" because the two composers "attempt to order materials through imposition of universal patterns of twelve-tone method and neo-classical form," "The Dry Salvages" reluctantly abandons its attempt to seek a cultural universal and acknowledges that "the past has another pattern" than that which one subsequently imposes on it (DS 86).[40] In fact, this other "pattern" is in direct opposition to the presumptions underlying the common cultural heritage to which the poem appealed in response to the national divisions of the Second World War. The falsity of this presumed common heritage derives from its inability to stop the wreckage and carnage of the battles at sea. The poem now rejects the notions of "sequence— / Or even development: the latter a partial fallacy / Encouraged by superficial notions of evolution" (DS 86–88). "Sequence," "development," and "evolution": all are necessary for the commonality which the poem initially attempts to establish, and their absence denotes a fundamental disparity that surfaces in the use of English as a catalyst for some greater imitation of the quartet form. Whereas a Haydn could make the string quartet the supreme form of chamber music and then be received open-armed in London, the reception not only has succumbed to time; it occurred in a domain that is alien to the political currents of military force and thus is powerless "When there is distress of nations and perplexity / Whether on the shores of Asia, or in the Edgeware Road" (DS 197–98).

As the universality of music proves to be increasingly unlike the potent "rages" of the river—in other words, as music proves to be an autonomous entity—the poem is forced into a dialectical reversal, and it reassesses the relation of music and language, basing the reassessment upon the knowledge that music is powerless as a counter-force to the tides of historical events. The poem consequently explores whether music, in its parallels with language, is any less culturally specific than language itself. Implicitly questioning the previous poem's conflation of musicology and etymology, "The Dry Salvages" places the abstract parallel between music and language into a more diverse conception of cultural history. Whereas "East Coker" critically exploits the etymology of the term "dancing" in order to highlight the history of the quartet form, "The Dry Salvages" challenges the unquestioned use of English etymology to illuminate the history of a musical form that came to fruition in German culture. Given, as Matthiessen has noted, "Eliot's belief that . . . [a poet's first duty especially in wartime] is still to the preservation and development of his 'native language'," "The Dry Salvages" situates *Four Quartets* between two contradictory allegiances: first to the cultural community unified by the English language, a community that in 1941 was at war with Germany; and secondly, to a decaying and impotent universality that persists in the autonomous realms of art and music (Matthiessen 103).

What the poem laments then is the collapse of culture as a gauge of human progress or as an effective force of enlightenment in history: the poem laments not only art's inability to circumvent the ravages of time but also its inability to circumvent its own autonomy. Indeed, the third movement of "The Dry Salvages" specifically rebuts the previous poem's attempt to conceptualize the temporal decay of music as a redemptive sacrifice. By asserting that "time is no healer," the third movement accentuates the insurmountable disparity between the domains of music and the substance of contemporary history. By positing "the future" as "a faded song" or "a Royal Rose . . . Pressed between yellow leaves of a book that has never been opened," the poem confines music to an aging realm of "what might have been" that has no influence over "what has been" or what is (DS 126–28). The third movement of "The Dry Salvages" thus redefines the "rose-garden" experience as the powerlessness of culture, and when the next movement concludes with a prayer "for those who were in ships, and / Ended their voyage" in death "Or wherever cannot reach them the sound of the sea bell's / Perpetual angelus," the prayer is for those who succumbed to the delusion that culture could serve as a point of universality or as a universal language (179–183).[41]

The poem is torn between the obligation that it feels to those who collectively sacrifice themselves at sea and the individual autonomous position that the poet must occupy in order to affirm a universal notion of culture. The assertion from the final movement of the poem, "you are the music while the music lasts" affirms this individual conception of culture (DS 211–212). But without a collective imperative the music is no match against the tide and "Ground swell" of history (DS 37).

"Little Gidding," Signification and the Marred Foundations "of Sanctuary and Choir"

Compared with the other poems of the *Four Quartets*, "Little Gidding" is the least explicit in its references to music. It is also the most deliberate in maintaining a disparity between poetic and musical form. For Eliot finds in this disparity a signifier for the growing social disparity and fragmentation that he incorporates into his poem. Ironically, in its signifying role, the disparity between music and language reconciles socio-historical experience and its signification and thus fulfills perhaps the most central project of all four poems. As if to rhetorically emphasize the relation that the disparity between music and language has with socio-historical context of the poem, Eliot situates the reconciliation amid the ruins of a community that antedates the autonomy of art and that recalls a period in the history of music when poetic and musical forms worked in unity and were an integral part of daily life. Rather than being an exercise in nostalgia, however, the recollection of this communal harmony is dialectically related to the contemporary destruction and ruin that Eliot confronts. Inasmuch as the contemporary fragmented relation of poetic and musical forms coincides with the actual fragmentation and ruin occurring while Eliot wrote the last of the *Four Quartets*, the sentiment of the poem is less a yearning for the old communal order of Little Gidding than it is a dialectical interpretation of its collapse. For in the parallel disparities within art and within society, the poem sees a dialectical reversal of Little Gidding that sustains order and meaning. Indeed, the emphasis on dialectical inversion accompanies the representation of each of the major images of the poem.

Preparing this dialectical interpretation, the opening movement of the poem initially conflates an inversion of seasonal characteristics with a Christian miracle and thereby introduces a conception of fire that unifies life (e.g., "a bloom more sudden / Than that of summer") and language in one temporal accord (Eliot LG 16–17). The poem attributes the seasonal anomaly of "Midwinter spring" not to "blaze of branch, or brazier" but rather to "pentecostal fire" (14; 9–10). The allusion to "pentecostal fire" allies the aberrational bloom with an ephemeral linguistic unity, equating the "Midwinter spring" with the descent of the Holy Spirit which temporarily provided the apostles with a heavenly language understood by all people from all nations. Like the "Midwinter spring," the unifying language of the Spirit is also marked by inverted characteristics that change its import: its "purpose is beyond the end figured / And is altered in fulfillment" (34–35). The "altered" purpose of the "pentecostal fire" emerges in the closing lines of the poem's first movement. In a radical departure from the traditional image of the Holy Spirit, the closing lines associate the fleeting "pentecostal" thaw with a "communication of the dead [that] is tongued with fire beyond the language of the living" (50–51). No longer is it the living who are filled with the

Spirit and speak in heavenly tongues, but the dead who "being dead" find "what . . . [they] had no speech for, when living" (49–51). Instead of conceding decline from present vitality into irredeemable decay and "worn-out poetical fashion," the poem's allusion to the anomalous "Midwinter spring" and its "pentecostal fire" thus suggests that the decayed state of the dead's speech has specific relevance to the contemporary socio-historical world, a relevance that is vastly different from the negative, "clang[ing]" warning of "the bell" in "The Dry Salvages" (EC 69; DS 47–48).

The inversion implicit in associating the tongues of fire with "the dead" dialectically historicizes the apostles' ability to convey the Word into the multiple discourses of their audience's diverse experience. The "altered" purpose that results from this dialectical inversion is evident in the poem's subsequent appropriation of the apostles' ability. The poem appropriates not the eternal Word spoken by the apostles but the signifying authority of the Word. According to tradition, the heavenly language of Pentecost bridged the chasm between the metaphysical and physical worlds and temporarily subordinated different languages to one unified transcendental code. Correspondingly, the language of "the dead" in its decayed and fragmented state signifies, so "Little Gidding" argues, contemporary "England and nowhere" in 1941 (LG 53). The former tradition articulates a life eternal, and the latter a life deceased and in disintegration. In "Little Gidding," the authority and "speech" that "the dead" now have "being dead" derives largely from what the poem posits as a course of history that has culminated in a correspondence between the disintegrated language of the deceased and the socio-historical situation of the living (49–50). This same disintegration is evident in an inversion of what the poem cites as a previous merging of language and music.

By affiliating the ("altered") heavenly tongues of flame with an historical site of prayer, the poem recalls a time when metaphysical discourse constituted an essential social organizing principle, a time when prayer and music were integrated into social life and music had not yet devolved as an art form into an autonomous realm unto itself. The imperative "You are here to kneel / Where prayer has been valid" refers specifically to the historical significance of "Little Gidding" itself, a Huntingdonshire village where in 1625 Nicholas Ferrar established an Anglican community that was visited both by George Herbert and Charles I ("a broken king") and where "prayer dominated the round of daily life" (LG 45–46; Booty 47). Peter Bürger has noted that in precisely such communities language and music were reconciled in a common concert of worship around which daily life revolved. This was a time when art and especially music were "wholly integrated into the social institution [of] 'religion'" (Bürger *Avant-Garde* 47). The poem subtly draws attention to this unity in its later allusion to "The marred foundations we forgot, / Of sanctuary and choir" (LG 75–76). While the allusion to "sanctuary and choir" recalls an architectural union of word and music, the forgotten "marred foundations" historicize the union and signal the disintegration of its base. Just as the poem inverts the significance of the tongues of flame, it also overturns the union of word and music. The breakdown of this union, however, like the dead who "being dead" find "what . . . [they] had no speech for, when living," becomes the catalyst for "altered" union; it becomes a reliable signifier of contemporary events.[42]

Once incorporated into the historical specifics of Eliot's wandering as a fire warden among the ruins left by the German air raids on London, the "tongues of fire," in their "altered" role, accentuate the historical chasm that separates the integrated community of Little Gidding and the ravaged city of London. Yet just as the "tongues of fire" change from being a source of unity to being one of destruction, destruction changes from being a source of discord to being one of modern paradoxical accord. The graphic historical imagery of the raids on London transposes the Christian discursive registers of an Anglican community (where discourse and daily life integrated in common devotional harmony) into the exhausted religious and poetical registers of a city in ruins (where discourse and daily life integrate in a common reduction to "a shell, a husk of meaning"). The inverted and now destructive character of the "tongues of fire" unifies Christian discourse and the city of London in common state of ruin.

Whatever reconciliation that the "worn-out" signifiers and a bombed-out signified might poetically achieve in a mutual state of ruin, the ruins upon which the reconciliation relies create what might be called a reconciliation in dissonance—and therein lies the poem's dialectical relation to musical form. Like "the polyphonic unity and harmony of a poem or musical work" in which, according to Richard Shusterman's comparison of the cultural criticisms of Eliot and Adorno, "the individual words and notes seem freely to bond themselves together in the whole without thereby losing their specific value and identity," the reconciliation among the ruins in "Little Gidding" "is an implicit condemnation of the failure of our social union and a model of what ideal society could be."[43] Indeed, the poem's continued reliance on the ruins of theological discourse and on allusions to previous Christian communities envelops the reconciliation among the ruins in an aesthetic acknowledgement of what reconciliation might have been. "In its very distinction from reality," this acknowledgement reflects an attitude which for Eliot and Adorno, as Shusterman has noted, is the definitive moment of art: the "very distinction from reality represents a protest against and an alternative to a reality that we are programmed to feel is inevitable" (Shusterman 388). In short, the poetic rendering of the destruction caused by German air strikes achieves an integrated fragmentation that introduces a reconciliation which the poem simultaneously rejects.

Nowhere is the dissonant echo of an alternative reconciliation more piercing than in the opening stanza of the poem's second movement where "the burnt roses" on "an old man's sleeve" who is buried beneath the rubble of a collapsed building give tragic specificity to the "unheard music hidden on the shrubbery" of the "rose-garden" experience in "Burnt Norton" (LG 54–55; BN 27). Indicative of the "What might have been," the individual victim of the fire raid maintains an accusingly "specific value and identity" which underscore the exclusions upon which the poem's reconciliations are based (BN 9). "The dark dove with the flickering tongue," to whose descent the "old man" succumbed, is also a victim, having lost its redemptive role in an inversion of the dove and flame of the Holy Spirit (LG 81). These two victims, man and Spirit, have already converged in the poem's earlier association of "the communication / Of the dead" with tongues of fire, and together they tell "what the dead had no speech for, when living" (49). Buried beneath the rubble, however, the "old man" does not communicate in words; his corpse is a necessary material counterweight to the subsequent apparition of the "compound ghost" who, in the most famous passages of the poem, speaks of and among the ruins of poetry and of London, "two worlds [he says] become much like each other" (95; 120).

The old man beneath the rubble underscores the awareness with which the "compound ghost" is able to find words he "never thought to speak / In streets . . . [he] never thought . . . [he] would revisit" (LG 123-24). For the "compound ghost," the most immediate reason for his new-found speech is that the current situation of London matches the status of his own poetic discourse. Both are in a state of ruin. But from the privileged position "at this intersection time," the "compound ghost" attempts what Adorno argued on behalf of shortly before his own death: "to shed light on all art from the perspective of the most recent artistic phenomena" (LG 124; Adorno *AT* 491–92). Speaking through the modern lyrical form of Eliot's composition, the "compound ghost" seizes the opportunity "to shed light" on poetry and speaks of the painful awareness "Of things ill done and done to others' harm / Which once you took for exercise of virtue" (LG 141–142). Not only does the "compound ghost's" work parallel the status of ravaged London; the "harm" done by the work in a mistaken "exercise of virtue" is symbolically manifest in the death of the "old man" that results from the descent of "the dark dove with the flickering tongue." Just as the fire-bombing of London announces "the death of water and fire" as discursive registers of religious discourse, so too does the "compound ghost" announce—in a path of immanent decay that began with the "figured leaf" of "Burnt Norton," became the "yellow leaves of a book" in "The Dry Salvages," and culminates with "the dead leaves still rattl[ing]" in "Little Gidding"—a regression of poetry into a state parallel to the horribly destructive force gilded beneath the traditionally unifying image of the pentecostal tongues of fire. In short, the "compound ghost" concedes that that which he once "took for exercise of virtue," what for a poet would be an advancement of culture and humanity through poetry, is as illusory and destructive as continued confidence in the traditional image of the Holy Spirit.

In a recent article entitled "Compound Ghost, Triple Devil, Terminal Books," Harvey Gross has likened the apparition of the "compound ghost" in

"Little Gidding" and the triple apparition of the devil in Thomas Mann's *Doctor Faustus*. Although the compound ghost in "Little Gidding" reflects on language and the devil in *Doctor Faustus* on music, Gross's comparison is consistent with the relation of language and music that exists throughout "Little Gidding." Coincidentally, Gross's comparison is also relevant for this present essay since the modern musicology articulated by the devil in *Doctor Faustus* derives largely from the manuscript of Adorno's *Philosophy of Modern Music*, which Adorno shared with Mann while they both were in exile in Los Angeles. Gross notes that in *Doctor Faustus*, Leverkühn the composer is able "with the devil's help" to supersede the exhausted conventions of harmony and tonality "with his 'invention' of the twelve-tone method of composition."[44] Unfortunately, however, Gross does not really explore the parallel between Leverkühn's "invention" (actually Schoenberg's invention) and the position that the poet in "Little Gidding" achieves with the help of the compound ghost.

The artistic positions developed in *Doctor Faustus* and "Little Gidding" are complementary: first of all, in the critical retrospectives that Leverkühn and the poet build into their respective art forms; and secondly, in inversions that challenge accepted notions of musical, linguistic, and social unity. Both the composer and the poet articulate aesthetic forms of dissonance, not only in their own creative realms but also in the relation of the two realms to each other.[45] In their stridency, the calculated cycles and patterns of serialism intone the historicity of traditional conceptions of harmony and resolution. A twelve-tone composition ends, as Adorno notes, in a precarious dissonant tension. Since it rejects any natural, transhistorical or transcendental harmony, only a deliberate and self-acknowledged imposition of serial structure holds together an otherwise fragmented musical material. As a poetic composition, "Little Gidding" ends in a comparable dissonance. Unlike the Anglican community at Little Gidding where language, music and social life all harmonized in a common object of devotion, in the poem "Little Gidding" language, music, and social life coincide in a common state of fragmentation. The unity of language and music is reduced to the "marred foundations . . . Of sanctuary and choir" (LG 75–76). As the poet concedes in historical reflections on Little Gidding: "We cannot revive old factions / We cannot restore old policies / Or follow an antique drum" (185–87). Distancing itself historically from the unities represented in Little Gidding, the poem acknowledges the dissonance underlying its constructed relation between words and music, and this dissonance becomes a signal representation of the greater disunities and fragmentation that the poem explores.

Moving beyond "The Dry Salvages," which posits its negative aesthetic in the image of a "tolling bell," the poet explains "It is not to ring the bell backwards" that he summons "The spectre of a Rose" (DS 35; LG 182–84). Like the poem's concluding line—"the fire and the rose are one"—this "spectre of a Rose" recalls the "the ash the burnt roses leave" on the "old man's sleeve" and also the fire-bombed ruins of the house under which the "old man" lies (LG 259; 54–55). The "ash the burnt roses leave" results in a chasm between poetry and music that cannot be traversed. Within the larger scope of *Four Quartets*, this "spectre" is allied with the "unheard music" in the rose-garden (BN 27). Given the growing dissonance between words and music in the poem, "The spectre of a Rose" and its association with the "Dust inbreathed [that] was a house" are haunting reminders of the "unheard music" that, reduced to ruins, can never be heard (LG 58). For the ruin of this house as a chamber is also the ruin of poetry as chamber music, and the structural relation of "Little Gidding" to the quartet form is thus one of a parity among ruins.

III

Adorno, Folk Culture, Commodification, and National Identity in Literature and Music

5

Adorno, Ellison, and the Critique of Jazz

All totaled, Adorno wrote seven essays on jazz: three in the thirties, two in the forties, and two in the early fifties. The portrait was never flattering and was highly idiosyncratic. In the thirties, Adorno's criticisms of jazz functioned as the negative critical movement in what can be described as his dialectical embrace of Walter Benjamin's classic essay "The Work of Art in the Age of Mechanical Reproduction."[1] For while a polemic against technology endures throughout Adorno's subsequent writing on jazz, extending well into the sixties and framing his discussion of jazz in *Dissonanzen* (1962), Thomas Levin has recently noted that even as far back as the thirties, Adorno was simultaneously calling for a reading of popular music that was "sensitive to both its reified and its utopian dimensions," and he began to acknowledge the didactic and "decidedly progressive" advantages offered by phonographs and radio programs.[2] Despite this call, Adorno lingered on the "reified" and never ventured into the "utopian dimensions" of jazz. Even Adorno's defenders concede that his criticisms are marked by an almost fanatical rigidity and that the criticisms tend to "flatten out the dynamic contradictions of popular culture" (Jay *Permanent Exiles* 122). Yet two comparable tendencies to "flatten out" surface in Adorno scholarship on jazz: those who criticize Adorno the strongest examine neither all of his essays on jazz nor the historical context of his arguments, and those who sympathize with Adorno ignore the vast amount of research on jazz that is at their disposal.[3] In both cases, jazz is handled as a homogeneous collective entity. The handling thus obscures the internal dynamics of jazz and attributes to it a privileged ahistorical status.

To understand Adorno's criticisms of jazz requires situating them in a social history that considers the internal (dynamic) tensions within the jazz tradition. One means of highlighting the socio-historical complexities of this tradition is to juxtapose Adorno's criticisms with the representations of jazz in Ralph Ellison's *Invisible Man* (1952). In his essays, Ellison has proven himself to be a formidable jazz critic in his own right. Bringing the two writers into the same discussion not only confronts Adorno's arguments with those of a critic who had first-hand experience of the formative years of jazz, but also, because of the important role that African-American musical traditions have in Ellison's novel, discussion of it side by side with discussion of Adorno places Adorno's criticisms within a context of the social complexities of the jazz tradition.[4] My goal in pursuing such considerations is to demonstrate Adorno's place in the history of jazz criticism and to give a much needed historical grounding to the debate on Adorno, jazz, and popular music. In particular, I want to focus on the pivotal position that Louis Armstrong plays in *Invisible Man*'s prologue and epilogue. What emerges from this focus is a surprising correlation between the attitudes of the narrator in Ellison's novel and of Adorno in his criticisms of jazz.

During the thirty years that span Adorno's writings on jazz, his only major discursive shift resulted from his encounter with two books which, save for numerous earlier discussions in Frankfurt with the jazz critic Mátyás Seiber, were to become the intellectual sources of all his subsequent writing on jazz: Winthrop Sargeant's *Jazz: Hot and Hybrid* (1938) and Wilder Hobson's *American Jazz Music* (1939). In one respect, the review Adorno wrote of these books in 1941, which is marred by misquotations and misrepresentations of Sargeant's and Hobson's arguments, only widens Adorno's frame of reference for opinions he already had about classical music and about jazz. Written roughly two years after Adorno's arrival in America, the review, interestingly enough, criticizes the defenders of jazz not because they equate jazz with classical music, but rather because in doing so—to invert Jay's phrase—they "flatten out the dynamic contradictions of" classical music. By reaffirming the internal disparities of classical music, Adorno begins in his review to dismantle what two years earlier he argued was an obsolete distinction between classical and popular music. Adorno believed that the culture industry had long since appropriated the distinction and thus undermined the presumptions of both Sargeant's and Hobson's arguments.

Jazz: Hot and Hybrid and *American Jazz Music* became fixed diametrical points of reference for Adorno, and the arguments Adorno formulated for his review resurface in his last three essays. Though critical of Sargeant's "naive" defense of jazz, Adorno admired him as a fellow musician and critic. Sargeant was a Viennese trained violinist with the New York Philharmonic, and his book was, according to Adorno, of "much more serious scientific intentions and . . . much more adequate to the subject matter" than Hobson's.[5] The fact that Adorno twists many of Sargeant's arguments against him did not stop Adorno from later frequently appealing to Sargeant as a "scientific" authority to substantiate his own arguments. The appeals span twenty years: from Adorno's short contribution to Runes's and Schrickel's *Encyclopedia of the Arts* (1946), to his article "Perennial Fashion" (1953) and his little-known published polemic with Joachim-Ernst Berendt (1953), to his *Introduction to the Sociology of Music* (1962).

Adorno's handling of Hobson, on the other hand, was curt if not abusive. He attacked Hobson's attempt to define jazz as America's classical music, reacted negatively to Hobson's understanding of how jazz had found its way into modern classical composition, and challenged Hobson's uncritical conception of modern classical music. In his equation of jazz and classical music, Hobson fails to distinguish between Viennese Schools which understood themselves in terms of rivalry and opposition. Adorno's disapproval derives in large part from the strong personal investment that he had in maintaining the clarity of these oppositions. By citing both Alban Berg's "*Wozzeck*" and Krenek's "*Jonny Spielt Auf*" (in the same sentence) as examples of jazz-influenced concert music, Hobson merges the avant-garde atonal school of Schoenberg with the "*Gebrauchsmusik*" of composers like Hindemith, Krenek, and Weill.[6] Adorno associated Hindemith's circle with "*Neue Sachlichkeit*" which was the subject of much of his aesthetic criticism and which was, temperamentally at least, incompatible with Schoenberg's atonal philosophy.

It is safe to say that as far as Adorno was concerned, if jazz was associated with "*Neue Sachlichkeit*" or "*Gebrauchsmusik*," so much the worse for jazz. Indeed, as early as his 1936 essay "On Jazz," Adorno had rejected jazz because of its association with "*Neue Sachlichkeit*," and the movement's ideological undertones.[7] It is no small coincidence then that after his review of *American Jazz Music*, Adorno subtly revises Hobson's argument in his contribution to Runes's and Schrickel's *Encyclopedia of the Arts* (1946). He cites all the examples given by Hobson, but replaces the reference to Berg with one to Stravinsky who, in *The Philosophy of Modern Music* (1949), was to become the central figure of contrast which Adorno used in his praise of Schoenberg. Four years later, in Adorno's published polemic with the German jazz critic Joachim-Ernst Berendt, "Für und Wider den Jazz" (1953), Adorno turns the tables on Berendt, who in defense of jazz notes the similarities it bears to the compositions of Stravinsky and Hindemith. Adorno responds that whoever believes Stravinsky and Hindemith to be the vanguard of the new and modern, clearly is unfamiliar with Viennese atonality.[8]

Aside from how the two books summon Adorno's investment in the rivalries of twentieth century European music, Hobson's and Sargeant's books are important to an understanding of Adorno's views on jazz because, while both books trace the migration of jazz musicians from New Orleans to Chicago, they were published prior to the advent of bebop. This is a source of enlightening irony in "Perennial Fashion," and also in *Introduction to the Sociology of Music*, since in both instances Adorno appeals to the authority of Sargeant when he rejects both swing and bebop.[9] Published when they were, Hobson's and Sargeant's books could provide no account of the period of musical innovation and philosophical redefinition that occurred in jazz during the forties. Hobson's and Sargeant's arguments precede the period which Adorno used them to reject, and Adorno's appeal to Sargeant in his rejection of bebop suggests that Adorno's opinions about jazz were already solidified before the rise of the movement he slights in passing reference. With the exception of his categorical rejections in 1953 and 1962, Adorno displays no knowledge of bebop whatsoever.

There is little question about the inexcusable disservice that Adorno did to jazz and to his own arguments by relying so heavily in the forties, fifties, and sixties on jazz histories published in the thirties. But what this disservice means for Adorno's critique is another question. His arguments precede what has often been called the second half of jazz history. If we can accept Miles Davis's claim that the history of jazz is summed up in four words, "Louis Armstrong Charlie Parker," then it is worth considering the place and the significance that Adorno's opinions have in relation to the first half of that history. Despite his condemnation of bebop, Adorno's criticism focuses primarily on the early history of jazz, and philosophically, his criticism coincides frequently with the underpinnings of the first major movement in jazz history after Louis Armstrong's migration to Chicago.

Inasmuch as Adorno maintains that, in the aftermath of the culture industry's rise, a serious distinction can still be made in classical music between "*Gebrauchsmusik*" and Schoenberg's avant-garde atonality, he concedes the possibility that other musical forms may sustain comparable critical disparities within the discourse of their own cultural traditions. Bebop's relation to swing, for example, can be understood in these terms, despite Adorno's having categorically rejected this interpretation. On this point, which is the logical baggage carried by Adorno's own arguments, it is helpful to apply to jazz Adorno's claim that works of art represent the last vestiges of critical resistance to social repression. Acknowledging the internal dynamics of the jazz tradition thus offers the possibility to heed Adorno's social and cultural critiques without succumbing to his penchant for totalizing concepts. Such an acknowledgement salvages Adorno's cultural theories by circumventing his monolithic conception of society and culture and by giving it a critical diversification and flexibility. To consider the dynamics of the jazz tradition facilitates an evaluation of jazz in terms of the "rigor," to follow Adorno, with which it established itself within a vast diversity of cultural contexts which Adorno passes over. The question thus arises concerning the extent to which jazz too is marked by dynamic disparities comparable to those whose integrity Adorno so vociferously defended with regard to modern European music. Pursuing this question provides a clear avenue into the workings of *Invisible Man* because Ellison draws heavily upon the disparities of jazz when constructing the essential tensions of his novel.

When Ellison's novel begins, the story has already ended, and the invisible man has retreated into hibernation, which he defines as "a covert preparation for a more overt action."[10] As a source of solace and inspiration, the invisible man listens to records by Louis Armstrong who, he says, has "made poetry out of being invisible" and who has already moved into a realm of "overt action" comparable to that for which the invisible man is preparing and which takes form in the poetic structure of the story he narrates (Ellison *IM* 8). For the invisible man, Armstrong's significance derives from an ability to create poetic meaning out of a situation with which the invisible man is only beginning to come to terms. Of central importance is the invisible man's distinction between the "covert" and "overt," because it is here that through literature he imitates Armstrong and develops what Deleuze and Guattari call a "minor literature" within the major cultural tradition which can afford him no visible recognition. In short, he begins to understand the revitalizing power of the vernacular amidst the dominant discourse which excludes him.

Briefly, Deleuze and Guattari argue that minorities (like the Czech/German Jews of Kafka's Prague) often construct a minor literature within a major language. Minor literatures emerge as a source of identity within an immediate political/cultural context. With regard to Adorno and the question of jazz, it is possible to modify Deleuze's and Guattari's arguments to accommodate a notion of a "minor culture" and to use this modification to examine two concurrent but disparate forms of cultural experience, what the invisible man calls the "overt" and "covert." The first instance falls under the scrutiny of Adorno's claim that resistance to uniformity demands the most rigorous critical activity. But the second becomes the minor cultural locus of identity and resistance which Deleuze and Guattari describe. A sense for the "covert" and "overt," or the "minor" and the "major," is implicit in the invisible man's act of self naming, i.e., in the identity that he assumes while in hibernation.

"Jack-the-Bear," the name which the invisible man assumes for himself in his secluded basement room, belonged to an actual jazz musician and in the context of the invisible man's hibernation alludes to what in criticism has been acclaimed as the most vital element of jazz culture. Ostendorf recounts that Louis Armstrong learned his art in private sessions where jazz musicians gathered, competed with one another, and forged musical innovations in improvised "cutting contests."[11] Jack-the-Bear was an avid participant in these sessions in Harlem during the thirties.[12] In his own essays on jazz, Ellison describes the sessions as "a retreat, a homogeneous community where a collectivity of common experience could find continuity and meaningful expression."[13] Even Winthrop Sargeant notes in his revised edition of *Jazz: Hot and Hybrid* that jazz historians have frequently discussed the double life of jazz, that a covert or subcultural form of jazz existed "for the enjoyment of the players themselves" beneath the popular commercialized version criticized by Adorno.[14] This duplicity in jazz culture is reflected in the name which the invisible man assumes for himself. Not only was Jack-the-Bear a legendary (covert) cutter, but his name later served as the title for one of Duke Ellington's greatest popular (overt) successes.[15]

The duplicity is also reflected in the structure of jazz music itself, and a momentary consideration of this structure suggests that the "covert" life of jazz is not merely a transitory respite to be discarded once the musician has prepared for "overt" action. The "covert" and "overt" exist concurrently, forming a social cultural parallel to the multilayered rhythms of jazz that are traceable to African influences and that are part of the religious cultural heritage of African-Americans.[16] In jazz a major beat in one line may simultaneously be a twelfth in another line, and thus jazz rhythm incorporates a notion of multiple meanings.[17]

Likewise, Amiri Baraka argues that in jazz improvisation the notes are not merely a departure from the score, but have multiple mediations and hence multiple meanings.[18] What in one setting constitutes the type of commercial exploitation for which Armstrong was later criticized by beboppers and Adorno alike, in another setting makes up the virtuosity upon which the legend of Armstrong firmly rests. Certainly, "the improvisatory skills of jazz musicians reflect the . . . flexibility and immediacy of response" which have been necessary for black American survival.[19] Later in the novel, this same type of flexibility enables the blues singer Trueblood, as Pancho Savery, Houston Baker, and Berndt Ostendorf have noted, to reaffirm "his [folk] identity" despite catastrophe, "translate his personal disaster into a code of blues," and resist the "centralized [cultural] monologue" which would condemn him.[20] The covert thus functions as a strategy for dealing with the deficiencies of overt social experience. More importantly, however, in jazz a double cultural life emerges, and in its parallels to the multilayered rhythms of African music, the duplicity of the jazz social experience is a distinctly African contribution to American culture. The duplicity is as much a part of the structures of the music itself as it is reflective of the lives of jazz musicians.

Given that Hitler's stigmatization of jazz as non-Aryan belonged to the same ideology that forced Adorno, a German Jew, to flee Nazi Germany, one would think that Adorno might have developed a sensibility for the struggles for freedom within African-American folk culture—or to follow Deleuze and Guattari that, as a member of one minor culture, Adorno might have felt strong affinities for the articulated struggles of another. In fact, Adorno claimed to have precisely such an affinity for black experience when, shortly after he published "Perennial Fashion," Joachim-Ernst Berendt accused him of implicit racism and suggested that Langston Hughes would be a more appropriate spokesperson than Adorno on behalf of black struggles for civil and cultural equality. The tag of racism has plagued Adorno since his earliest writings on jazz. Adorno reminds Berendt quite accurately that he (Adorno) co-authored the most significant study of racism in America in recent times, *The Authoritarian Personality* (1950). Adorno explains to Berendt that he desires merely to point out where blacks are being exploited as "eccentric clowns" and where jazz subtly makes entertainment out of what has been done to African Americans (Adorno "Wider" 892-93). In this respect, Adorno's response to Berendt corresponds with criticisms voiced in the African-American community itself. In fact, Adorno's argument coincides almost verbatim with Ellison's argument in "Change the Joke and Slip the Yoke," where he claims that "the entertainment industry . . . [debases] all folk materials" and reduces blacks to grotesque comedy (Ellison *Shadow* 48). For Adorno, however, understanding of debasement and racism is inseparable from the forced experiential lessons he learned amidst the fascist rise to power in Weimar Germany. The seemingly racist undertones of his criticisms of jazz are a combination of abhorrence to both the culture or entertainment industry and the implementation of Nazi ideology.

Given the historical context of Nazi cultural politics, one can read, for example, the often criticized grounds that Adorno uses for rejecting jazz in his first article on the subject, "Abschied vom Jazz" (1933), as a subtle defense of it. Adorno wrote this first article shortly after the Nazis outlawed the broadcasting of jazz on the radio. When one places Adorno's claims that jazz is "not Black, not powerful, not dangerous . . . [nor] emancipatory" in the context of fascist Germany, Adorno's arguments refute point by point the hysteria to which the Nazis appealed when they banned jazz music. As Marc Weiner has argued, it is thus "possible that [Adorno] intended . . . [his claims] to be read as a strategic response to the conservativism discernible in his contemporaries' reaction to the music."[21]

The problem with Weiner's reading of "Abschied vom Jazz" is that, unless the article is placed within the general schema of Adorno's critique of fascist cultural ideology, it is equally possible to read "Abschied vom Jazz" as a defense of high culture, a reading which is encouraged by Adorno's scathing review of Wilder Hobson's book. This is the most frequent criticism of Adorno, typified by critics like Lorenzo Thomas, William Nye, or Peter Townsend who argue that, as a Eurocentric cultural elitist, Adorno had a deaf ear when it came to vernacular cultural expressions. Fredric Jameson subscribes to a similar position, although with a more apologetic tone, by simply redefining Adorno's writing on jazz as a critique not of "serious jazz" but of "Paul Whiteman" and by comparing Adorno's criticisms with a rejection of a "standard Hollywood Grade-B genre film" (Jameson *Late Marxism* 141). In Adorno's defense Martin Jay, Ulrich Schönherr, and Jamie Owen Daniel have argued that Adorno's controversial opinions on jazz employ the identical dialectical methodology that, a year after he published "On Jazz," Adorno used when criticizing Wagner in *In Search of Wagner* (Jay *Adorno* 119; Schönherr 86; Daniel 40).[22] Two years later in "On the Fetish-Character in Music and the Regression of Listening" (1938), Adorno suggested that the Nazis' banning of jazz was as disgusting as their subsequent programmatic attempt to "cultivate" the masses by broadcasting the greatest achievements of German classical music.

The importance of "On the Fetish-Character in Music and the Regression of Listening" to any understanding of Adorno's concerns in his criticism of jazz cannot be underestimated. It undercuts the charges that Adorno was defending a high cultural elitism, because in it he asserts that "the differences in the reception of official 'classical' music and light music no longer have any real significance."[23] For Adorno "the real dichotomy . . . was not between 'light' and 'serious' music—he was never a defender of traditional cultural standards for their own sake —but rather between music that was market-oriented and music that was not."[24] According to Adorno, the culture industry (and fascism is implicated here as well) had gained control of both classical and folk or popular music and employed similar mechanisms in both cases to manipulate the market. Although Adorno's favorable comments on music always refer to European music, to argue that Adorno's criticisms of jazz are a defense of high culture is to ignore his focus on the socio-historical tendencies which have rendered "the organization of culture into 'levels' . . . patterned after low, middle and high-brow," not only obsolete but also "reprehensible" (Adorno "Perennial" 127).[25] Adorno's general critique of the commodity character of music as it has evolved under late capitalism challenges the survival of both classical music and jazz as forms of entertainment.

In *Adorno's Aesthetic Theory*, Lambert Zuidervaart argues that in the early stages of capitalism "music was produced to be purchased, and it was purchased to be enjoyed." Adorno's objection was not against enjoyment, but rather that at the hands of the late capitalist culture industry the use value of enjoyment had been supplanted, and exchange value was now presented as "as an enjoyable use value" (Zuidervaart 77–78). When Adorno speaks about the necessity of jazz's constantly promising "its listeners something different [to] excite their attention," Adorno is not so much talking about jazz itself as the industry that props it up (Adorno "Perennial" 126). But as a consequence, this industry seriously compromises the possibility for critical assessments of the quality of the entertainment provided by the music, whether jazz or classical. On this point Adorno is no voice in the wilderness. In *Black Nationalism and the Revolution in Music* (1970), Frank Kofsky notes the conflict of interest resulting from the fact that the critics of jazz are by and large "dependent on the recording industry for their livelihood."[26] They cannot afford to be critical because they are the same people who earn their living by writing record jackets. More recently, John Gennari has explained that early jazz critics would have had trouble avoiding these conflicts, that anyone "trying to make a living as a jazz critic in the 1930s . . . would have had a hard time *not* looking for the most remunerative possibilities available in the practice of his craft."[27] To say that "Jazz, like everything else in the culture industry, gratifies desires only to frustrate them at the same time" refers to the advertising hype which redirects "enjoyment" to the actual purchase, and the often misleading thought that one is getting something "new" and "innovative" (Adorno "Perennial" 126).[28]

Although Adorno's criticisms of modern music hinge on a dichotomy between market orientation and resistance to commodification, his reservations about jazz folk culture as a locus of struggle and liberation cannot entirely be linked to the abuses of the entertainment or culture industry. They are also "tied . . .

to his revulsion with Nazi pseudo-folk culture" (Jay *Adorno* 120). Martin Jay has noted that for Adorno:

> Folk music was no longer alive, because the spontaneous *Volk* had been consumed in a process that left popular music, like all popular culture, the creature of manipulation and imposition from above (Jay *Imagination* 185).

Inasmuch as the manipulations "from above" can be associated with the entertainment industry, so too are Adorno's criticisms of jazz inseparable from an intellectual opposition to the conditions which he believes led to the election of Hitler (Daniel 40). Adorno's apprehensions about jazz culture stem from his having observed the Nazis manipulate folklore to their own propagandistic ends.

Adorno's concern that jazz culture lends itself to appropriation does not appear to have been groundless. Scott DeVeaux observes in "Constructing the Jazz Tradition" that the history of jazz is a "struggle for possession of that history and the legitimacy that it confers."[29] The struggle is often waged through definition by exclusion. Jazz has so frequently been coopted by groups with contradictory agendas that Amiri Baraka complained that white critics who seek to define "jazz as an art (or folk art)" often do so without giving consideration to the intelligent "socio-cultural philosophy" from which it stems (Baraka *Black Music* 14). During different periods, jazz has been embraced across the political spectrum. Cold Warriors and the State Department have used it as an avatar of American cultural values (Kofsky *Nationalism* 31, 111; DeVeaux 526; Gennari 478). In the twenties and thirties, the Left too vied for possession of the jazz tradition in accordance with Lenin's general wishes that all branches of the party render

> direct aid to all the revolutionary movements among the dependent and underprivileged nations (for example, Ireland, the American Negroes, etc.) and in the colonies.[30]

Citing S. Frederick Star's *Red and Hot*, James Lincoln Collier has noted that in 1928 "the Comintern decided . . . to treat American blacks as a 'colonized nation'" and that consequently critics like John Hammond, Otis Ferguson, Charles Edward Smith and B.H. Haggin represented jazz in Left-oriented presses "as the 'folk music' of . . . [a] colonized race."[31] Incidentally, Collier himself has been the subject of much deserved criticism for his own selective revision of the jazz tradition.32 But his argument on the subtleties of the Left's interest in jazz offers some provocative insights into how *Invisible Man* questions the substantial theoretical support that black nationalists historically received from the Communist party. Lenin's insistence on "the right of subjugated peoples to self-determination" takes the ironic form of the Brotherhood's concern that the invisible man might not be black enough to represent their interests in Harlem and in the invisible man's being given "freedom of action" while remaining "under strict discipline to the committee" (Berry and Blassingame 416; Ellison *IM* 351). Here, the irony emerges as it becomes increasingly evident to the invisible man that the Brotherhood will tolerate only its own limited preconception of what is black and what constitutes legitimate ethnic expression.

In his article "The Signifying Modernist," William Lyne observes that when the invisible man is asked by another member of the Brotherhood to sing a "Negro work song," the invisible man's mentor Jack rifles his ability to respond, subsumes it beneath the monologic interests of the Brotherhood and thus disarms the "double-voiced tools [in jazz] that are supposed to undermine and transform . . . official hierarchies." In short, Jack, whose own expressions occasionally regress into a European tongue, appropriates "one of the most important parts of African American expressive culture" (Ellison *IM* 304).[33] He can only understand enjoyment of African American musical traditions as degrading and as a remnant of racist attitudes. Collier's arguments suggest that a similar procedure marks the Left's manipulation of jazz for its own political ends. On this point, he is in agreement with other historians, except that it is euphemistic to describe their view of jazz merely "as the 'folk music' of . . . [a] colonized race." Jack's disapproving retort, "the brother *does not sing*!," differs from the left's provisional embrace of jazz only in its frank rejection of the value of jazz traditions.

Scott DeVeaux has argued that Star and Collier mis-perceive jazz and see it as a crippled articulation of a repressed people. Yet the same can be said of the Left whose appreciation of jazz in the thirties was as often scurrilous as it was supportive (DeVeaux 534). Examples abound. John Hammond was subjected to severe criticism in the *Daily Worker* when, after his "Spirituals to Swing" concert (1939), he claimed that "jazz music is uniquely American, the most important cultural exhibit we have given to the world."[34] Following the benefit given the next year for the Spaniards who were fighting against fascism, Hammond was so infuriated with the party's patronizing response to Fats Waller and Cab Calloway "that he demanded, and received an apology from the *Daily Worker*" (Naison 3–4; 15). The source of the Left's criticism of Hammond and of their patronizing attitudes toward jazz musicians lies in their assessment of jazz itself, an assessment which treated black folklore and jazz not as "important cultural exhibits" but rather as Eugene Gordon depicted them at the American Writers' Congress in 1935: "as a 'national psychosis' resulting from repression."[35] In this respect, Jack's blunt rejection of the request that the invisible man sing "a Negro work song" parallels the Left's view of jazz: that it needed to be overcome.

At first glance Adorno's own position on jazz would appear to coincide with that expressed by Eugene Gordon and by the character Jack in Ellison's novel. In "Perennial Fashion," he argued that a "real unadulterated jazz" could not be distinguished from "the abuse of jazz" because abuse was an innate dimension of jazz itself. Negro spirituals, he argued, "were slave songs and as such combined the lament of unfreedom with its oppressed confirmation" (Adorno "Perennial" 122). To celebrate "Negro spirituals" now was also to celebrate the un-freedom that they confirm. However, Adorno's position differs from the Left's provisional support of jazz specifically with regard to the question of abuse. Gordon's reservations about the aesthetic virtue of jazz did not hinder the Left's appropriation of it as a tool for its own agenda.

Of particular interest to the Left was the desire to dampen rivalries with black nationalists who had described themselves "as a nation within a nation" some seventy years prior to the Comintern's decision to adopt a similar line (Berry and Blassingame 397). In terms of improving the living standards of the African-American community, the gains brought about by the Left's activism in the 1930s had weakened support for black nationalist ideologies of Garveyism. Ellison portrays this competition in the Brotherhood's rivalry with the black nationalist, Ras the Exhorter (Naison 2; Strout 82). Jazz fell within the scope of this agenda, in part, because the Nazi denouncement of it as degenerate galvanized black civil rights activists and the Left in a common fight against the racist attitudes of fascism (Naison 3). But jazz was not supported for jazz's sake. Rather the Left's embrace of jazz further undermined black nationalism by coopting what Mary Berry and John Blassingame have called its cultural nationalistic program (Berry and Blassingame 388).

Ellison's novel parallels the Left's use of jazz when, on the advice of the invisible man, the Brotherhood attempts to gain a consensus for its overall agenda by forging one on a specific community issue, the resistance to evictions. The strategy is to force Ras and his black nationalist followers into a position where the only way for them to keep from contradicting their own rhetoric is to give their support to the Brotherhood. Having gained community support for this specific goal, Jack then shifts focus from local issues to international ones (Ellison *IM* 355; 418). Likewise, specific support by the Left for jazz music in the thirties was an attempt to gain consensus for a larger political agenda. Insofar as the Left capitalized on the opportunity presented by the Nazi denouncement of jazz, their interest in jazz was as "unadulterated" as the Brotherhood's interest in pushing the issue of unjust evictions in Harlem; both serve to divert support from black nationalism and build consensus for their own program; both are part diversion and ploy.

In contrast to such political stratagems, Adorno's criticisms evince an unwillingness to pay disingenuous lip service, i.e., to abuse jazz, as a political strategy for forging consensus. Having witnessed how easy it was for the Nazis to manipulate folklore in a similar manner, Adorno approached jazz with apprehension and caution, recognizing that out of their element the artifacts of folk culture can become powerfully dangerous rhetorical tools. In this regard,

Adorno's apprehensions have a subtle correspondence with the arguments of those whose defense of jazz emphasizes a cultural nationalism over the celebrated double life of jazz. Like Adorno, jazz critics who tend toward cultural separatism are most vehemently critical of the degrading abuse that jazz and jazz musicians have suffered and are skeptical of programmatic attempts to integrate them into a larger communal system.

Unlike Adorno, however, separatist critics attempt to circumvent the abusable dimensions of jazz by asserting its purity and value vis-á-vis environments that are prone toward abuse. Jazz becomes a music of "doing," whose vitality is lost in the recordings that document it.[36] Or the vitality of jazz diminishes "the further jazz move[s] away from the stark blue reality of the blues continuum and the collective realities of Afro-American and American life."[37] In a new context, jazz becomes re-coded, vitiated, reified. The vital literally becomes an object, manipulatable and marketable. The separatist project, then, is to shelter jazz from abusive environments—except the problem with blaming abuse entirely on socio-historical mediations (i.e., the social context), exempting jazz itself, is that the two cannot be neatly separated. The fact that jazz readily glides from one context to the next would suggest that it is fundamentally not as separatist as those who would "protect" it.

In reply to the unsympathetic analyses of black cultural nationalism that have dominated scholarship, Mary Berry and John Blassingame counter that, given the abysmal failures of integration, black separatism is no more "pathological," fantastic, or "unrealistic" as an idea than is integration (Berry and Blassingame 396). Yet neither is it any less problematic. If it were possible for jazz to thrive within a social vacuum, then perhaps apprehension would not have dominated Adorno's critique—and it is here that he parts ways with the majority of separatists. Whereas separatist critics often attack the abusers of jazz, Adorno pursues a radical critique aimed at eliminating the potential for abuse within cultural artifacts. His arguments presume that the potential for abuse (not just of jazz but of any cultural artifact) is one of the few areas of potential whose realization is virtually inevitable. This is no less true of jazz in the hands of the white jazz establishment than it is of Communism in the hands of Stalin. The same is true of the Enlightenment philosophies which underlie the Brotherhood's ideology in Ellison's novel, and which Adorno and Horkheimer subjected to a rigorous critique in *Dialectic of Enlightenment* precisely because, like jazz, the potential for abuse was part of their structure. For Adorno, the project of cultural criticism—however dubious its prospects might be—is to develop a discourse at whatever cultural level (high or low, aesthetic or philosophical) that cannot be appropriated, that cannot be abused. Not only do Adorno's criticisms of jazz link it with the culture industry; but, insofar as jazz purports to be a voice of liberation (separatist or otherwise), it also falls within the scope of Adorno's dialectical critique of Enlightenment philosophy. In both cases the issue for Adorno is to point out where discourses of liberation perpetuate the domination that they ostensibly eliminate, to show where they generate the abuse they are supposed to prevent. To criticize jazz is simultaneously to criticize the social structures from which it seeks (or purports) to disentangle itself, structures which inevitably absorb, appropriate, and alter jazz almost as quickly as it appears.

Unlike those paying lip service, the invisible man's interest in jazz is not a strategy for building consensus. He turns to jazz and the recordings of Armstrong in disillusionment with the Brotherhood, once he realizes that their "words [can] no longer teach him anything."[38] At first one might argue that the turn coincides with sentiments of many jazzmen who, "unable to convey . . . [their] deepest emotions in the received idiom . . ., invented terms of . . . [their] own."[39] The correspondence between Armstrong's voice and his horn would suggest that in Armstrong's musical riffs the invisible man seeks what the "Brotherhood's" idiom precludes.[40] Or along these same lines, the invisible man's shift from the Brotherhood to Armstrong coincides with Larry Neal's classic argument that Ellison is a counter-Marxian black nationalist, who develops, as Houston Baker has added, "a theory of culture able to lend clarity to the quest for Afro-American liberation."[41] But in Ellison's novel, the recordings of Louis Armstrong are not merely a reinstatement of the "double-voiced" tools repressed by those whose interest in the black community was never more than a calculated ploy in a larger struggle for power. The invisible man's relation to Armstrong is far more ambivalent and coincides with Adorno's own apprehensions about jazz—particularly with regard to the critique of jazz as a discourse of liberation.

Kimberly Benston argues that in his plight for recognition, the invisible man "is drawn into . . . the Marxian (or more accurately, Hegelian) historical myth of progress through linear, spiralling development," in short, progress toward a teleological goal.[42] According to Benston, the invisible man's movement toward freedom necessitates a recognition that teleological history is a myth (Benston "Historicism" 91).[43] Yet this myth is precisely what the invisible man finds repeated in Armstrong's music. In "The Poetics of Jazz," Ajay Heble explores how early jazz musicians, like Armstrong, relied on a diatonic scale. Structurally, the music resembles the "linear, spiralling development" cited by Benston. Armstrong's music drives toward resolution. Always evolving towards a goal, viz., the tonic, the music "begs for completion," fosters the illusion of *telos* and "produce[s] a semblance of [the] sociality" that has been denied the invisible man in his own experiences.[44]

The *telos* reflected in Armstrong's music may explain why the invisible man listens to "What Did I Do To Be So Black And Blue," rather than to Armstrong's legendary "West End Blues" or "Weather Bird." Like Adorno himself, the invisible man recognizes that "in music, the concept of representation or imitation as a way of correlating art and reality is not particularly fruitful" (Hohendahl *Reappraisals* 66). Adorno is as apprehensive about jazz culture as he is about Enlightenment philosophy—so too is the invisible man as ambivalent with Armstrong's teleological diatonic music as he is with the Brotherhood's teleological, dialectical ideology.

The myth of progress has beaten and excluded the invisible man. In the novel's epilogue he says he is uncertain whether his disillusionment "has placed him in the rear or in the avant-garde" (Ellison *IM* 599). This question of historical position, whether he is behind or ahead, reiterates the invisible man's relation to Armstrong. The position that he develops in relation to Armstrong not only resembles the ambivalence to jazz that Adorno expresses in his rejection of folk culture. It also expresses an attitude that only in retrospect has been called part of jazz history.

As is the case with Charlie Parker and bebop, the invisible man's personal history begins with his ambivalent relation to the diatonic music of Armstrong. When the invisible man says that he likes Louis Armstrong because "he's made poetry out of being invisible," his subsequent explanation of his "own grasp of invisibility" is a paraphrase of Charlie Parker. The invisible man explains: "Invisibility . . . gives one a slightly different sense of time, you're never quite on the beat. Sometimes you're ahead and sometimes behind" (Ellison *IM* 8). This is an explanation of the musical structure that Parker developed and that became the signature of bebop (Collier *Making* 350; 353–4). Upon its arrival, bebop was called everything but jazz. The musical dimension of bebop responded to a long history of repression, and the rejection of bebop by contemporary jazz critics fueled its momentum as a sub-cultural phenomenon. The subsequent placement of bebop in the jazz tradition was possible only by an improvised concept of history which, like the music of bebop itself, "denies system, closure, purity, abstract design" (Ostendorf 154). Like Schoenberg's own rejection of Late Romanticism's organic development, continuity and closure, bebop marks a departure from the organic musical structures that Adorno observed in the early forms of jazz. Insofar as the invisible man aligns himself with bebop's temporal and rhythmic revisions of Armstrong's music, he is also shifting conceptual modes of history. He shifts from a repressive systematic teleology to the unsystematic and to un-totalizing historical improvisation.

Critics have argued that, viewed from its social aspect, bebop was a "manifesto of rebellious black musicians unwilling to submit to further exploitation" and "was a deliberate attempt to avoid playing the role of the flamboyant black entertainer, which whites had come to expect" (Kofsky *Nationalism* 57; Collier *Making* 360). In this regard, Adorno's most vociferous attacks on the commercial jazz industry are contemporaneously as well as philosophically in harmony with the temperament of bebop. His criticisms coincided with a growing self-consciousness that occurred within African-American communities as bebop was on the rise. Baraka argues that during the forties African-Americans began to "consciously analyze and evaluate American society in many of that society's own terms." The crucial realization was that being black was not the only liability but rather that the society itself was also lacking. As the African-American community grew increasingly self-conscious and confident, the general deficiencies of American society became more apparent.[45] Like Adorno during his exile in the United States, black artists began to recognize the presence of these deficiencies, specifically in entertainment, and they sought art forms in which they could distance themselves "from a cultural tradition that . . . [had] been integrated into the culture industry" (Hohendahl *Reappraisals* 65). Bebop was actively engaged in this search. So was Ellison.

For all its emphasis on racial identity and on resistance to exploitation, bebop still succumbed to the debasement which it tried to avoid. The reasons for this are complex and not, as Frank Kofsky has argued, solely because whites controlled the "jazz establishment," found bebop's black nationalist undertones incompatible with their business interests and forced jazz musicians to conform.[46] Rather, the debasement resulted from dialectical tendencies in American society which were able to blunt "the sharp, ugly lines of . . . [the bebop] rebellion" (Ellison Shadow 204). In short, black nationalist or anti-capitalist sentiment has proven to be a lucrative product in the marketplace. "The culture industry can diffuse . . . rebellious sentiment . . . by repeating the same ideas and themes, even if they speak to the deepest contradictions of capitalism, until they lack all meaning."[47] Just as the invisible man turns to jazz when the Brotherhood's words of liberation and freedom prove to be the contrary, so too does the revolutionary promise of the jazz idiom accommodate, indeed contain, its opposite.

The presence of this opposite is most immediately apparent in bebop's point of departure, i.e., its attempted break from the traditions that Armstrong was said to embody. Through the figure of Armstrong in his novel, Ellison exposes the delusory, even contradictory, idealism that seethed beneath the beboppers' "rejection of the traditional entertainer's role" (Ellison *Shadow* 225). In his essays, Ellison expresses understanding for the desire of Parker's contemporaries to move beyond the "heritage from the minstrel tradition," viz., the tradition carried on by Armstrong, but at the same time he notes that the beboppers were caught up in the contradiction of trying to get "rid of the role they demanded, [striving] in the name of their racial identity . . . [for] a purity of status which by definition is impossible for the performing artist" (Ellison *Shadow* 225). Against the backdrop of "the thrust toward respectability exhibited by the Negro jazzmen of Parker's generation," the invisible man points out that Armstrong has not been superseded (Ellison *Shadow* 225). The break up of a linear teleological history has preserved him. Armstrong, the invisible man says, "is still around with his music and his dancing and his diversity, and I'll be up and around with mine" (Ellison *Shadow* 225; *IM* 568). Though clearly not Armstrong's, neither is the invisible man's diversity that of the beboppers.

An awareness of these contradictory tendencies—or deficiencies—pervades the writings of both Adorno and Ellison, and it is the search for a form in which to critically articulate the awareness of them that finally places the two writers dialectically at odds with both the deficiencies in American society to which bebop responded and to bebop itself. While Ellison's novel alludes sympathetically to bebop, the novel is no mere apology for it—any more than the unflattering portrayal of the Brotherhood is merely a criticism of the deficiencies of the communist party. First of all, inasmuch as bebop carries either a revolutionary or black nationalist agenda, it too falls within the scope of Ellison's critical presentation of the Brotherhood and of Ras. The invisible man does after all spear the black nationalist in the jaw. Secondly, to argue that bebop has superseded the pitfalls into which Armstrong fell is to grant to jazz the teleological history with which the invisible man is at odds. Correspondingly, the more one examines where and how Adorno's arguments diverge from the general similarities that they bear to bebop, the more Adorno's arguments converge with the attitude that Ellison develops toward jazz and bebop in his novel.

In particular, the beboppers were "resentful of Louis Armstrong," as Ellison was later to argue, "confusing the spirit of his music with his clowning" (Ellison *Shadow* 211). If Ellison's depiction of the beboppers is accurate, then Adorno's association of jazz with the antics of an "eccentric clown" at first appears to have fallen into the same trap.[48] In terms of general disposition, Adorno certainly had more in common with beboppers than he either realized or was willing to admit. How far this convergence extends beyond general disposition is another matter. Recently, Ulrich Schönherr has suggested implicitly that the convergence extends a great deal. Although Schönherr does not pursue the historical similarities between Adorno's arguments and those of bebop, he does argue that the contributions of musicians who followed in the wake of bebop have "largely fulfilled what Adorno had not seen realized in jazz" (Schönherr 93). But Schönherr has not gone unchallenged.

In the introduction to the volume in which Schönherr's article appears, Russell Berman and Robert D'Amico challenge Schönherr on the grounds that "to continue to defend jazz . . . through its later exponents and more 'artsy' performances vastly underestimates the force of Adorno's suspicion of emancipatory appearances."[49] Although it sounds as if Berman and D'Amico are addressing one issue and Schönherr another, i.e., as if Berman and D'Amico are reaffirming Adorno's dismissal of the notion that jazz is a source of liberation and Schönherr is merely concerned with musical innovations, the two are in fact intimately related, because the area in which jazz's most significant innovations have occurred is also the area in which jazz has traditionally expressed its emancipation: improvisation.

Schönherr's claim presupposes the position of critics like Bruce Baugh who argues that Adorno relies too heavily on musical notation and thus fails to recognize the significance of the unscorable subtleties of jazz and blues improvisation (Baugh 73–4). Yet, such assertions, which are standard criticism of Adorno, are premised upon a fundamental mis-perception about musical scores. Adorno points out that rather than producing mechanical acts, classical score establishes a sophisticated context for interpretation, the subtleties of which scoreless improvisations cannot provide and which are not part of notation anyway. Indeed, Adorno argues that "a performance of a Beethoven quartet that conveyed exclusively what was prescribed in the music would not make sense" (Adorno "Review" 168). "Inner transfiguration" and "paraphrases," traits which André Hodeir cites as hallmarks of improvisation, occur in every act of playing from the score.[50] The point is this: reading a musical score is already an improvisatory act, just as reading a text is an act of construction. The inevitable improvisatory movements within the context established by the score may in fact be the only prospects of liberation which music offers. For Adorno, the exploitative, abusive wherewithal of the culture industry is so pervasive that only the most concerted effort can circumvent it (in this case only the musician's interpretative response to an already orchestrated context of resistance).

Adorno's defense of scored music coincides with his general views on the critical function of art and culture as a whole. Each genuine cultural artifact facilitates an interaction that in turn cultivates critical resistance. This is not to say that, collectively, cultural artifacts lead to a unified concept of resistance or even of liberation. Rather they comprise a diverse array of critical contexts, the individual mastery of which impedes abuse and appropriation in specific repressive situations. Nor is this to say that jazz music has never achieved the level of critical sophistication to which Adorno refers; it is merely the false dichotomy of "free" improvisation and "constrictive" musical notation that is reductive.

Adorno's position on context, resistance, and cultural artifacts helps to explain the disparate cultural repertoire that the invisible man employs in order to break the rhetorical bind that Jack places him in with the contradictory statement: "You will have freedom of action—and you will be under strict discipline to the committee" (Ellison *IM* 351). The diverse field of reference in Ellison's novel provides "the resources of consciousness and imagination . . . [which the invisible man] brings to bear against the pressures of a changing environment."[51] For the invisible man, the "changing environment" is reflected in the evolution of Jack's sentence, in the casual (almost un-observable) glide from "freedom" to "strictness." Perhaps the invisible man's single most significant accomplishment lies in marshalling his diverse interaction with cultural artifacts in a grand unmasking of the latent "strict" repression in each of the discourses of liberation in the novel.

Armstrong belongs to the invisible man's cultural repertoire and to his process of unmasking repressive "strictness" masquerading as liberation. Insofar as the invisible man is able to use Armstrong in this regard, Ellison provides a positive dialectical compliment to Adorno's claim in "Perennial Fashion" that "the organization of culture" in levels of high, middle, and lowbrow is anachronistic and "reprehensible." Most importantly, Ellison uses Armstrong to read bebop against the grain. He uses what Adorno describes as the obsolescence of high and lowbrow distinctions in order to undercut bebop's attempt to obtain liberation through a recognition by "high" culture. To undercut this appeal to high culture, Ellison embraces Armstrong and places improvisation in the most debasing light (Ellison *Shadow* 225). The most explicit example of this is to be found in the factory hospital attendants who, while trying to give the invisible man an electronic lobotomy, tell him—like fans encouraging a jazz player to improvise—to "Get hot, boy! Get hot!" (Ellison *IM* 232). The hotter he gets the more effect the lobotomy will have. Ellison thereby creates a position sensitive to the criticisms Parker and his contemporaries levied against Armstrong while at the same time subjecting bebop to critical scrutiny. In this respect, the invisible man is able to transform his original ambivalence for Armstrong into a critical negative dialectic.

This dialectic is manifest in the hospital scene as well because the scene can also be read as an allusion to the degrading side of the jazz tradition that Parker and his contemporaries were trying to circumvent. They sought to avoid not merely the entertainer's role but also the association of this role with the tradition of minstrelsy. Adorno shared this sentiment, repeatedly drawing attention to the continued presence of minstrelsy in modern jazz. In 1938 he echoed the stock Leftist interpretation of jazz and argued that "the European-American entertainment business" had such control over jazz that its "triumph[s]" were "merely a confusing parody of colonial imperialism" (Adorno "On Jazz" 53). Nowhere was this colonial attitude more played out than in minstrelsy. Houston Baker has noted that in minstrelsy white Americans "conceptualized a degraded, subhuman animal as a substitute for the actual African" (Baker *Blues* 193).

The only way out of this degrading role is for Baker, like Ellison, to maintain that the private session of jazz and blues singers—when the white oppressor is absent—is where the real playing occurs (Baker *Blues* 193–94). Baker's argument is compelling so long as one is of the opinion that there are adequate opportunities for the mask to be cast aside and so long as earlier role playing does not impair or constrain the player when he or she is alone. In these presumptions, Baker follows the arguments previously articulated by Robert B. Stepto in *From Behind the Veil* (1979). Both critics rely on an idealistic conception of the self whose integrity is immune from impairment despite the repeated "self-humiliation" and the "symbolic self-maiming," which according to Ellison is enacted by the minstrel (Ellison *Shadow* 49). Stepto, for example, claims that one of the great achievements of *Invisible Man* is "its brave assertion that there is a self and form to be discovered beyond the lockstep of linear movement within imposed definitions of reality."[52] Not merely the advent of post-structural theories of the self challenges Stepto's and Baker's claims. So too does the invisible man's relation to minstrelsy. His "improvisation" at the factory hospital questions the extent to which the formation of a vernacular theory compensates for the "maiming."

In "On the Fetish-Character in Music . . .," Adorno begins his critique with an argument on the dissolution of the subject, a dissolution which arguably takes "humiliation" and "symbolic self-maiming" seriously and interprets such tendencies as having lasting debilitating consequences (Adorno "Fetish" 276). According to these arguments, vernacular theory is purchased at great cost. More recently, Eric Lott has explored how blackface minstrelsy enacted a complex symbolic castration of black males.[53] An allusion to this disturbing aspect of the jazz tradition occurs in the invisible man's dream when he is in the coal pit at the novel's end. Not only does he dream of castration, but he does so sleeping atop the material used to blacken faces in minstrelsy (Ellison *IM* 557). While Lott's exploration provides historical documentation for Adorno's infamous assertion that jazz has an "eunuchlike sound," the invisible man's dream graphically depicts what for Adorno were the most disturbing aspects of the blackfaced minstrelsy out of which jazz emerged. Indeed, Adorno was never able to see a function of jazz beyond the minstrelsy which he criticized in 1936 and 1938.

That the legacy of minstrelsy lies at the foundation of the jazz tradition is hardly subject to debate, but whether one can equate the colonialistic prejudices embodied in the figure of the minstrel with the late capitalist enterprise embodied in the jazz musician is another question. What Adorno does in his reading of jazz is to presume that the interest of capital in culture is tantamount to the gross sub-human parodies of African-Americans in minstrelsy. While the two are historically related, they are not the same, and to imply that they are succumbs to a blinding ahistoricism—with regard to minstrelsy but more significantly with regard to the historical consequences of late industrial capitalism. To undo this conflation is simultaneously to place Adorno in historical context and to uncover the dialectic at play in Ellison's novel. It is to apply the invisible man's break with the teleological historicism of the Brotherhood, his break with Armstrong's diatonic music, and his break with bebop's supposed evolution beyond swing; it is to apply all of these ruptures to the supposed continuity between minstrelsy and jazz. The question that jazz raises with regard to Adorno is whether the interest of the culture industry can really be reduced to a kiss of death for all cultural expression.

Scott DeVeaux has argued that jazz implicitly challenges traditional *agoraphobia*, the fear of the marketplace, which in cultural issues has manifested itself within an inflexible dialectic between "commercial" versus "artistic." Jazz challenges this dialectic because it "developed largely within the framework of modern mass market capitalism" (DeVeaux 530). Insofar as jazz has maintained a double life, this is perhaps where it is most readily to be found: in the forging of a space which is simultaneously commercial and aesthetically interesting. In fact, Adorno provides the basis for this argument in the peripheries of "On Jazz," where he concedes the need for high quality jazz in order to promote mass consumption and to "allow the upper class to maintain a clear conscience about its taste" (Adorno "On Jazz" 51). In his novel, Ellison moves Adorno's argument from periphery to center and explores the history of jazz as a securing and expanding of the parameters of the limited space for the quality (jazz or hibernation) that Adorno allows for marketing purposes.

Instead of merely dismissing Adorno as a cultural elitist, it is far more fruitful to address the evolution of his own terms—in other words, to consider whether the encroachment of technology and the culture industry is a process which halts once uniformity is supposedly reached. Florindo Volpacchio has argued that technical advances in market machinery were in direct response to the need to accommodate an increasingly diverse and fragmented consumer public. For its own survival the entertainment industry has had to accommodate heterogeneity.[54] Given Adorno's own pessimistic concerns regarding the momentum behind the culture industry, it is difficult to imagine how it would come to a standstill or avoid diversification in its own interest. There is an inkling of this awareness in a peripheral reference to jazz late in *Aesthetic Theory*, but whether the covert spaces of jazz would have attained visibility in the final version of Adorno's unfinished manuscript is a matter of speculation.

6

Cultural Identities, Commodities, and Myth: Adorno and Baraka on Wagner and the Flying Dutchman

For scholars sympathetic to Adorno's cultural criticisms, his unflattering critique of jazz has long been a source of discomfort because it so readily suggests a Eurocentric predisposition against American musical culture. Repeatedly, critics ease the harshness of Adorno's criticism of jazz by subordinating it to his general critique of the culture industry, an industry that, according to Adorno, neutralizes all cultural value and difference (whether high or low) and that has its beginnings with Richard Wagner. Ulrich Schönherr, for example, has described Adorno's views on jazz as a "failed encounter," but he, like Jamie Daniel and Martin Jay before him, is quick to note the parallel between Adorno's criticisms of jazz and his criticisms of Wagner (Schönherr 86; Daniel 40; Jay *Adorno* 119). Unfortunately, while it is true that there are important similarities between these two critiques—especially with regard to the culture industry—scholars have only mentioned them in passing, as an immediate reply to charges that Adorno's views on jazz are evidence of his cultural elitism.

By not examining the details of the comparison between Adorno's criticisms of Wagner and of jazz, scholars inadvertently pass over the real opportunity offered by the comparison. For Adorno, Wagner is not only the pivotal figure in the birth of the culture industry, but, as Andreas Huyssen has noted, Wagner is "the pivotal figure in Adorno's prehistory of the modern" (Huyssen 29). Thus, to scrutinize the similarities between Adorno's separate critiques offers the opportunity to consider the extent to which Adorno's analysis of jazz falls within his conception of modernism itself. Such considerations also begin an investigation into what Huyssen says is sadly lacking in Adorno's thought.

Huyssen criticizes Adorno for "never asking himself" whether the limited resistance to the culture industry which Adorno allows "could be located in the mass cultural commodities themselves" or whether the positions wrought by "gender, class and race" could significantly contribute to resistance (Huyssen 28). Although the criticism is particularly important to an examination of Adorno's critique of jazz—because as a cultural phenomenon jazz has traditionally been a meeting ground for questions regarding both "mass cultural commodities" and "race"—Huyssen is only partially correct in his criticism of Adorno. As the coming arguments will show, race has a central position in the conception of modernism which Huyssen convincingly demonstrates to be inseparable from Adorno's opposition to the culture industry. By locating the beginning of the culture industry with Wagner, Adorno takes issue with Wagner's anti-Semitism and challenges those who blame the commodification of culture on the Jews.

Inasmuch as Adorno's arguments on Wagner and the culture industry implicitly counter Wagner's racism, a comparison of Adorno's critiques of Wagner and of jazz cannot be limited to the negative influence of commodification. The comparison also unavoidably raises the questions of race and repressed cultures. As the following arguments will show, the issue in Adorno's critique of jazz is not so much whether he defends high culture against low culture, but whether the sophistication of his conception of repressed cultures is equal to the sophistication of his conception of the culture industry. Tracing the direct parallels between Adorno's critique of Wagner's music and of jazz, as I will do in the first section of this essay, is thus a preparation for a greater inquiry into Adorno's thoughts on ideology and race.

In order to assess the extent to which Adorno's critique of the culture industry intertwines with a critique of racism, it is also necessary to investigate the larger constellation of ideas with which Adorno was concerned following the first publication of his essays on Wagner and his earliest essays on jazz. At this time, he and Max Horkheimer were working out theoretical arguments on the culture industry, formulating a dialectic of myth and Enlightenment, and developing a general theory of prejudice from discussions of anti-Semitism. Historically, these separate arguments, all included in *Dialectic of Enlightenment* (1947), had the unspoken anti-fascist agenda of splintering the mainstays of Nazi ideology, especially the Nazi association of Jews with the negative influence of capital. These arguments also bear upon Wagner, an avid supporter of nineteenth-century "revolutionary anti-Semitism." I will argue in the second section of the essay that, in the context of Adorno's ideological critique of Wagner, the thematic divisions of the *Dialectic of Enlightenment* implicitly respond to a racist conflation—of myth, anti-Semitism and anti-capitalism—that is not only evident in Wagner's political pamphlets (especially his infamous "Jews in Music") but in his operatic adaptation of the myth of the Flying Dutchman as well. Drawing upon Wagner's own concession that the Flying Dutchman is a variation of the Wandering Jew, I will argue that Wagner's *Flying Dutchman* falsely unifies, under the guise of myth, all of the anti-Semitic epithets that the thematic divisions of *Dialectic of Enlightenment* meticulously dismantle.

Wagner's cultural chauvinism figures prominently in the theory of authoritarian normative values that Adorno developed in response to anti-Semitism, and Adorno extended this theory to account for the repression of minority cultures in general. The extension marks a crucial disruption in the parallels often drawn between Adorno's critiques of Wagner and jazz. Whereas Wagner's music and jazz occupy similar positions in relation to the culture industry, jazz culture belongs more appropriately to the domain of those who, like the Jews, have had to suffer the repressive chauvinism of people like Wagner. Yet where the parallels between Adorno's critiques of Wagner and jazz break down, a far more contentious one emerges: namely, the parallel that Adorno implicitly draws between the repression of the Jews and the repression of minority cultures in general.

The goal of the essay is thus to show how Adorno's critique of jazz is locked in a dialectic between two contradictory pulls: on the one hand, he uses jazz to argue that exchange value reduces all culture (whether high or low) to a repressive undifferentiated equivalence; and on the other, he himself understands repressed cultures only in their relation to the dynamics of anti-Semitism. In this respect, *The Flying Dutchman* is an ideal piece for inquiry—and not merely because the mythical figure of the Dutchman exemplifies Wagner's anti-Semitic chauvinism. Coincidentally, the African-American writer and jazz critic Amiri Baraka (LeRoi Jones) also uses the mythical figure in his drama *Dutchman* (1963). For Baraka, the Dutchman becomes the voice for an unapologetic assertion of a sublimated, violent Black jazz aesthetic. Since Baraka uses the Dutchman not only as a tool for interpreting jazz but also as a catalyst for dramatizing the complex relationship between racism and cultural values, his drama accommodates a critical examination of the parallel Adorno draws between repressive anti-Semitism and prejudice in general.

By stressing neglected aspects of the Dutchman myth, Baraka's *Dutchman* vigorously attacks the assumption that African-American experience corresponds to Jewish experience. Although a close examination of Wagner's libretto and Baraka's drama reveals that Baraka's character, the young black male Clay, echoes crucial lines from Wagner's character the Dutchman—and would thus suggest an affirmation of the parallels Adorno draws between the plight of the Jews and that of other repressed cultures—the two figures, I argue, are mutually exclusive. Unlike Wagner's emphasis on the myth's derivation from the Wandering Jew, Baraka underscores the myth's association with the slave trade and stresses versions of the myth in which the outcast figure of the Dutchman is black.

The differing emphases of Wagner and Baraka elucidate the fundamental contradiction that constitutes the Flying Dutchman's identity, and this contradiction maintains the distinctness of the experiences of Jews and African-Americans as members of repressed cultural minorities. In a genealogy of the myth, I point out that the Dutchman is accompanied by two specters—one white and one black—casting dice for the Dutchman's soul. The two are not reconciled but are suspended in dialectical opposition. For when the die is cast, one specter can win only at the other's expense. The myth of the Flying Dutchman thus contains a concept of difference and particularity that lends support to Adorno's analysis of Wagner's anti-Semitism but that in doing so simultaneously undercuts the compatibility of this analysis with an analysis of the plight of African-American culture, a plight that includes jazz history. It is not enough, however, to say that the myth of the Dutchman highlights the blindness of Adorno's conception of repressed cultures. The rivalry implicit in the two specters casting dice is reflected in the repressive foils that Baraka employs in forwarding his own aesthetic agenda.

While Baraka's *Dutchman*, in its evocation of long neglected allusions to Africans within the legend of the Flying Dutchman, forces a dialectical polarization in the unity upon which much of Wagner's anti-Semitic image depends, Baraka nonetheless succumbs to a cultural chauvinism that is comparable to Wagner's. His use of the Flying Dutchman to assert a black jazz aesthetic parallels Wagner's use of the same myth to assert high German culture. Similar to Wagner, Baraka posits cultural value by using a Jewish stereotype as a foil for his own black aesthetic. He thus falls prey to the dialectical course posited by Adorno and Horkheimer in *Dialectic of Enlightenment*, following a path from myth to enlightenment that regresses back again into repressive myth.

The ideological similarities between Wagner and Baraka ultimately expose how Adorno's sensitivity to the reductive tendencies of commodification obscures his lack of sensitivity to the internal dynamics of repressed cultures. By demonstrating how both Wagner and Baraka isolate and use the Jewish aspects of the Dutchman legend as a foil for their own cultural agendas, I intend to show, in the last section of this essay, how the anti-Semitic attitudes in Baraka's early writings (attitudes he has since publicly denounced) strain Adorno's efforts to use his critique of Wagner and his general discussions of anti-Semitism as a paradigm for a general theory of prejudice and racism.

Of Wagnerians and Jazz Enthusiasts

The similarities between Adorno's critiques of Wagner's music and of jazz are less the product of a conscious effort on Adorno's part to link the two forms of music than they are reflective of Adorno's recurrent methodological strategies. They derive from Adorno's opposition to an historical trend beginning in the late nineteenth century that he believes now impedes the ability to make legitimate assessments of cultural value: a gradual reification that has reduced all culture to its commodity value. What links his critiques of Wagner's music and of jazz is a belief that neither possesses the aesthetic wherewithal to combat this situation. They merely feign an opposition to a repressive system of commodification whose stagnancy they leave intact. Indeed, nowhere are the similarities between Adorno's critiques of Wagner's music and of jazz more similar than in assessments which depict both as relying on structural forms that counterfeit change, evolution, and temporal development within a system whose unchanging state they perpetuate.

Adorno comes closest to a deliberate parallel between the two musical forms in *Introduction to the Sociology of Music*, where he argues that popular music (which for Adorno includes jazz) merely extends the same commodified appeals that mar Wagner's compositions. Both appeal to a specific type of listener, the "cultural consumer," and cater to his/her fascination with "an exorbitant and, so to speak, measurable performance—breakneck virtuosity . . . wholly in the sense of the 'show' ideal."[1] According to Adorno, this listener, for whom "the joy of consumption . . . outweighs . . . [the] enjoyment of the music itself as a work of art," first posed as "a Wagnerian" in the nineteenth century, even "though today he is more likely to call Wagner names" (Adorno *SM* 7). Historical and aesthetic boundaries between Wagner and popular music give way to an unchallenged privileging of showmanship, whose "aesthetic appearance," exists solely "in order to further the cause of exchange value."[2] At the center of this commodity character in Wagner's work is, according to Adorno, a "failure at the level of technique" which results from "the fact that" in Wagner's music "eternal sameness presents itself as the eternally new" (Adorno *Wagner* 62). This same argument is of course the touchstone of Adorno's critique of jazz. He challenges its "timeless" or "perennial fashion," and its appearance of "perpetual novelty within perpetual sameness," arguing that these are mere marketing techniques as were the "wild antics of the first jazz bands" (Adorno *SM* 33; "Perennial Fashion" 119; *SM* 203; "Perennial Fashion" 121). For Adorno, the technical failure in Wagner's music and in jazz is a stagnancy that touts itself as fluidity, movement and change. At best an intoxicating "ersatz satisfaction" and at worst an empty false promise and a "rip-off," "perennial fashion" promises a novelty that it cannot deliver—a promise that was first practiced "on a grand scale" in Wagner's works (Adorno *SM* 27; 45).

Adorno locates a similar stagnancy in the very temporal structures of both musical forms. As later is the case with jazz, Adorno is exceptionally harsh with Wagner's reliance on beat. He argues that, historically, the reliance constitutes a regression back to when "conductors used a heavy stick to beat out the rhythm" and that Wagner's reliance on beat harks "back to . . . barbaric origins" (Adorno *Wagner* 32). More importantly, Wagner's use of beat as "a kind of abstract framework" falsifies mastery of "the empty time with which he begins, since the measure to which he subjects time does not derive from the musical content, but from the reified order of time itself" (33). In measures not derived "from the musical content"—what Adorno later also describes as jazz's "inability to conceive music dynamically . . . as something freely evolving"—Adorno sees a repressive imposition, an abstract assertion of temporal evolution that is in fact inertia: a sameness that presents itself as new (Adorno *SM* 13). The music betrays history and time by positing regression as progress.

Underlying Adorno's concern with the temporal inertia of these musical forms is an implicit equation of artistic merit with a work's ability to achieve, in aesthetic realms, a dialectical negation that exposes the thwarted and regressive evolution of late capitalistic society. Adorno thus interprets the "abandonment of properly motive-thematic work, the triumph of the compulsive repetition over the productive imagination of unfolding variations" in Wagner's work as a "resignation of a collective consciousness that can see nothing ahead anymore" (*SM* 63). He is also highly skeptical of the purported spontaneity in Wagner's music and of the free improvisation in jazz. For Adorno, Wagner's spontaneity and jazz improvisation are evidence of the un-dynamic randomness wrought by entropy. Wagner is "anxiously . . . intent," he argues, "upon making his music appear spontaneous, immediate and natural and upon concealing the controlling will" (*Wagner* 50). His "spontaneity" is but a facade decorating decline into uniform duress. Likewise, Adorno speculates that the freedom of improvisation is staged, that "what is served up as improvisation outside the innermost circles of jazz experts will have been rehearsed" (*SM* 31). For Adorno, such "spontaneity" and "improvisations" are the greatest betrayal of an aesthetic freedom that can only be achieved through a temporal development in the music itself, a freedom that manifests itself in overt opposition to the existing restrictions of present socio-historical conditions, whether these conditions be cultural, political, or both.

When one examines the presumptions underlying Adorno's comments on "breakneck virtuosity," "eternal sameness" and the "abstract [temporal] framework" of beat, an image emerges of Wagner's music and of jazz that, in Adorno's arguments, places their point of commonality in a two-fold illusory relation to temporal passage. Their musical structures, which abstractly assert a temporal development that they do not unfold, coincide with the music's illusory *engagements*, which abstractly assert a cultural and political agenda that they can only pretend to fulfill. Both musical forms, although "believed to be above the capitalist marketplace[,] remain tied to it, and to its underlying structure"—not only with respect to their musical techniques but also with respect to their socio-cultural agendas (*SM* 119).

Even their nationalistic programs, like their musical techniques, have marketable commodity value and are thus appropriated by the very forces they ostensibly oppose (*SM* 13). With Wagner, the appropriation ironically coincided with what was supposed to be the culmination of his cultural scheme. Adorno notes that "the social reality of [Wagner's] Bayreuth" was "a mockery of the national community concept" that was its impetus: the visitors who supported Bayreuth were of an "international set that the Teutonic nationalist could not but despise" (118). Similarly, as Houston Baker has pointed out, when black critics chastise the African-American community for its failure to "sustain modern jazz as 'legitimate' artistic expression," the logical conclusion is that the white community has been sustaining it and that modern jazz thereby cannot wholly be the artistic property of African-Americans (Baker *Afro-American Poets* 150). The pattern follows that of Wagner's Bayreuth in that both musical forms rely on seemingly radical cultural appeals whose susceptibility to being defused and packaged keeps them "captive of the culture industry and thus of musical and social conformism"(*SM* 34).

While Adorno's fixation on the temporo-structural dimensions of music evinces, in both of his critiques, an assessment of art based upon its relation to the (pro- or regressive) movement of history, the parallels in Adorno's analyses of the socio-cultural dimensions of Wagner's music and of jazz reveal a conception of history as that which, under the influence of capital, has regressed into a virtually unsublatable intransigence. With regard to issues of cultural value, the two musical forms succumb to the historical dialectic that Adorno and Max Horkheimer formulate in *Dialectic of Enlightenment*: both Wagner's music and jazz rely on gestures toward liberation that merely strengthen the repressive structures they oppose. Both fall prey to a dialectic in which "the circumstances of production . . . gain primacy over the productive forces" (*SM* 223). For Wagner, this dialectic quickly commodifies his anti-capitalistic sentiment and reduces his gestures toward freedom to an attempt to "warm up the alienated and reified relations of men and make them sound as if they were still human" (*Wagner* 100). Adorno argues that jazz faces a similar fate: while its "productive forces" might derive from black nationalist and radical sentiment, ultimately the "circumstances of production" mediate the structures through which these sentiments appear, and, as is also the case with Wagner's music, the "circumstances of production" turn identification with the sentiments of the "productive forces" into identification with the oppressor.

By focusing on the antinomies of "productive forces" and their "circumstances," Adorno sustains a rigorous dialectical materialism in his assessment of aesthetic import. Rather than appraising Wagner's music and jazz by the quality, potential or "inner abundance" that the marketplace—presumably for reasons of expediency—does not convey, Adorno maintains that potential (as "inner" or "subjective abundance") can only be understood as "the transmuted form of an experienced objectivity" (*SM* 48). In other words, aesthetic potential follows from objectification rather than the other way around. Adorno's critiques adhere to a materialist dialectic not only insofar as he subordinates potential to objectification, but also insofar as his arguments imply that to separate a work's "productive forces" from the actual "conditions" of its material manifestation posits an idealistic notion of art that both plays into ideology and fabricates history.

Adorno measures the aesthetic potential of both Wagner's music and jazz against the realities of the exchange principle. Unable to defy the rule of exchange and achieve a functionlessness "in a society that has been functionalized virtually through and through," their aesthetic value diminishes (*SM* 41). Especially in jazz, the dialectic of "productive forces" and "conditions of production" generates a "history of a heresy that has been received into mass culture." Caught in this dialectic, the history of jazz cannot be divided into the separable realms of heresy and commodified appropriation. Its history is rather that of "a protest against the official culture that has been socially captured and rendered harmless" (*SM* 33; 12–13).

As he rejects an idealistic separation of the potential of jazz from its manifest social realities, Adorno subtly lays the foundation for an argument that jazz alludes to something irretrievable and non-existent: that it evinces "those things which were not embraced" and "which fell by the wayside" in the movement of dominant socio-historical trends (Adorno *MM* 151). Lyotard, in an argument indebted to Adorno, has explained the notion of falling "by the wayside" as an incessant state of being forgotten: "The Forgotten is not to be remembered for what it has been and what it is, because it has not been anything and is nothing, but must be remembered as something that never ceases to be forgotten." Lyotard's comments are especially helpful in assessing what Adorno gains by emphasizing the manifest social reality of jazz; they suggest that a separation of jazz from its commercial manifestations obscures the irreparable absence and unrestorable theft of potential that commercial jazz signifies. When Adorno describes jazz as having been reduced to providing "tired businessmen" with vicarious compensation "for what they must deny themselves otherwise," he argues that commercial jazz is evidence of the potential that the rule of the commodity renders irretrievable (SM 9).

Given Adorno's belief that Schoenberg and the Viennese school successfully resisted the rule of the commodity, it is important not to misunderstand Adorno's criticisms of Wagner and of jazz as a complete rejection of any non-identity with market forces. What substantially increases Wagner's and jazz's susceptibility to commodification is what also constitutes perhaps their most important parallel in Adorno's criticism: their nationalistic agenda, which, Adorno notes made Wagner "an article for export like Hitler" (*SM* 167). The agenda is marketable because it offers radical but easy solutions by asserting its own identity through a process of exclusions, a process which, as the next section demonstrates, relies on a reductive conception of commodification.

Of Wagner, Culture and "Revolutionary Anti-Semitism"

Adorno's views on Wagner and jazz coincide regarding the relation of art to history and commodification. But taking his arguments on commodification out of the context of the larger scope of his analysis of Wagner greatly reduces the analysis' dialectical quality. For the question of commodification reverses a central tenet of Wagner's revolutionary cultural agenda. An exploration of this reversal is absolutely crucial to assessing how Adorno's critiques of Wagner and jazz overlap. The reversal even effects the structure of *Dialectic of Enlightenment*.

Adorno and Horkheimer carefully organize *Dialectic of Enlightenment* to maintain a clear distinction between their critiques of the culture industry and of anti-Semitism. The book's structure can be seen both as a response to the racism of the Nazis and as a response to a long tradition within German socialism, the leaders of which often equated Jewishness with capitalism and the profit motive. Marx's "On the Jewish Question" is the model for this type of writing. Wagner also penned a major polemic against the Jews. As Adorno noted a decade before *Dialectic of Enlightenment*: "Wagner's anti-Semitism is something he shared with other representatives of what Marx called the German Socialism of 1848" (*Wagner* 23). Like Marx's essay, Wagner's infamous "Jews in Music" reflects this "revolutionary" anti-Semitism.[3] But instead of discussing the profit motive in general, Wagner focuses on the influence of capital on culture and blames the decline of German culture on a process of commodification spearheaded by Jewish financial interests. He argues that "Jewish egoism exploits and dominates nature," and he "used the term art-commodity-exchange [*Kunstwarenwechsel*] to suggest that the relation of the Jews to art was identical to their relation to wares and commerce."[4] What is striking about Wagner's "revolutionary" anti-Semitism is the extent to which its concepts and even its terminology foreshadow the critique of the culture industry that Adorno and Horkheimer developed a century later.

In many respects, Wagner's "Jews in Music," because of its particular concern with the commodification of culture, looms in the shadows of *Dialectic of Enlightenment*. When Horkheimer and Adorno separate the discussion of anti-Semitism from the discussion of the culture industry, they not only dismantle the conflated strands of Wagner's argument; they also fulfill what for them is a necessary prerequisite to anti-fascist thought. Indeed, in the same year that Adorno and Horkheimer first published *Dialectic of Enlightenment*, Adorno argued that the lack of distinction between Wagner's anti-capitalism and his anti-Semitism reflected proto-fascist tendencies:

> Many of Wagner's specifically Fascist traits, particularly his antisemitism [sic.], are due to his opposition to the commercialization of culture, the socio-economic roots of which he was as incapable of realizing as was Nietzsche. But Wagner himself was not protected against the culture industry to come.[5]

Crucial to understanding the implicit fascism of Wagner's "revolutionary" writings are his "opposition to the commercialization of culture" and his inability to recognize its "socio-economic roots." For it is not "the Marxian idea of the social emancipation of the Jews . . . [being] the emancipation of society from the profit-motive" that is fascist in Wagner's arguments, but rather Wagner's appropriation of this formula for a nationalistic cultural agenda (*Wagner* 27). For Adorno, Wagner's use of the formula to defend the purity of German culture from the so-called "un-German" influence of the Jews reduces the "criticism of the culture market . . . [to] an apology for barbarism" (*MM* 152).

Ten years prior to his collaboration with Horkheimer, Adorno had already laid the theoretical groundwork for *Dialectic of Enlightenment* in the essays he later republished in *In Search of Wagner*. He criticized Wagner for failing to differentiate between "the Marxian idea of the social emancipation of the Jews" and for the general call for "the destruction of the Jews themselves" (*Wagner* 27). He argues that Wagner's anti-Semitism only superficially coincides with the Marxian critique of the profit motive. A "private idiosyncracy" motivates Wagner's anti-Semitism (*Wagner* 23).6 It is merely "an outlet" for "anger . . . discharged on defenseless victims" (*DE* 171). But most damning of all is Adorno's conclusion that the same Wagner, who was so concerned that Jewish influences were commodifying German culture, was himself "intertwined with the origins of the culture industry" (*Wagner* 107). Adorno counters Wagner's scorn for "art-commodity-exchange" with the argument that the "leitmotif" has "a commodity-function, rather like that of an advertisement" (*Wagner* 31). Evoking the same dialectical methodology that he and Horkheimer would soon apply to the Enlightenment, Adorno argues that Wagner's attempt "to escape the market requirements of the commodity known as opera. . . . paradoxically . . . only leads him more deeply into the commodity" (*Wagner* 82).

By linking Wagner to the culture industry, Adorno lays the foundation for the first of two strategies that he and Horkheimer developed in their analyses of anti-Semitism. The first of these strategies was to rigorously counter the reductive "equation of the modern money-hungry world with 'Judaism'" and to demonstrate how much more complex the logic of the commodity and the commodification of culture are than the anti-Semitic stereotypes allow (Rose *Race and Revolution* 38–39). In the case of Wagner, Adorno demonstrated how "the rule of the commodity," as the organizing principle in bourgeois society, could appropriate even Wagner's attempt to escape market requirements. Furthermore, whereas Wagner scorned the Jew because he "stands in correlation with none but those who need his money; and never yet has money thriven to the point of knitting a goodly bond 'twixt man and man," Adorno takes Wagner's slur as "an early example of the changing function of the bourgeois category of the individual."[7] The money-minded characteristics which, Wagner argues, "tore asunder" the Jew's "connection with the former comrades in his suffering" (Wagner "Jews in Music" 53), are, according to Adorno, the plight of every individual (including Wagner) not only in nineteenth-century liberal capitalism but especially in the advanced stages of twentieth-century monopoly or late capitalism:

> In his hopeless struggle with the power of society, the individual seeks to avert his own destruction by identifying with that power and then rationalizing the change of direction as authentic individual fulfillment. The impotent petitioner becomes the tragic panegyrist (*Wagner* 17).

Within a society organized according to the "rule of the commodity," money-mindedness is essential for survival, and the society's concomitant ideology of "individual fulfillment" rationalizes the contradictory pursuit of securing individual survival through a perpetuation of the very system that threatens one with destruction.

Like Wagner, Adorno and Horkheimer "argued for an egoism that is more than the self-interest of *homo oeconomicus*," something that would (re)instate the "goodly bond" to which Wagner refers.[8] But this "goodly bond," insofar as it is the mark of "serious art" and culture, has succumbed to the competitive struggle to survive: "Serious art has been withheld from those for whom the hardship and oppression of life make a mockery of seriousness" (*DE* 135). Adorno praises Wagner for belonging "to the first generation to realize that . . . [the] world . . . has been socialized through and through" (*Wagner* 119). What Wagner failed to realize, however, was that the pervasiveness of this socialization was exemplified in the reified conscious structures that blinded him to his own participation in the commodification which he attempted to resist by personifying it in the Jews.

The second strategy that Horkheimer and Adorno employ in their analysis is to open "Elements of Anti-Semitism," the chapter in *Dialectic of Enlightenment* that follows their critique of the culture industry, with a conditional acceptance of the seemingly contradictory views that Jews are a race and that they are merely a group with a shared tradition, having "no national or racial characteristics" (*DE* 168). Stressing the notion of a shared tradition, Adorno and Horkheimer posit anti-Semitism as an instance of a wider social phenomenon that coincidentally has victimized the Jews and that originates not out of Jewishness but rather out of authoritarian normative attitudes. So little does anti-Semitism have to do with Jewishness-as-such and have rather to do with repressive and authoritarian social norms that its "victims are [not only] interchangeable according to circumstance" and could alternately be "gypsies, Jews, Protestant, Catholics, and so on," but any one of its victims "may take the place of the murderers, with the same blind lust for blood, should they be invested with the title of the norm" (*DE* 171). These comments on interchangeability, so unsentimental about the frailty of common traditions in the face of authoritarian normative agendas, parallel Adorno's de-personification of commodification—in this instance, the victimization of Jews having nothing essentially to do with Jewishness and rather stemming from the establishment and enforcement of a general social norm.

The question of race becomes relevant only when Adorno and Horkheimer consider the history of the Jews' restricted interaction with other Europeans, in particular their interaction with Germans. Whether the Jews constitute an actual race is less important than the fact that their "Aryan colleagues" considered the Jews to be a race and controlled the terms of its definition: "the most compelling anthropological proofs that the Jews are not a race will, in the event of a pogrom, scarcely alter the fact that the totalitarians know full well whom they do and whom they do not intend to murder" (*MM* 102). In order to interact successfully with the Germans, the Jews had to accept the designation of race and abide the racial stereotypes that structured the way society perceived them. They "were only allowed to retain their . . . [high positions in industry and in the administrations of German emperors] if by their behavior they tacitly accepted or confirmed the verdict pronounced on other Jews" (*DE* 174). This self-defeating necessity created a situation in which Jewish assimilation meant not so much a personal denial of a problematic concept like their "true Jewish identity" as much as it did an acceptance of a clearly false, stereotypical, and alienating identity.[9]

Because assimilation meant acceptance of a reductive and anti-Semitic identity, the Jews—even those who maintained some semblance of assimilation—"could not be absorbed into European nations; they were not allowed to put down roots and so they were dismissed as rootless" (*DE* 175).[10] The Jews who resisted the stereotypes and would not assimilate anti-Semitism found themselves trapped nonetheless. European society had developed a stereotype of the Jews that accounted for its exclusionary practices against them: the Jews who resisted a false assimilation demonstrated their "rootlessness" and those whom the Germans excluded and expelled supposedly didn't want to be absorbed anyway.[11]

In terms of its structure, Adorno's and Horkheimer's argument on anti-Semitism and race echoes their argument on anti-Semitism and the commodity. In the latter, the stereotype of the money-minded Jew becomes the reified economic contradiction faced by all individuals who, in their struggle for survival, perpetuate a system that is essentially hostile toward them.[12] With regard to anti-Semitism and race, the contradictory dynamic is the same. The Jews who historically resisted the reductive anti-Semitic stereotypes prevalent in European society succumbed to them nonetheless: resistance was reduced in stereotype to another example of Jewish rootlessness. Similarly, the Jews who assimilated accepted the very anti-Semitic attitudes—as part of their assimilation—that their assimilation attempted to circumvent. Most importantly, the figure of the Jew becomes in Adorno's and Horkheimer's argument the embodiment of non-identity with the norm, and the fate of the Jews at the hands of the Nazis becomes the quintessential illustration not only of the cost of non-identity but of forceful integration as well.

Ironically, the general ideological structures with which, according to Adorno and Horkheimer, all individuals who fall out of the norm must contend, parallel Wagner's analysis of the plight of the Jew: "the educated Jew" stands "alien and apathetic," "his whole artistic bent . . . [being] a mere luxurious, needless thing" in a society "with whose tastes and aspirations he does not sympathize, whose history and evolution have always been indifferent to him" (Wagner "Jews in Music" 53). By separating their discussions of the culture industry from anti-Semitic stereotypes and by conceiving anti-Semitism as a principle that potentially attacks all forms of non-identity, Adorno and Horkheimer dialectically counter the racist components of Wagner's essay and arrive at the threshold of a full-blown modernist aesthetic.

Bryan Magee in *Aspects of Wagner* argues that Wagner's description of the Jews is "substantially correct," but that this same condition has become the condition articulated in modern art.[13] In Adorno's argument, the condition is beyond that articulated in modern art; it is, as Adorno noted much later, the condition of art itself in a free-market society, deliberately without function but appropriable by the society it resists: "Profit takes [the] functionless [of art] into its service and thereby degrades it to meaninglessness and irrelevancy" (*SM* 41). The functionlessness, the indifference and lack of sympathy, that Wagner ascribes to the Jews becomes the characteristic of autonomous modern art in Adorno's aesthetics. The fear expressed by Wagner concerning the commodification of culture through a so-called negative influence of the Jews, if separated from its anti-Semitism, becomes a prophetic description of the fate of autonomous culture in the shift from nineteenth-century liberal capitalism to the reunification of culture with the economic in "the new technological media of reproduction and dissemination [of] monopoly capitalism" (Huyssen 21).

Of Paintings, Projections, Ballads, and Blues

Since Adorno counters Wagner's vilification of the Jews with a general theory of authoritarian normative agendas, initial considerations would suggest that his criticism of Wagner provides a framework through which to understand the fate of jazz in an America dominated by white normative values. If the issue in Adorno's critique of Wagner's anti-Semitism is not Jewishness-as-such but rather the authoritarian dispositions of those who single out Jews for repression, then jazz culture would appear to have more in common with those who are the object of Wagner's authoritarian attitudes than with Wagner's cultural ideology. The movement from the particular example of anti-Semitism to a general theory of normative values ought, on one level, to set Adorno's critique of Wagner at odds with his critique of jazz. But the contrast never occurs in Adorno's writings—in part because in both critiques Adorno devotes very little attention to specific pieces or works. Ideally, then, what is needed in order to examine the similarities between Adorno's critiques of Wagner and of jazz is a context which simultaneously considers whether Adorno's general analysis of Wagner sustains application to a specific opera and whether his theory of authoritarian normative agendas applies to rather than defends jazz.

The suitability for such considerations of Wagner's *The Flying Dutchman* derives above all from its representation of the Dutchman. In this representation, the opera initially appears to embrace an attitude that not so much confirms

Adorno's criticism of Wagner but rather coincides with the position from which Adorno articulates his critique. In other words, the opera initially appears to use the Dutchman to challenge normative agendas. Though this appearance ultimately functions as an ideological diversion for a more repressive cultural program, it also suggests that the opera incorporates tensions that reconcile the seeming incompatibility—with regard to normative values—of Adorno's critiques of Wagner and of jazz. In its apparent challenge to normative values, the opera assumes a position that for Adorno is characteristic of the illusory challenges offered by jazz.

What intensifies the suitability of *The Flying Dutchman* is that the African-American jazz critic and playwright Amiri Baraka appeals to the same myth as Wagner in order to posit a black jazz aesthetic in his drama *Dutchman.* In fact, Baraka's use of the myth of the Flying Dutchman as a defense of jazz ultimately succumbs to the same ideological patterns observable in Wagner's opera. In both pieces, however, the ideological program emerges only after they first articulate an apparent challenge to normative values. While Baraka's views on jazz are certainly subject to debate, they are nonetheless significant in this context because he uses jazz as a catalyst for challenging the normative values of white America. Exploring the ideological parallels between these two pieces thus facilitates an examination of the nature of the parallels between Adorno's critiques of Wagner and of jazz.

In both the opera and the drama, the challenge to normative values results from a subtle and gradual disclosure of repressive mis-perceptions, foreshadowed even in the earliest encounters between the central characters (viz., between the Dutchman and Senta in the opera and Clay and Lula in the play). Both Wagner's Dutchman and Baraka's Clay express a delighted confusion about the immediate interest that the female characters take in them. Whereas Senta's spontaneity spurs on an inquisitiveness in the Dutchman that supplants confusion, with Clay the confusion only gradually dissipates and manifests itself first in his being "a little surprised and maybe stiff" when Lula approaches him on the subway.[14] The Dutchman, on the other hand, probes unsuccessfully for the source of Senta's interest in him. Though he asks, "Could deepest sympathy for my suffering penetrate you," he does not learn that the source of Senta's "sympathy" is his similarity to a painting and a ballad about him.[15] Senta's entire attachment to the Dutchman, an attachment which precedes ever having seen him, derives from her emotional fixation on these representations, and she quickly places him within the framework that they provide.

Wagner's stage directions emphasize that Senta is moved not by the unfolding of the Dutchman's character but rather by his correspondence to her constructed image of him. Rather than examining how closely the representations correspond to the actual Dutchman, Senta pursues the contrary course. The second act introduces Senta "leaning back in a large armchair . . . sunk in contemplation of the picture on the wall" (Wagner *Flying Dutchman* 58), and, when the Dutchman arrives with Daland, her father, Senta's excitement results from his resemblance to the painting she has of him:

> The door opens and the Dutchman and Daland appear. The Dutchman enters at this moment. Senta's gaze turns from the picture to him and she gives a violent cry of surprise, after which she remains transfixed without taking her eyes off him (Wagner *Flying Dutchman* 65).

The initial movement from "picture" to person is indicative of Senta's entire interaction with the Dutchman. From the picture and the ballad of the Dutchman, Senta constructs a system which mediates all her responses and from which she will not allow the Dutchman to diverge. Later, in the third act, for example, when the Dutchman believes that Senta has been unfaithful to him with Erik and bids Senta farewell, Senta responds to the Dutchman's explanation of his fate with the claim: "I know you well! Well I know your fate. I knew you when I first saw you! The end of your suffering is here" (Wagner *Flying Dutchman* 76). While Senta's statement reaffirms her commitment to the Dutchman, it also rebukes his attempt to explain who he is. In other words, Senta tells the Dutchman that she doesn't need his explanations, for she knows the recorded legend about him.

Baraka interprets the Dutchman's relation to Senta's fixation on the ballad of the Flying Dutchman as a paradigm of an individual's struggle to break out the normative values through which others perceive him or her, and in Baraka's play these subtleties of Wagner's opera have been shaped into the pivotal dramatic tensions of *Dutchman*. Senta's statement "I know you well!" becomes Lula's statement to Clay" "I know you like the palm of my hand"—extensions of her earlier assertions: "you're a well-known type" and "I know the type very well." Lula makes these statements while "humming snatches of [a] rhythm and blues song," and thus Baraka transposes Senta's fixation on the ballad of the Flying Dutchman into a general fascination with jazz and blues. Out of this fascination Lula constructs an image of African-American culture that provides her with the "type" she claims to recognize in Clay (Baraka *Dutchman* 17; 12). Indeed, much of the dramatic tension results from Clay's thwarted attempts, at the play's end, to break out of the categories into which Lula has forced him. Senta has done much the same thing with the Flying Dutchman. Her statement that she knows him "well!" is really a statement that she knows the ballad and the painted image of the Dutchman well.

Senta's reduction of the Dutchman to the ballad of him is of no small consequence. The reductiveness blinds Senta to the very real peril to her own person that her constructions generate. While the ballad acknowledges that only a faithful woman can redeem the Dutchman from his fate, nowhere does it remark on the fate which the Dutchman himself later explains awaits those unfaithful to him: "eternal damnation." Nor does the ballad give a full account of what faithfulness entails: a profession of fidelity "before the Eternal One"—which, although somewhat vague, is another way of saying that subsequent infidelity to the Dutchman will cost a woman her life. Senta's fixation on the ballad obstructs her understanding that infidelity to the Dutchman makes him a jealous executor of the sentence of "eternal damnation." The Dutchman reiterates this threat when, after having discovered Senta with Erik the Hunter, he alludes to the fate of "numerous victims" who "have fallen to this sentence through" him (Wagner *Flying Dutchman* 76). Since the unfaithful enter into (a damned) eternity "through" him, when the Dutchman tells Senta that "ten-fold death would be to me a desired pleasure," the statement cannot wholly be understood as an exaggerated longing for his own death—especially since the Dutchman has just heard Erik remind Senta of her promise to remain true to him (74). He is in fact threatening to place Senta "before the Eternal One." Erik fully understands the threat to Senta's life, and, "in wild anxiety," he calls "to the house and to the Norwegian ship" for help. As the Dutchman departs—having resisted the temptation to kill Senta—he replies to her claim "I know you well" with "you do not know me, you have no idea who I am!" (76).

The Dutchman's decision to leave without killing Senta suggests that her life has been spared on a technicality: not she, but the image she has constructed of the Dutchman is unfaithful to him, and she remains constant to a reductive attempt to make the Dutchman faithful to the constructed image. At the center of tension is a ballad that inadequately represents the full complexity of the Dutchman's experience. It is the source of Senta's projections. Inadequate representation offset by an obsessive constancy to and misdirected embellishment of that representation constitutes the underlying tension of Wagner's opera—and also of Baraka's *Dutchman*. Like the opera, the drama revolves around the representational limits of a musical form (jazz) that is the product of a vast and complex socio-historical experience.[16] The reductive image of African-Americans that Lula constructs from jazz's representation of their experience parallels Senta's relation to the ballad of the Flying Dutchman. In fact, Lula's implied presumptions about blues and jazz culture provoke Clay's most eloquent expressions of how little she knows or understands either about jazz or what he calls "the pure heart, the pumping black heart" (Baraka *Dutchman* 34). In Baraka's drama, however, Lula's projections more clearly reinforce a preexisting system of repressive normative values. The discursive structures of this system are so pervasive that Clay can only combat Lula's understanding of jazz with terms that imply the illegitimacy of jazz and African-American literature.

In a scene patterned after the closing act of Wagner's opera, Clay not only echoes the Dutchman's threat-laden correction of Senta's mis-perception of his situation. He also clarifies the latent dispositions of jazz that are obscured by Lula's system of values. Just as the Dutchman tells Senta that she has no idea who he is, Clay finally responds to Lula's claim to know his "type" by telling her: "You don't know what you're talking about. You don't know anything" (Baraka *Dutchman* 33). Though more directly, Clay's counter to Lula's presumed knowledge of African-Americans repeats the Dutchman's ambiguous threat to Senta. He openly tells her: "I could murder you now." The echoes of Wagner culminate when Clay places the Dutchman's desire for "a ten-fold death" at the heart of Charlie Parker's creative genius. The maneuver coincides with Adorno's own claim that "every work of art is an uncommitted crime" and reflects a desire with which Clay subsequently identifies (Adorno *MM* 111):

> Bird would've played not a note of music if he just walked up to East Sixty-seventh Street and killed the first ten white people he saw. Not a note! And I'm the great would-be poet. Yes, that's right. Poet. Some kind of bastard literature . . . all it needs is a simple knife thrust. Just let me bleed you, you loud whore, and one poem vanished (Baraka *Dutchman* 35).

By recasting the Dutchman's desire for a "ten-fold death" in racial terms, Clay radically intensifies the charge of blindness against Lula. Like Senta and the ballad, Lula's familiarity with jazz and blues leads her to false conclusions about African-Americans. At best, Lula could be said to have an "appreciation" rather than "an understanding of the attitude which produced" jazz (Baraka *Black Music* 13). Her "appreciation" stems from a system of values whose embrace of jazz multiplies the very rage it does not see because the embrace withholds an unconditional recognition of legitimacy. Clay's reference to "bastard literature" alludes to his own and jazz's insurmountable illegitimacy within the normative values that govern even Lula's liberal attitudes. Lula's "appreciation" reflects a system of values that, despite whatever accuracy one might attribute to Clay's account, has rendered the rage of jazz innocuous and marketed it for profit.

In one respect, Clay's references to Charlie Parker and Bessie Smith momentarily divert the scrutiny that Lula has so skillfully focused on him. But even the diversion merely shifts attention to a cultural phenomenon, the denial of whose legitimacy reflects the course of Clay's own experience. For though Clay may be "a well-educated, well-dressed, [and] well-adjusted young man," his adjustments preclude the legitimacy that they seek—as is graphically illustrated by Clay's final act of identification with jazz.[17] His decision to follow the example of Charlie Parker and to opt for alternatives to murder prompts his own murder.[18] With regard to dramatic function, the decision serves as an accelerated illustration of the gradual course that Clay has pursued all along.

As he seeks legitimacy by assimilating "his values to those of a materialistic and rationalistic culture"—an assimilation that is necessary for his own survival—Clay encounters the contradictions through which normative values regulate difference.[19] Either his difference excludes him altogether or assimilation forces him into vulnerability. Rather than leading to full acceptance, his assimilation opens him to charges of wearing a jacket and tie "from a tradition . . . [he] ought to feel oppressed by," of being "full of white man's words," and of being "just a dirty white man" (Baraka *Dutchman* 18; 31).

The tense exchange about Clay's clothing and ethnicity occurs under the implicit pressure generated by the other passengers' presence and derives from the fact that Clay, in his individual efforts to succeed, must ignore the racist oppression that helped to build and structure the society whose values he must espouse for his own advancement.[20] As is the case with the normative values which, according to Adorno, structure anti-Semitism, opportunity for Clay depends upon a tacit acceptance of the larger institutional or structural exclusions of African-Americans in white America. Individual necessity forces Clay in his own interest to perpetuate a system that collectively works against his own interest. As Sherley Anne Williams has noted:

> Assimilationism seems to mean that one accepts the various stereotypes which bolster the white supremacist's image on a group basis while one rejects them on an individual basis, particularly if that individual is one's self.[21]

Williams's description of Clay's assimilation is an almost exact parallel of Adorno and Horkheimer's description of Jewish assimilation. Both equate it with absorption into an essentially hostile community of discourse. Ironically, the hostility does not diminish with an individual's acceptance of the norm, because the norm needs aberrations for its own identity.

If Lula were merely a homicidal psychopath seeking victims, the conclusion of *Dutchman* would not achieve the dramatic force that it does. What gives the conclusion its force is the tension generated from Lula's concomitant espousal of liberal ideals and expression of homicidal tendencies, the former functioning as an umbrella for the latter. Though somewhat crudely put, the disparity between these two inclinations illuminates the regressive moment in attitudes which ostensibly are progressive. In this respect, Baraka exploits perhaps the most significant parallel between Lula and Senta, for Senta too bases her fixation on the Dutchman on what she believes to be a progressive comprehension of his plight, a comprehension that she attempts to pass on to Erik. When in the second act of Wagner's opera, Erik reminds Senta of the promise of marriage she has made to him, Senta remains elusive and, instead of reaffirming her promise to Erik, portrays her attraction to the Dutchman as a general expression of human compassion. She asks Erik equivocally: "Shouldn't the pitiful fate of terror move me?" In her effort to distract from the personal quality of her emotions, Senta "leads Erik close to the picture to explain her meaning" and then asks him whether he doesn't also feel "the pain" and "deep remorse" that is represented in the Dutchman's portrait (Wagner *Flying Dutchman* 64). Yet by using the portrait as the basis for a general appeal for compassion, a portrait that later proves to be an inaccurate depiction of the Dutchman, Senta's appeal becomes an abstract force of repression. For the compassion she solicits inherently excludes the person on whose behalf it is voiced.

In Baraka's play, these abstract sympathies are represented in an eroticized form of white liberal attitudes which Clay, after having been provoked by Lula, attacks on two fronts.[22] First of all, Clay points out the repressive unacknowledged dimension of Lula's liberal ideals. When Clay points out that "Western rationalism" teaches men and women to murder with "sober," "pious," and "very rational explanations," Lula, grossly offended and in a "different, more business-like" tone, indignantly tells Clay "I've heard enough" and takes the first opportunity to kill him (Baraka *Dutchman* 36). Furthermore, Clay points out to Lula—just as the Dutchman points out to Senta—that her ideals are misconstrued anyway. Just as Senta bases her infatuation on a flawed constructed image of the Dutchman, so too does Lula base her interaction with Clay upon a naive understanding of what it means to be black in America. In one of the most oft cited lines of the play, Clay tells Lula: "You don't know anything except what's there for you to see. An act. Lies. Device. Not the pure heart, the pumping black heart" (Baraka *Dutchman* 34). With this assertion, Clay establishes a fundamental delineation between Lula's perceptions of him and his own identity. What the nature of this delineation is, however, has been the subject of much debate.

Kimberly Benston has interpreted Clay's statement as an assertion about whites in general, who, according to Benston, "believe they can penetrate the pure, pumping black heart by learning a few of black culture's symbols and venerating a few of its more obvious leaders." To follow Benston's arguments, whites are like Senta constructing a sentimental image of suffering from the portrait of the Dutchman: "they cannot truly go behind the mask and discover the ground of suffering and wisdom that is the necessity of this culture, the home of Clay's true identity."[23] It is difficult enough to understand the logic of how Benston is able to penetrate the white heart deeply enough to know that whites cannot penetrate the black heart. But the generalizations about whites are not nearly so problematic as Benston's final claim about "Clay's true identity." Indeed, much of the criticism of Baraka's play hovers around essentialist concepts like "one's true self," "the notion of an authentic self," and "white America" being "blind to the real Clay."[24] Unfortunately, this tendency in criticism is at odds with the deeper subtleties of Baraka's drama.[25]

The play accommodates a delineation between "an authentic" and "unauthentic" black self only at the level of Clay's angry response to Lula's offensive presumptions about who and what he is. Indeed, his more focused attack on Western rationalism challenges the very tradition from which "the notion of an authentic self' comes. As Andreas Huyssen has noted, the notion of a stable or authentic self' is a product of "the bourgeois age," a product coincidentally enough, of Wagner's age (Huyssen 23). "The notion of the authentic self' derives from the tradition which Lula rightly tells Clay he "ought to feel repressed by" (Baraka *Dutchman* 18). The fact that Clay, in the heat of his anger, appeals to the abstract categories of the very tradition he rejects, is a profound illustration of what Horkheimer in "Egoism and the Freedom Movement" has described as the difficulties of maintaining a separate cultural identity in a social environment that is fundamentally and historically hostile:

> In the historical process in which the individual attained abstract consciousness of his own self, the abolition of slavery ended one form of class society, but not classes themselves, and so it did not only emancipate man but also enslaved him internally at the same time.[26]

The enslavement to which Horkheimer refers is that of "the superficial independence of economic subjects," whose freedom is consumed by the need to sustain themselves economically. In its consideration of the relation of African-Americans to white culture, Baraka's drama develops a similar notion of internal enslavement. Werner Sollors has argued, in contrast to Benston and the "true self' school, that Lula and Clay "are not fully individualized 'characters' in the sense of realistic drama, but reified types" (Sollors 118). It is against this reification that Clay must struggle, a struggle that pulls him simultaneously between "Lula's ethnocentric white culture" and "the black ethnicity represented by the blues."[27] Clay's reference to "the pure heart, the pumping black heart" is not so much a reference to a separate "authentic self' as it is a negative dialectical rejection of the reified mode through which Lula perceives him.

Dutchmen, Dialectics, and Difference

Adorno's critiques of Wagner and jazz overlap in his assertion that both rely on structural forms that counterfeit resistance and evolution within a system whose un-changing state they perpetuate. In *Dialectic of Enlightenment*, Adorno and Horkheimer make similar claims about the path of Enlightenment philosophies out of myth: in pursuit of their ideals, these philosophies inevitably regress back into myth. Since the Dutchman in Wagner's opera and the jazz aesthetic in Baraka's drama can be assessed in terms that suggest resistance to authoritarian normative values and since both rely on myth as their point of departure, the question that arises is whether, in their deployment of myth, *The Flying Dutchman* and *Dutchman* regress back into the practices of exclusion which they promote themselves as having dialectically opposed. With regard to the dialectical and temporal evolution which Adorno argues is lacking in both Wagner's music and in jazz, the issue in *The Flying Dutchman* and *Dutchman* is whether their posited enlightened ideals and evolution are mythical precisely because the opera's and drama's movements rely on false unities.

Scholars writing on Baraka's drama almost inevitably note that Baraka appeals to the same myth that Wagner uses in his opera. Yet the few who have discussed this allusion have never really explored the sense in which Baraka's use of this specific myth challenges an entire tradition of literary and cultural exclusions, and in particular the sense in which Baraka uses the character of Clay to expose Wagner's selective use of myth.[28] In fact, an exploration of how Baraka summons the rich tradition out of which the myth comes illuminates the exclusions upon which Wagner relies in order to posit a redemption of the Flying Dutchman at the end of his opera. Initially, then, while Wagner's Dutchman and Baraka's Clay overlap in their relation to Senta and to Lula, Baraka's use of the myth of the Flying Dutchman develops in opposition to Wagner and formulates an alternative, indeed mutually exclusive, claim to the same myth. This alternative claim functions on two levels. For while Baraka exposes the selective use of myth in Wagner's opera, he does so in order to formulate a black jazz aesthetic, and thus each step toward a more comprehensive understanding of the myth of the Flying Dutchman carries an implicit rebuttal to the historical reception of jazz.

In one respect it is wholly consistent with the myth of the Flying Dutchman itself that both Wagner and Baraka vie for possession of it. John Livingston Lowes, in his classic study of Coleridge's adaptation of the same myth, notes that the legend of the Flying Dutchman derives from an oral tradition in the Netherlands about a Captain Falkenberg who is condemned to the seas because of a murder that he committed. Lowes adds that Falkenberg is "accompanied by two spectral forms, one white, one black" and that "the two forms play at dice for the wanderer's soul."[29] It is not a matter of coincidence that the image of the white and black "spectral figures" parallels the implicit competition between Wagner and Baraka to claim the myth for their own creations and their own cultural agendas, especially as the parallel concerns Baraka's defense of jazz. A close examination of the registers used by both artists in summoning the myth reveals that Baraka is largely involved in an act of recovery and is actively reinstating dimensions of the legend discarded not only by Wagner but also by numerous previous literary representations of the Flying Dutchman. By refocusing attention on long neglected aspects of the legend of the Flying Dutchman, Baraka defines jazz within a context of polarized competition for its possession.

The critics who address the legend of the Flying Dutchman in Baraka's play note that the title *Dutchman* alludes to the type of ship, a Dutchman or Dutch man-of-war, that first brought black slaves to the American continent (Williams *Brightness* 106). Although critics have focused primarily on the title, the allusion coincides with the legend. The Flying Dutchman's ship is indeed a slave-ship, and the captain's fate results from the murder of two hundred slaves who perish while penned in hatches below the deck and who, like Clay in Baraka's drama, are thrown overboard.[30] By staging his play "heaped in modern myth," Baraka's act of recovery simultaneously passes a verdict on the selective mythology of his literary predecessors. By recalling the myth's own judgement against a concealed massacre of slaves, Baraka indicts his predecessors with collusion and posits a definition of jazz as an artistic voice against bondage and repression. He equates his predecessor's own literary practices with the brutal act that leads to Falkenberg's damnation.[31]

Baraka uses Clay to dramatize the harsh contradictions of black entry into a system of values whose assessment of African-American culture comes out of the same tradition that rationalized the repression of it: a system whose history is based upon exclusion. In response to these realities of African-American experience, Baraka turns to the myth of the Flying Dutchman. Werner Sollors has noted that "Baraka's view of the slave trade as an original sin, and of the legacy of slavery as a curse upon America, makes plausible the relationship of *Dutchman* to the Flying Dutchman" (Sollors 131). But the relationship is more than that. As an aesthetic context, the myth is useful to Baraka both in terms of its structure and in terms of the history of its representation in literature. As important as recovering the myth's indictment of the slave trade is the image of the white and black specters casting dice for the soul of Falkenberg. Since the image pits black and white against one another in a game that only one can win, it generates a tension that is not recognizably resolvable, and simultaneously freezes the tension in an image of the moments before the final deciding die has been cast. This frozen tension produces the aesthetic illusion of a synthesis or a resolution that remarkably maintains the integrity of two mutually exclusive positions.

While Baraka recreates this competition in the exchanges between Lula and Clay, the conclusion of *Dutchman* asserts that in American history the coexistence of contradictory white and black interests only exists in the realm of myth. In a manner of speaking, the die has long been cast, both for African-Americans in general and for jazz in particular. The frozen tension between white and black specters gives way to Lula's murder of Clay. While the reception of jazz has been indicted, the death of Clay leaves the reception intact but exposed. In this respect, Baraka's drama coincides with Adorno's claim that revolutionary art and philosophy allow "themselves to be guided by an existing, but now questionable, totality whose immediate right to exist they dispute while they indirectly reproduce it" (Adorno *Wagner* 48). On the most immediate level, Baraka's disputation manifests itself in an attempted strict division between myth and empirical reality. He contrasts the experience of African-Americans with the coexistence of the black and white specters aboard Falkenberg's ship. But even in the realm of myth, as is also implicitly the case with jazz, the coexistence of white and black interests has not proven to be secure—no matter how suspended or frozen the tensions might be. Baraka's drama not only contrasts African-American experience with the structural tensions of the myth of the Flying Dutchman. His focus on the black dimensions of the myth exposes the repressiveness of all previous literary representations of the Flying Dutchman.

Dutchman follows a long line of adaptations that have consciously or unconsciously excluded either the indicting allusions to the slave trade, the black specter, or both. Unlike the frozen moment of tension that precedes the settling of the specters' dice, the constructed resolutions in the literature recreating the myth of the Flying Dutchman have been counterfeited, creating an ideological appearance of resolution obtained by pushing the black specter completely out of the picture. Samuel Taylor Coleridge's *Rime of the Ancient Mariner* is a dramatic case in point, particularly appropriate because Coleridge originally structured both the white and black specters into his poem. Originally, a white female figure with "lips [that] are red" like Lula's and whose "looks were free" was accompanied by a "*Jet-black* and bear" figure who was later discarded and replaced with Death.[32] In the historical sub-stratums of Coleridge's poem, a black figure resides whose record is no longer given.

For Baraka, to accept the exclusion of the black figure in the myth of the Flying Dutchman is ultimately to suffer the same fate—just as Clay's pragmatic disregard of America's racist past makes him, according to Baraka, its ultimate victim.[33] On an aesthetic level, Baraka refuses to be reconciled with the contradictory path that his drama suggests Clay is forced to follow in American society. With the refusal he also rejects the course of jazz's reception. Baraka's use of the white and black specters playing dice for the Dutchman's soul is not merely a parallel to the struggle reflected in the character of Clay who is torn between white mainstream values and African-American ethnic identity. The competition for the Dutchman's essence parallels the competition for the essence of jazz that is reflected in the divergent interpretations of it by Lula and Clay.

That this struggle actually constitutes the Dutchman's identity is evinced in variations of the myth where the captain aboard the Dutchman's phantom ship is not white but black (Bassett *Sea Phantoms* 352).[34] Indeed, recent productions of Wagner's *The Flying Dutchman* have capitalized on this very aspect of the myth. At Bayreuth during the 1980s the director Harry Kupfer gained controversial but wide acclaim for his decision to cast the black operatic singer Simon Estes in the role of the "Dutchman."[35] Kupfer's production forcefully accentuated the grounding that the Dutchman's identity has in contradiction, an accentuation that otherwise is not immediately apparent in Wagner's libretto. In this respect, Baraka and Kupfer have much in common, not only in their interest in the black strands of the Dutchman legend but also in their implicit concurrence with Adorno's argument that Wagner's compositions often function as "agent[s] of ideology" because his music simulates a "unity of the internal and external, of subject and object, instead of giving shape to the rupture between them" (Adorno *Wagner* 38).

Kupfer's productions of *The Flying Dutchman* were especially successful at achieving this "rupture" because of the wild disparity between his casting and the public's expectations. Baraka's drama, on the other hand, achieves the "rupture" in a dramatic tension that is generated by alternating Lula and Clay in the role of the Dutchman and by opposing their interpretations of jazz. Although their respective genders would cast Clay as the Dutchman and Lula as Senta, it is Lula, for example, who like the Dutchman in Wagner's libretto, is responsible for the death of her suitors. In criticism, this has been the standard reading of Lula. Buttressed by arguments that the passengers on the subway who assist Lula on command parallel the Dutchman's ghostly crew, critics have argued that Lula and not Clay assumes the role of the Dutchman. But both Lula and Clay evince the murderous traits that are part of the Dutchman's character: Lula, in the actual killing of Clay; and Clay, in his confession that his poems, like the mesmerizing notes from Charlie Parker's saxophone, are sublimated acts of murder. Although Lula does vie at times for the role of the Dutchman, the death of Clay is not enough to give her exclusive claim to the Dutchman's role. Senta is as responsible for the Dutchman's death as Lula is for Clay's—even though the Dutchman's death is touted as "redemption." Furthermore, when Clay vies for the role of the Dutchman, Lula's character is by no means suspended without function. Read as a variation of Senta, Lula quickly exposes some surprising equivalencies among Wagner's characters that are subtly buried in his libretto.

Lula's nonchalant discovery of another black man, a seeming equivalent to the one she has just killed, finds its closest parallel to Wagner's opera in Senta's vacillation between Erik the Hunter and the Dutchman.[36] Despite Adorno's belief that Erik is a mere "dramatic prop," Erik and the Dutchman are actually mythological equivalents who are only dramatically posed as rivals (Adorno *Wagner* 88). As Bassett has noted, the Flying Dutchman is a "nautical manifestation of the same spirit that wanders on the shore as the wild huntsman" (Bassett *Sea Phantoms* 362). Insofar as the presence of Erik in *The Flying Dutchman* alludes to this parallel mythological figure, he establishes the second half of a pair whose dialectical counterparts are found in the connection between Clay and the young black man who appears in the final scene of *Dutchman*. While the wild hunter may be an equivalent to the Dutchman in terms of circumstance and condition, his presence constitutes the closest that Wagner comes to directly representing the black and white specters who vie for the Dutchman's soul in the legend of Falkenberg: for in mythology—though, as might be expected, not explicitly in Wagner's opera—the wild hunter is black.[37]

Insofar as Clay's comparison of himself with Charlie Parker lays claim to the role of the Dutchman—because through literature Clay is able to suppress his desire to kill Lula just as the Dutchman suppresses his desire to kill Senta—Clay's comparison also establishes an affinity with Wagner's main character that leads to a dialectical dismantling of the presumptions underlying the Dutchman's identity. But the dismantling only really begins with the knowledge that Wagner conceived his image not so much in accordance with its relation to the wild huntsman per se, but rather with its connection to a similar, archetypical figure: the Wandering Jew.[38] Wagner emphasizes this point by relocating Erik (the wild huntsman) to a minor position—in one sense because he detracts from the Flying Dutchman's derivation from the more prominent figure, the Wandering Jew. In both general lore about the Dutchman and in especially Wagner's own writings on him, the Dutchman is synonymous with the Wandering Jew, a point not missed by Nietzsche's acerbic pen in *The Case of Wagner*.[39]

In addition to the formal similarities wrought through the use of the same myth, Baraka's character Clay parallels Wagner's nautical variation of the Wandering Jew on two interrelated thematic counts. First of all, both Wagner's Dutchman and Baraka's Clay "face the constant threat of commoditization" which, according to Adorno "ultimately contaminates . . . Wagner's heroic models" (Adorno *Wagner* 105). In the case of *The Flying Dutchman*, the contamination arguably comprises an aspect of the opera's plot since Senta's father Daland, reaffirming Jewish stereotypes, is so unable to assess the Dutchman in terms other than his financial wherewithal that he fails to inquire who or what he is bringing home to his only daughter. Daland's presumptions put Senta in considerable peril, and the actual danger associated with the Dutchman further denigrates the image of the Jew. A similar situation is depicted in the image of African-American artists that Clay defends in *Dutchman*, in particular in the image of the jazz musician Charlie Parker whose contribution to African-American culture is, to follow Clay's argument, so exploited and reduced to its market value that white America is ostensibly unable to see the genuine rage and latent violence it contains. Clay likens himself to the Dutchman in that he finally makes clear to Lula that her provocations place her in great peril and that he could easily kill her.

Thematically, Wagner's and Baraka's main characters also overlap in that both are ostracized as a result of their ethnicity. Not only does Clay indict the reified structures of the white society that lead to the exploitation of black artists whom that same society simultaneously shuns, but entry into that society is premised upon a willing submission to exploitation. For Wagner, too, the ostracism intertwines with a threat of commoditization projected into the Dutchman's character. Wagner's Dutchman is implicitly stigmatized as an exploiter and usurer, which in turn serves as a rationalization for his being ostracized. For Wagner's Dutchman is a composite of that circular logic which ostracizes individuals because they behave in accordance with the demands of the position in which they are forcibly held.

Clay's and Wagner's Dutchman also overlap in that they both fall prey to a seeming release from their position as outcasts that in actuality merely exacerbates their situation. In Wagner the exit takes the form of a so-called "redemption." Nietzsche recognized quickly that the allusion to the Wandering Jew in Wagner's opera *The Flying Dutchman* coincided with an obsession with redemption that permeates all of Wagner's work: "There is nothing about which Wagner has thought more deeply than redemption: his opera is the opera of redemption." For Nietzsche, however, the significance of *The Flying Dutchman* resides in its inadvertent betrayal of how Wagnerian redemption is no redemption at all, and is so compromising that the "redeemed" Wandering Jew is "of no further concern to us" (Nietzsche *Case of Wagner* 160–61). He is "of no further concern" because he no longer exists. He dies. His redemption follows the same ideological pattern which, historically, appealed to the image of the Wandering Jew in order to justify the forcible expulsion of Jews.[40] Just as the Jews supposedly longed for the exodus forced upon them, so too does the Dutchman supposedly long for the death he receives in the closing moments of Wagner's opera. As Adorno was later to add in polemical terms: "Redemption, in Wagner, is tantamount to annihilation," characters being redeemed "the same way in which the Gestapo may claim to have redeemed the Jews" (Adorno "Wagner, Nietzsche and Hitler" 161). In this same respect, the murder of Clay by Lula exposes the "redemption" of the Dutchman for what it is: murder. Even the symbol of this redemption bears out its contradictory effect. In legend, the Wandering Jew is singled out by a mark on his forehead that he shares with Cain, the mark of a burning cross.[41] Given the violence that this symbol signifies in America, Clay and the Wandering Jew find an odd unity beneath a symbol whose supposed signification of redemption in reality represents terror.[42]

Far from being inconsistent with his "well-known anti-Semitism," Wagner's "redemptive" appropriation of the Wandering Jew is a logical and ideological extension of deep-seated racial resentment.[43] Ironically, Baraka succumbs to a very similar form of anti-Semitism in an inverted (chiastic) deployment of the rhetorical structures that Wagner uses when isolating strands of the Dutchman legend which are incompatible with his dramatic vision.[44] Just as Wagner isolates the myth of the wild huntsman (a black allusion) in the minor character of Erik so that attention focuses on the Wandering Jew instead, Baraka isolates the myth of the Wandering Jew when Clay speculates that Lula—rival for the role of the Dutchman and interpreter of jazz—"must be Jewish" (Baraka *Dutchman* 29). Although Baraka blurs Lula with Senta so that attention focuses on the blackness of the Dutchman which Wagner has discarded, he like Wagner also vilifies her Jewishness.

In the split between Lula and Clay, Baraka attempts to dismantle the hybrid that exists between Clay's and Wagner's Dutchman. But the attempt is not entirely successful and establishes as its consequence a disturbing connection between Wagner and Baraka instead. In short, not only do Clay's and Wagner's Dutchman coincide in their positions as outcasts and in their positions as victims of an imposed self-destructive redemption; these thematic affinities produce a hybrid image of the Flying Dutchman that is ideologically unified in the shared anti-Semitic attitudes of Wagner and Baraka. To follow Nietzsche, Wagner's redemption compromises the integrity of the Wandering Jew—a figure which already compromises the Jews because it is a stereotype that comes not from Jewish but from Christian traditions. Baraka's drama, on the other hand, in its vilification of Lula implicitly argues that the Wandering Jew compromises the integrity of the blackness, the Dutchman, and jazz. In both works, Jews are singled out either in a redemption akin to "annihilation" or in a condemnation that charges them with repression.

The mechanisms of this ideological affinity between Baraka and Wagner can be seen in a short critique of Wagner that Adorno wrote directly after the Second World War—at a time when Adorno was perhaps his most direct in singling out the proto-fascist tendencies in Wagner's corpus and character. Adorno criticizes Wagner's having bated his conductor Herman Levi so that he would seem to bear the responsibility for Wagner's subsequent insulting dismissal of him. This, for Adorno, is a classic example of blaming the victim. The anti-Semitic sub-text to the dismissal, viz., that as a Jew Levi supposedly desired and brought the dismissal upon himself, "bears witness to the existence of one of the most sinister features of the Fascist character even in Wagner's time: the paranoid tendency of projecting upon others one's own violent aggressiveness and then indicting, on the basis of this projection, those whom one endows with pernicious qualities" (Adorno "Wagner, Nietzsche and Hitler" 158). A similar strategy is observable in the countless provocations that Lula thrusts at Clay before murdering him in a brutally orchestrated act of "self-defense." Ironically, Lula, whom Clay considers to be Jewish, becomes the manipulative provocateur who projects upon Clay her "own violent aggressiveness," accuses him of being a "murderer" and passes sentence on him. In short, Baraka uses Lula in a reversal of the bating-the-victim strategy that Adorno identifies in Wagner. Baraka—to follow Adorno's logic—turns the Jew into a fascist oppressor. In one respect, the reversal that turns Lula into an oppressor would appear to be consistent with Adorno's arguments that the victims and victimizers of authoritarian normative values are interchangeable—except that the image of the Jew in Baraka's drama, being a derivative of the Wandering Jew, is in fact already a repressive stereotype of Jews.

The historical context to the extremity of Baraka's attempt to dismantle the hybrid image of the Wandering Jew and the black captain of the phantom ship is a contradictory one. Shortly after *Dutchman* was produced, Susan Sontag wrote in a review of the play that we "tend to choose our images of virtue from among our victims" and that "in just a few short years, the old liberalism, whose archetypal figure was the Jew, has been challenged by the new militancy, whose hero is the Negro."[45] In Baraka's drama, however, the militancy takes the form not of a mere succession in historical archetypes, but rather of an internal division: an accusation that one archetypical victim has succumbed to victimizing. The anti-Semitic undertones of Baraka's militancy—which place him on an ideological par with Wagner—effectively force a polarization that leaves Wagner's Dutchman and Clay (or jazz) in a dialectical opposition that seethes beneath the more general unified image of the Flying Dutchman. Despite the shared position as ethnic outcasts that the two have in the image of the Dutchman, the Wandering Jew and the black captain of the phantom ship are pitted against one another in Baraka's drama—both casting dice for the Dutchman's soul. An African-American is a victim of stereotypes forced upon him by a Jew who is also a product of stereotypes.[46]

The real irony in Baraka's agenda is that, in his effort to recover the black strands of the legend of the Flying Dutchman and to use the recovery as a defense of jazz, he finally succumbs to the same dilemma as his character Clay. Although Baraka ostensibly refuses to accept the censorious exclusions that have predominated in representations of the Flying Dutchman and jazz, Baraka's own representation reproduces, in the domain of myth, Clay's pragmatic disregard of America's racist past. Specifically, by (re)asserting the myth's black allusions as an opposition to the Wandering Jew, Baraka perpetuates the very exclusions he seeks to avoid—and not merely because the Wandering Jew is a product of stereotyping. For in myth, the connection between the Flying Dutchman and the Wandering Jew surpasses their both being victims forced into permanent transience, and thus there is an implausibility in Susan Sontag's reference to Baraka's use of the Flying Dutchman as a mere historical succession in archetypes of victims. The two figures are related because they both are internally and structurally at odds with themselves; both are a contradictory hybrid, a false unity. Not only is the Dutchman a hybrid of the wild huntsman and the Wandering Jew, black and white specters, and Clay and Lula, but the genealogy of the Wandering Jew follows an almost identical pattern. To assert a black jazz aesthetic by opposing the black strands of the Flying Dutchman to the Wandering Jew can only be achieved by repressing the black strands that are present in the legend of the Wandering Jew.

In much the same way that the soul of Falkenberg relates to the black and white specters throwing dice for his soul, in legend and history the figure of the Wandering Jew derives from a composite image of the mythical figure of Cain and the historical Persian king Ahasuerus, whose kingdom spanned from Ethiopia to the river Indus and whose name the Wandering Jew later inexplicably received.[47] Insofar as the Wandering Jew is an extension of the earlier mythical figure of Cain, he carries with him remnants of this earlier figure's characteristics. Hurwitz notes: "In the Apocalypse of Moses, he [Cain] is referred to as *Adiophotos*, 'the one without light', 'the dark one', but at the same time as *Diaphotos*, 'the enlightened'" (Hurwitz 219). Just as Cain, Ahasuerus's predecessor, is described as being both light and dark, the Flying Dutchman is sometimes white and sometimes black. In terms of his relation to the myth of Cain, both the white and black references are present in the Wandering Jew. In terms of history, a similar although not so pronounced disparity is observable. The history of the king Ahasuerus, recounted in the book of Esther, is that of being caught in a rivalry between, on the one hand, his top advisor Haman, a dark-skinned Persian who, after casting dice (Pur) to determine the most propitious time, seeks the king's authority to annihilate the Jewish population, and, on the other hand, his Jewish Queen Esther, who seeks and finally wins the king's favor in a bid to save her people, a bid that ultimately leads to Haman's execution. In their rivalry, Haman and Esther compete for Ahasuerus's soul, like the black and white specters competing for the soul of Falkenberg and for that of jazz.

Not only in his appeal to the anti-Semitic stereotype of the Wandering Jew but also in his failure to recognize the black strands within the legend of the Wandering Jew, Baraka posits his black jazz aesthetic only at the expense of other repressions. His drama is thus comprised of two contradictory dialectical movements, the first progressive and the second regressive. In its first movement, the drama offers a counter-force from within the myth of the Flying Dutchman that breaks "the spell of collective powers," a spell which, by disregarding the Dutchman's black traits, asserts a false unity in his character. The counter-force and defense of jazz appear as a form of enlightenment which *Dutchman* offers through a contradiction of the myth of unity in the figure of Falkenberg. The play "contradicts myth and thereby escapes its violence."[48] The escape through contradiction is the crux of Baraka's dialectical relation to long-standing literary and cultural traditions. By recovering the black attributes of the Flying Dutchman, Baraka's drama punctuates the contradictions that comprise the Dutchman's and jazz's character. In the second movement of its dialectic, Baraka's drama pursues an opposite course. As he recovers, he discards, perpetuating stereotype and foregoing, in the legend of the Wandering Jew, the very allusions he so meticulous summons in the legend of the Flying Dutchman.

Normative Values, Contradiction, and Theories of Repression

Adorno claims that both Wagner's music and jazz rely on a fabrication of temporal movement. Both Wagner's *The Flying Dutchman* and the jazz aesthetic articulated in Baraka's *Dutchman* lend credence to his claims. Wagner offers the Dutchman a redemption that leaves intact the system with which the Dutchman is at odds—a redemption that is no progression. In his drama, Baraka perpetuates the anti-Semitic stereotype upon which Wagner relies, using it as a foil for his recovery of repressed black allusions within the myth of the Flying Dutchman. In the process, Baraka succumbs to a stagnancy because he reasserts black mythical allusions only by repressing others. In this respect, both the opera and the drama become trapped in what Adorno calls the dialectic of Enlightenment. Their opposition to normative values ultimately reinstates the systems which they resist. With regard to Wagner, it is perhaps almost predictable that the example of *The Flying Dutchman* coincides with Adorno's critique of authoritarian normative values, because Wagner occupied a crucial position in Adorno's formulation of the critique. The critique is in one sense "Wagner-specific" and exposes anti-Semitic undertones in Wagner's work that have often been noted. With regard to Baraka, the issue is not so simple because his drama cannot be reduced to an anti-Semitic diatribe, even though anti-Semitism is observable in his work. The more pertinent questions with regard to Baraka are whether the parallel contradictions between Wagner's opera and Baraka's drama adequately account for the complexities of jazz that Baraka dramatizes in his play, and whether these complexities expose the limits of an attempt to defend Adorno's critique of jazz by citing its similarity to his critique of Wagner.

For Adorno, the threat of commodification derives from the reductive uniformity that it imposes on all cultural phenomenon, a uniformity that obstructs historical evolution and progress because it nullifies aesthetic difference and diversity. The same is true of anti-Semitism. The threat it embodies derives from the authoritarian uniformity it enforces, a uniformity that is reactionary and resistant to the change which inevitably results from the dynamic interaction of diverse social groups. In both instances, the issue for Adorno is the embattled position of the particular which he defends by transforming the specific phenomenon of anti-Semitism into a general critique of the oppressiveness of normative values. Insofar as the separate arguments on commodification and anti-Semitism relate to Jews, both are crucial to Adorno's analysis of the normative values which govern Wagner's work because Wagner personifies the threat of commodification in a stereotype of the "money-minded" Jew. Adorno's separate critiques of the culture industry and normative values are the product of a negative dialectic in which he dismantles the false, stereotypical unities of European anti-Semitism. Thus to position African-American culture within the framework of Adorno's critiques of the culture industry and normative values is, on one level, to tacitly and mistakenly assert that the stereotypes of Jews and African-Americans are the same. But this point is easily lost in the increasing prominence that the critique of the culture industry took in Adorno's thought after the publication of *Dialectic of Enlightenment*. Indeed, Adorno's fundamental opposition to the unities wrought by commodification obscures the forced unity through which the similarities between his critiques of Wagner and jazz are maintained: a generalized theory of authoritarian normative agendas that is based upon a paradigm which Adorno derives from European anti-Semitism.

The Eurocentrism of this paradigm suggests the need to consider not only what is gained but also what is sacrificed by reading Baraka's drama through the framework which Adorno provides. On two contradictory counts his drama would appear to confirm Adorno's arguments. First of all, in its focus on the

Dutchman as a figure who falls outside normative values (the metaphor of Baraka's jazz aesthetic), Baraka's drama initially affirms Adorno's and Horkheimer's argument that the victims of what has traditionally been called anti-Semitism are interchangeable. From the beginning of *Dutchman*, the conflation of both Lula and Clay in the role of the Dutchman forces a recognition that the captain of the phantom ship accommodates a plurality of readings in the Dutchman's status as outcast, both as Jew and as African-American. But this affirmation is at odds with Adorno's rejection of jazz as an aesthetic locus of opposition, a rejection which asserts that jazz feigns an opposition that it never formulates. In contradistinction to this first affirmation, a reading of *Dutchman* against *Dialectic of Enlightenment* exposes the ideological flaws in Baraka's apparent affirmation of Adorno's theory of normative values: by building its black jazz aesthetic in opposition to the myth of the Wandering Jew, Baraka's revised version of The Flying Dutchman "reverts [again] to mythology" because it perpetuates an exclusion of the black mythical allusions it sets out to recover (*DE* xvi). This reading coincides with Adorno's critique of jazz in that he repeatedly argued that the resistance attributed to jazz merely provided cover for continued exploitation of African-Americans.

Despite these ideological problems, Baraka's drama raises legitimate questions concerning the adequacy of the defense of cultural particulars in a generalized theory of "the Other." Although *Dutchman* gives presence to both of the contradictory tendencies in the Flying Dutchman's character and aesthetically reconciles them within the framework of the play itself, the play forcefully resists the violence caused by any attempt to build an abstract theoretical unity beyond the dramatic structure of the play. In this respect, the drama remains true to the actual structure of the myth of the Flying Dutchman in a manner that Wagner's opera never does. For Baraka structures both contraries—the competing white and black specters—into his drama in order to accentuate their mutual exclusiveness, an accentuation that ultimately challenges Horkheimer's and Adorno's attempt to defend the oppressed particular with a generalized theory of anti-Semitism. The game of dice between the white and black specters positions jazz within two concurrent spheres, neither of which can be dismissed without undermining the social contradictions that jazz exposes and neither of which wholly subsumes the other.

While the similarities between Adorno's critiques of Wagner and of jazz appear to provide a rebuttal to charges that Adorno defends high European culture against popular or low culture, the Eurocentrism of his critiques functions on a more subtle level: specifically, within the privileged position that he grants to European Jewry when formulating his conception of authoritarian normative values. Nowhere is this more evident than in his (in)famous statement that "to write poetry after Auschwitz is barbaric," and even when Adorno later recanted this statement in *Negative Dialectics*, the retreat is enmeshed in nightmarish pangs "that he is no longer living at all, that he was sent to the ovens in 1944 and his whole existence since has been imaginary, an emanation of the insane wish of a man killed twenty years earlier."[49] No one seriously questions the significance that the horrific persecution of the Jews by Nazi Germany has had for culture in general and for Adorno in particular, but "it is a gross error and political over-simplification to maintain that anti-Semitism and anti-Negroism are two sides of the same coin."[50] For whom does Adorno speak when he claims that Auschwitz has made the practice of poetry an act of barbarism? How was it possible to write poetry after America's three hundred year involvement with slavery? Comparable questions led James Baldwin to argue that "The Jew's suffering is recognized as part of the moral history of the world and the Jew is recognized as a contributor to the world's history: this is not true for blacks."[51]

With regard to Adorno's assessment of normative values, the fate of Clay in Baraka's drama almost literally follows the sentiments of Harold Cruse who "balked" at the notion that "both Negroes and Jews were 'in the same boat'."[52] But Clay's death is not the play's conclusion, and as ominous as is Lula's approach toward her next potential victim, Baraka ends his play with a reinstatement of both of the specters vying for the Dutchman's soul. In doing so, he reasserts the plurality of readings of the Dutchman. The conclusion of the play opens up a conception of history that is grounded in irreconcilable diversity and the movements of which are based in a sorting out of difference. Insofar as the conclusion of Baraka's drama is the last note of his jazz aesthetic, the closing scene is dialectically opposed to Adorno's description of jazz as an avatar of "eternal sameness."

Notes

Introduction

1. Robert Hullot-Kentor has attempted somewhat to correct this situation with his recent translation of the "Odysseus Essay" from *Dialectic of Enlightenment* (*New German Critique* 19.2 [1992]), but the dissatisfaction with previous translations of Adorno's work extends to C. Lenhardt's rendering of *Aesthetic Theory* (New York: Routledge, 1984). Criticism of Lenhardt's translation was so strong that it is no longer in print.

2. Albrecht Wellmer, *The Persistence of Modernity* (Cambridge, MA: MIT Press, 1991) vii.

3. Jean–François Lyotard, *Heidegger and "the jews"*, trans. Andreas Michel and Mark S. Roberts (Minneapolis: University of Minnesota Press, 1990) 43. Hereafter *Heidegger*.

4. Jürgen Habermas, "Modernity—An Incomplete Project," *The Anti-Aesthetic* (Port Townsend, WA: Bay Press, 1983) 12, 9.

5. Paddison's book would seem to have alleviated Michael Steinberg's "fear that Critical Theory in general and the critique of Adorno in particular will proceed into the future without appropriate understanding of the cultural—material and textual—world which grounded Adorno's lifelong confrontations with theory, and that is music" ("The Musical Absolute," *New German Critique* 19.2 [1992]: 39). Interestingly enough, Paddison's analysis of Adorno's musicology, especially with regard to the historicity of musical material, is at odds with Steinberg's assertion that for Adorno "musical knowledge occurs through the ability of music to make reference to an absolute by way of a particular utterance" (22). Although the examples of Paddison's analysis are numerous, see for instance his chapter "The Immanent Dialectic of Musical Material" (149–158).

6. Max Paddison, *Adorno's Aesthetics of Music* (New York: Cambridge University Press, 1993) 14.

7. In "A Matter of Tradition," a critical review of Jameson's controversial reading of Adorno in *Late Marxism* (1990), Eva Geulen criticizes Jameson, in part, for having adopted the exact opposite strategy for his book, a strategy which on a structural level he shares with Zuidervaart and Paddison. She argues that any critique of *Late Marxism* needs to begin with Jameson's "privileging of the whole—a condition reinforced by the book's very structure; *Late Marxism* is not a loose collection of essays but a tightly knit

construction." As Geulen notes, Jameson's "privileging of the whole" ultimately breeds an incompatibility between Adorno's conception of history and the conception of history that Jameson attributes to him:

> In contradistinction to Adorno, who took a particular interest in what had fallen from the predominant historical narrative, Jameson's concept of *ouevre* reflects his concept of history (as such); a whole unfolding via a narrative structure. The simple solution to the problem of how to engage what is historically no longer current—to retain and preserve those elements in Adorno that are still useful today and to jettison others that history has rendered obsolete—presupposes what Jameson is not willing to grant, i.e., that parts can be broken loose at the expense of the whole (*Telos* 89 [1991]: 156, 158).

Robert Hullot-Kentor arguably extends this observation on Adorno's "interest in what had fallen from the predominant historical narrative" a step further. Noting that dialectics attempts "to grasp time in concepts," Hullot-Kentor argues that Jameson's desire to "celebrate the dialectic as such" mis-represents "Adorno, for whom dialectics is the wrong state of things and negative dialects its presentation." ("Suggested Reading: Jameson on Adorno," *Telos* 89 [1991]: 171, 173).

8. Russell Berman, *Cultural Studies of Modern Germany* (Madison: University of Wisconsin, 1993) 12.

9. Peter Uwe Hohendahl, "The Displaced Intellectual?: Adorno's American Years Revisited," *New German Critique* 19.2 (1992): 90, 78–79, 91.

10. Theodor W. Adorno, *Minima Moralia*, trans. E. F. N. Jephcott (New York: Verso, 1974) 150. Hereafter *MM*.

1. Historical Dialectics and the Autonomy of Art in Adorno's *Aesthetic Theory*

1. For a brief definition of the term "materialist," I would recommend Lambert Zuidervaart's discussion of Marxist aesthetics in his book *Adorno's Aesthetic Theory* (Cambridge, MA: MIT Press, 1991)—in particular, his statement: "Marx's historical materialism implies that conflicts within art must be examined in terms of conflicts within the technological and economic base" (69). For the whole of Zuidervaart's argument see pages 68–77. This section substantially revises arguments first formulated in his "The Social Significance of Autonomous Art: Adorno and Bürger," *Journal of Aesthetics and Art Criticism* 48 (1990):61–77. Insofar as the term "materialist" is associated with the disappointment that marked the reception of the *Aesthetic Theory*, it is worth tracing the term back to Marx's "Thesen über Feuerbach," in which "materialism" is "sinnlich menschliche Tätigkeit" and in which "materialism" is concerned with changing the world. See *Marx-Engels Werke*, vol. 3 (Berlin: Dietz Verlag, 1956) 5–7. For a more thorough discussion of the Left's disappointment with Adorno's *Aesthetic Theory*, see Peter Uwe Hohendahl, *Reappraisals* (Cornell, NY: Cornell University Press, 1991) 1–21 and especially 75–98. The latter section is a reprint of his "Looking Back at Adorno's *Ästhetische Theorie*," *German Quarterly* 54 (1981): 133–148.

2. Hohendahl maintains that with the formation of the Brandt government "radical [political] reform seemed to be possible" (*Reappraisals* 9), and the Left abandoned what they interpreted as Adorno's pessimistic aesthetics of hibernation—what Peter Bürger describes as Adorno's succumbing to the historical bourgeois separation of art from the context of practical life. See *Theorie der Avant-Garde* (Frankfurt am Main: Suhrkamp, 1974) 63; trans. Michael Shaw (University of Minnesota Press, 1984) 46. Bürger maintains this same position in his more recent article "Adorno's Anti-Avant-Gardism," *Telos* 86 (1990–91): 49–60.

3. Adorno's revision of dialectics preceded *Aesthetic Theory*, having already occurred in *Negative Dialectics*, where, as Martin Jay has pointed out, drawing upon the ideas of Benjamin, Adorno replaced the Hegelian conception of synthesis with that of the constellation of ideas. See *Negative Dialectics* trans. E.B. Ashton (New York: Continuum, 1973) 156–166. Hereafter *ND*. For Martin Jay's account see *Marxism and Totality* (University of California Press, 1984) 241–275, especially 246–252. These revisions and their relation to Adorno's aesthetics will be discussed later in this work.

4. Jay Bernstein, "Art Against Enlightenment," *The Problems of Modernity*, ed. Andrew Benjamin (New York: Routledge, 1989) 62.

5. For further discussion of this last issue see Jochen Schulte–Sasse, "Theory of Modernism versus Theory of the Avant-Garde," Forward, *Theory of the Avant-Garde* xviii; see also Elizabeth Wright, *Postmodern Brecht* (New York: Routledge, 1989), pp. 68–89. For a specific discussion of the effect of Adorno's negativism on his reception see the *Telos* editors' "Introduction to Adorno," *Telos* 7 (1974): 2–3.

6. Jean–Fançois Lyotard, "Adorno as the Devil," *Telos* 7.1 (1974): 137.

7. The most recent assessment of this unique form of dialectics can be found in Fredric Jameson's discussion of Adorno's aversion to positivism: see *Late Marxism* (New York: Verso, 1990) 89–90.

8. For an analysis of the aesthetics of Kant and Adorno see Lambert Zuidervaart, "The Artefactuality of Autonomous Art: Kant and Adorno," *The Reasons of Art*, ed. Peter McCormick (University of Ottawa Press, 1986) 256–263.

9. "Kunstwerke sind Nachbilder des empirisch Lebendigen, soweit sie diesem zukommen lassen, was ihnen draußen verweigert wird, und dadurch vom dem befreien, wozu ihre dinghaft–auswendige Erfahrung sie zurichtet." [translation corrected] Theodor Adorno, *Ästhetische Theorie* (Frankfurt am Main: Suhrkamp, 1973) 14; trans. C. Lenhardt (Boston: Routledge & Kegan Paul, 1984) 4. Hereafter *AT*.

10. "soll dem Nichtidentischen beistehen, das der Identitätszwang in der Realität unterdrückt." [translation corrected] Adorno *AT* Suhrkamp 14; Routledge 6.

11. "altern, erkalten und sterben" [translation corrected] Adorno *AT* Suhrkamp 14; Routledge 6.

12. "Was einmal in einem Kunstwerk wahr gewesen ist . . . [ward] durch den Gang der Geschichte demontiert." [translation corrected] Adorno *AT* Suhrkamp 67–68; Routledge 60.

13. The controversy regarding Adorno's seemingly contradictory application of the term "reification," a controversy pursued by Gillian Rose and picked up by Martin Jay, is explained by Adorno's argument on the inadequacy of synthesis as a means of accounting for historical passage. As later discussion will show, Adorno replaces sublation with the idea of constellations. While "constellations" maintain the dimension of the socio-historical, they avoid the illusion of resolution that Adorno argues is inherent to the notion of sublation. It is this illusory resolution that Adorno combats and that constitutes what he deems as reification. See Gillian Rose, *The Melancholy Science* (London: Macmillian, 1978), pp. 40–47 and Martin Jay, *Marxism and Totality*, pp. 266–272.

14. "Gerade als Artefakte aber, Produkte gesellschaftlicher Arbeit kommunizieren sie auch mit der Empirie, der sie absagen, und aus ihr ziehen sie ihren Inhalt." [translation corrected] Adorno *AT* Suhrkamp 15; Routledge 6–7.

15. Bruce Baugh uses this lack of comprehensiveness for a convincing revision of Adorno's aesthetics. Baugh argues that an art work's non-identity is addressed to specific groups and is much more contextualized than Adorno allows. See "Left-Wing Elitism: Adorno on Popular Culture," *Philosophy and Literature* 14 (1990) 65–78.

16. The term "*Bewegungsgesetz*" will be explored in the sections that follow.

17. In his article "Karl Popper and the Frankfurt School," Robert D'Amico observes the emergence of similar arguments in Horkheimer's late writings. D'Amico maintains that for Horkheimer and the Frankfurt School, moral commitments and theoretical agendas "followed different logics of analysis" (41). See *Telos* 86 (1990–91): 33–48.

18. "Ästhetischer Ausdruck ist Vergegenständlichung des Ungegenständlichen, und zwar derart, daß es durch seine Vergegenständlichung zum zweiten Ungegenständlichen wird, zu dem, was aus dem Artefakt spricht, nicht als Imitation des Subjekts." (Adorno AT Suhrkamp 170; Routledge 163). A small note on the translation is in order because in the original it is not the expression that becomes "a second non-objective substance," but the objectified "non-objective." The "artefact" is the aesthetic expression, and it consists of more than the objectification of the non-objective. Otherwise negation would not occur, and the "artefact" would remain an "imitation of the subject." That the objectified non-objective becomes a "second non-objective" acknowledges its role in the dynamic or dialectic of aesthetic negation.

19. The placement of these arguments in an appendix may be the consequence of editorial decisions made after Adorno's death. But this is not explicit in the afterward to the *Aesthetic Theory* written by Gretel Adorno and Rolf Tiedemann. Indeed, the editors mention the paralipomena (appendix I) that Adorno wished to incorporate into the final draft of the text and the introduction (appendix III) that Adorno had planned to revise. No mention is made of the excursus "Theorien über den Ursprung der Kunst," the only

appendix to which Adorno gave a separate title and which he called an "Exkurs," i.e., a digression from the main issues of his concern.

20. "Sie muß gegen das sich wenden, was ihren eigenen Begriff ausmacht, und wird dadurch ungewiß bis in die innerste Fiber hinein." [translation corrected] Adorno *AT* Suhrkamp 10; Routledge 2.

21. While Hohendahl is correct in distinguishing Adorno from this position, his associating Lukács with it is somewhat sweeping and obscures the diversity of positions Lukács defended during his life.

22. In an essay entitled "Adorno and the Metaphysics of Modernism: The Problem of a 'Postmodern' Art," Peter Osborne has pointed out that this de–stabilization is not a phenomenon unique to works of art. He argues that aesthetics itself experiences this crisis and that the attempts to circumvent the exhaustion of aesthetics is at the center of Adorno's project. He writes:

> If art had reached a point at which it must 'revolt against its essential concepts' in order to survive, it none the less remains inconceivable without them. All modern art, according to Adorno, is inscribed within the terms of the contradiction. Under such conditions, aesthetics can have only one goal: 'to foster the rational and concrete dissolution of conventional aesthetic categories' in such a way as to 'release new truth content into these categories' by confronting them with the most recent forms of artistic experience. (24)

See *The Problems of Modernity*, pp. 23–48.

23. Eugene Lunn, *Marxism and Modernism* (University of California Press, 1982) 230.

24. Peter Dews, "Adorno, Post-Structuralism and the Critique of Identity," *Problems of Modernity* 14.

25. "Kunst hat ihren Begriff in der geschichtlich sich verändernden Konstellation von Momenten." [translation corrected] Adorno *AT* Suhrkamp 11; Routledge 3.

26. Rainer Nägele, "The Scene of the Other: Theodor W. Adorno's *Negative Dialectics* in the Context of Poststructuralism," *Boundary 2* 11 (1982–3): 68.

27. In *Marxism and Totality*, Martin Jay attributes Adorno's questioning of sublation to the influence of Benjamin, for whom also "dialectical mediation with its goal of *Aufhebung* (sublation) too quickly forced a unity where none in fact existed." Jay argues that Adorno drew heavily on Benjamin's *Der Ursprung des Deutschen Trauerspiels* in this instance and with regard to "constellations" as well. See *Marxism and Totality* 248.

28. Martin Jay, *Adorno* (Cambridge: Harvard University Press, 1984) 248.

29. "eine dem kategorialen Gefüge enthobene Objektivität." [translation corrected] Adorno *AT* Suhrkamp 488; Routledge 453.

2. *Aesthetic Theory* and Fragmenting the Unities of Negation

1. Albrecht Wellmer, "Truth, Semblance, Reconciliation: Adorno's Aesthetic Redemption of Modernity," *Telos* 17.4 (1984–85): 103. This same argument is repeated in "On the Dialectic of Modernism and Postmodernism," *Praxis International* 4.4 (1985): 357.

2. Max Horkheimer and Theodor Adorno, *Dialectic of Enlightenment*, trans. John Cumming (New York: Continuum, 1991) 7. Hereafter *DE*.

3. Theodor W. Adorno, "Theses Upon Art and Religion Today," *Kenyon Review* 7.4 (1945): 678.

4. "Begriff in der geschichtlich sich verändernden Konstellation von Momenten." [translation corrected] Adorno *AT* Suhrkamp 11; Routledge 3.

5. David Roberts, *Art and Enlightenment* (Lincoln: University of Nebraska Press, 1991) 62.

6. Peter Osborne, "A Marxism for the Postmodern?" *New German Critique* 19.2 (1992): 175.

7. Peter Uwe Hohendahl, "Adorno Criticism Today," *New German Critique* 19.2 (1992): 7.

8. Shierry Weber Nicholsen, "Toward a More Adequate Reception of Adorno's *Aesthetic Theory*: Configurational Form in Adorno's Aesthetic Writings," *Cultural Critique* 18.2 (1991):55.

9. Albrecht Wellmer, "Reason, Utopia and the Dialectic of Enlightenment," *Praxis International* 3.2 (1983): 90.

10. Adorno *AT* Suhrkamp 69 / Routledge 62. A note on the translation is in order. Lenhardt radically alters the meaning of the sentence by changing its original punctuation. The punctuation in the original text suggests that the social idea of art is to sacrifice to the social universal an example or illustration of how particularity is possible at all. "Opfern," the German verb "to sacrifice," is included as part of art's social idea. The original reads: "Wäre selbst einmal die atomistische Struktur der Gesellschaft verändert, so hätte die Kunst nicht ihre gesellschaftliche Idee: wie ein Besonderes überhaupt möglich sei, dem gesellschaftlich Allgemeinen zu opfern: solange Besonderes und Allgemeines divergieren, ist keine Freiheit. Vielmehr würde diese dem Besonderen jenes Recht verschaffen, das ästhetisch heute nirgendwo anders sich anmeldet als in den idiosynkratischen Zwängen, denen die Künstler zu gehorchen haben."

11. Adorno "Progress," trans. Eric Krakauer, *Benjamin: Philosophy, History Aesthetics*, ed. Gary Smith (Chicago: University of Chicago Press, 1989) 86.

12. Adorno repeatedly defines art as occupying a position which responds to this dialectic: "By definition, art works are socially culpable. But the worthy ones among them try to atone for their guilt" (Adorno *AT* 333).

13. Andreas Huyssen, *After the Great Divide* (Bloomington: Indiana University Press, 1986) 22.

3. Trying to Understand *Godot*: Adorno, Beckett, and the Senility of Historical Dialectics

1. Though the examples from critical essays are numerous, perhaps no other work has done as much to institutionalize the discussion of Adorno's views on Beckett than the publication of the anthology *Aesthetics and Politics* ed. Ronald Taylor, et. al. (New York: Verso, 1977). Ironically, the valuable service done by the editors in anthologizing the polemical writings of Bloch, Brecht, Benjamin, and Adorno has also rigidly structured the subsequent critical discourse on Adorno.

2. Originally published as "Versuch das Endspiel zu Verstehen" in *Noten zur Literatur II* (Frankfurt am Main: Suhrkamp, 1961); English translation, "Trying to Understand Endgame" *New German Critique* 9.2 (1982): 119–50; hereafter TUE. For the most recent Anglo–American discussions of Adorno and Beckett see: W. J. McCormack, "Seeing Darkly: Notes on T. W. Adorno and Samuel Beckett," *Hermathena: A Trinity College Dublin Review* 141.2 (1986): 22–44; Jay Bernstein, "Philosophy's Refuge: Adorno in Beckett," in *Philosopher's Poets*, ed. David Wood (New York: Routledge, 1990), 177–91; Lambert Zuidervaart, *Adorno's Aesthetic Theory* 150–77.

3. Jack Zipes, "Beckett in Germany / Germany in Beckett," *New German Critique* 9.2 (1982): 156. In all fairness to Zipes, this is not the goal of his article. He is interested in providing a much needed account of the reception of Beckett in Germany, and argues that in terms of influence Beckett is as towering a figure as Brecht.

4. Adorno notes that waiting is based on expectation, i.e., the anticipated fulfillment of some sort of goal. But he warns that it is easier to take idle waiting for a phenomenal absolute than to see its historical determination (*ND* 375).

5. Jean Hyppolite notes that the first appearance of the dialectic of "lordship and bondage" in Hegel's thought occurs in his early discussions of the Jewish faith: *Genesis and Structure of Hegel's Phenomenology of Spirit*, trans. Samuel Cherniak and John Heckman (Evanston: Northwestern Unive. Press, 1974), 172; hereafter *Genesis*. See G. F. W. Hegel, *Early Theological Writings*, trans. T. M. Knox (Philadelphia: Univ. of Pennsylvania Press, 1971) 68–69, 205; hereafter *ETW*. The difference between this first and Hegel's final version of "lordship and bondage" dialectic will be discussed later in this work.

6. In one respect, Adorno's efforts to revise dialectics is typical of post–war post–Hegelian philosophy. As Judith Butler has noted, scholars like Alexandre Kojève and especially Jean Hyppolite were actively engaged in a historical revision of Hegelian dialectics. Of Hyppolite's *Genesis and Structure of Hegel's Phenomenology of Spirit*, she writes in *Subjects of Desire* (New York: Columbia University Press, 1987):

Hyppolite makes use of the principle of retrospective wisdom to criticize the *Phenomenology* for its presumptions of progressivity, elaborating the reflexive structure of Hegel's narrative transitions to effect a transition beyond the *Phenomenology* itself. That the *Phenomenology* requires a commentary at all indicates the problem of reading this text within an historical experience that can no longer support the optimism of Hegel's ever-buoyant narrative (80).

7. For this split see Susan Buck-Morss, *The Origin of Negative Dialectics* (New York: The Free Press, 1977), 24–62. But the argument was not limited to Adorno and Lukács. Adorno's position coincides with the simple question which George Kelly, in his classic article "Notes on Hegel's 'Lordship and Bondage'," *Review of Metaphysics* 19 (1966): 780–802, posed to the dominant Hegelian–Marxists of his day: "Where did Hegel ever say," he asks, that the "future is with the slave"? (783). Kelly's question—which is in direct response to Alexandre Kojève's claim that "if History must be *completed* . . . only the Slave . . . can do it" (*Introduction to the Reading of Hegel*, ed. Allan Bloom, trans. James Nichols, Jr. [Ithaca: Cornell University Press, 1980], 47)—rejects any possibility of using Hegel as a defense of the proletariat. But Adorno, as the coming arguments will show, challenges the master-slave dialectic even in the non-Marxist form embraced by Kelly.

8. See Jean-François Lyotard, *The Postmodern Condition*, trans. Geoff Bennington and Brian Massumi (Minneapolis: University of Minnesota Press, 1984), 27–31. Ironically Adorno, who belongs to those whom Lyotard discredits, actually develops an argument for rejections which Lyotard posits only through assertion.

9. Günter Anders, *Die Antiquiertheit des Menschen* (München: Verlag C.H. Beck, 1956), 213–32.

10. Adorno's criticism of Anders coincides with the arguments of Ernst Fischer, who in *Art against Ideology* (London: Penguin, 1969) argues that Lucky transposes the master–slave dialectic, but "the revolution . . . alters none of the essential nature of power" (8). Given the fact that Pozzo is still in control of Lucky when the two appear, it is difficult to understand where exactly Fischer sees a transposition.

11. Hohendahl, *Reappraisals* 156. Hohendahl uses these parallels to contextualize Adorno's reading of Beckett within a constellation of Sartre, Lukács, and Brecht.

12. Thomas Kuhn, "The Route to Normal Science," *The Structure of Scientific Revolutions* (Chicago: University of Chicago Press, 1962), 12.

13. See Adorno, *Minima Moralia*, 146. W. Martin Lüdke formulates a similar summary–analysis as part of his discussion of Adorno and Beckett ("Der Kronzeuge," in *Theodor W. Adorno*, ed. Heinz Ludwig Arnold. 2nd ed. [Munich: Edition Text + Kritik, 1983], 139). W. McCormack does as well in "Seeing Darkly: Notes on T.W. Adorno and Samuel Beckett." The relation between Adorno's understanding of Beckett and his arguments in the *Dialectic of Enlightenment* is generally accepted. Yet both Lüdke and McCormack neglect to consider what Martin Jay has argued so convincingly about the focus of the *Dialectic of Enlightenment*: that Adorno and Horkheimer "situated anti-

Semitism at the culmination of a process at once social, psychological, and philosophical, a process which was the dialectic of the Enlightenment itself": "The Jews and the Frankfurt School: Critical Theory's Analysis of Anti-Semitism," *Permanent Exiles* (New York: Columbia University Press, 1985), 99.

14. One might ask how it is then that, based on the all-inclusiveness of his own arguments, Adorno is able to criticize the society of which he is a part. The question misconstrues, it seems to me, the greater issue addressed by the *Dialectic of Enlightenment*. The issue is not whether one can posit authentic criticism, but rather whether critical thought can realistically effect change and, perhaps more importantly, whether it can be formulated such that it resists appropriation.

15. Horkheimer and Adorno formulate a similar argument in their "On the Critique of the Philosophy of History," which belongs to the notes and drafts section of the *Dialectic of Enlightenment*, 222–25.

16. Janelle Reinelt has aptly pinpointed this facet of Adorno's thought as that which has opened him to the charge of being a "cultural mandarin." In "Approaching the Postmodernist Threshold: Samuel Beckett and Bertolt Brecht," in *The Aesthetics of the Critical Theorists*, ed. Ronald Roblin (Lewiston, NY: Edwin Mellen Press, 1990), she argues that Adorno's "insistence on form and rejection of content as the location of any politics in art makes him a cultural mandarin, elitist in his preference for difficult, complex artists like Beckett and his dismissal of didactic, message-laden work, even including Brecht. He shifts the locus of resistance from the representation of agency to the impact of the total work" (343).

17. Lüdke describes this negative shadow as a "permanent connection with catastrophe" (*permanenter Katastrophen-zusammenhang*): "Der Kronzeuge" 145.

18. As Buck-Morss has already noted, Adorno's convictions here resulted in large part from his observation of the evolution of the Party under the leadership of Stalin: "theory, when transformed into an instrument of revolution, manipulated truth according to the needs of Party strategy" (*Origin of Negative Dialectics* 29, 31).

19. Illuminating that which one seeks to avoid, viz., meaning's susceptibility to appropriation, is a difficult fence to skirt because it easily falls into resignation or ideological complicity with oppression. Bernstein examines how Adorno uses the autonomy of art as a response to the critique that "art's forms are not sufficiently autonomous from the dominant modes of societal reproduction for them to avoid complicity with what they deny" ("Philosophy's Refuge" 181–82).

20. Adorno was fully aware of the precariousness of the argument. Indeed he argues that successful works of art transcend blame for "the context of culpability" of which they are inevitably a part. Yet their ability to transcend blame leaves them "having to atone for trying to escape." Insofar as all works are, as Beckett claims, a "desecration of silence," they have to atone for the expression that reinstates silence, the expression that transcends the fray so that transcendence is neither justifiable nor any longer possible (*AT* 195).

21. For a variation of this same argument which highlights its basis in a critique in capitalist society, see Lüdke 140.

22. Bernstein has argued that, in Adorno's aesthetics, art works achieve a synthesis whose meaningful purpose cannot be conceived in practical or discursive terms. They enact a synthesis whose meaning evinces "a semblance of truth without domination" (180). But this is only partially true because the abstract synthesis to which Bernstein refers is at odds with synthesis, and in particular with the undercurrents of domination which accompany every instance of synthesis. Thus the achievement of Beckett is his ability to have expressed an "unswerving negation" at an historical moment in which the possibility for such expression appeared to be eclipsed by universal domination. Beckett's uncompromising stance concurs with Adorno's life-long inquiry into the catastrophic effects of imposing the universal on the particular. Rather than achieving an abstract synthesis, Beckett reinstates the particular. Beckettian irreconcilability attests to Adorno's belief that history moves not through synthesis but rather by forcefully covering over its contraries, by imposing domination on them in the form of apparent progressive resolution or the promise thereof.

23. In the formation of this specific point in and of this section in general, I am indebted to insightful conversation with Deborah Chaffin.

24. Jean Hyppolite, *Studies on Marx and Hegel*, trans. John O'Neill (New York: Basic Books, 1969) 71.

25. Karl Marx, "On the Jewish Question," *Marx-Engels Reader* 2nd ed., ed. Robert Tucker (New York: Norton, 1978) 26–52.

26. For additional reading on Adorno's embrace of this position see Zuidervaart 161–66.

27. Samuel Beckett, *Waiting for Godot* (New York: Grove, 1954) 28–9; 53; 22; hereafter *WG*.

28. "Commitment," *Aesthetic and Politics* 184–85.

29. In "*Modern Times* in the Light of Adorno and Beckett," in *Charles Chaplin: His Reflection in Modern Times*, ed. Adolphe Nysenholc (New York: Mouton de Gruyter, 1991), Yvan Bamps and Ralph Heyndels have suggested a thematic correspondence between Didi and Gogo and the tramp in Chaplin's *Modern Times*. The film offers "a highly graphic representation of . . . reification" (119), which, they argue, helps "to negate the presumed absence of message" in *Waiting for Godot* (120). Their argument, which is a provocative interpretation of *Modern Times*, seems to me, in its point of departure, to have overcome reservations about Hollywood which Adorno himself never could. On the one hand, this gives Bamps and Heyndels much freedom in their argument. But, on the other, the connection they cite could equally well coincide with a pernicious unifying element which seethes beneath Beckettian clowning.

30. Adorno notes that according to psychoanalysis, clownish humor is "a regression back to a primordial ontogenetic level." Insofar as Hegel's philosophy can be

considered "organic"—and I realize that this is not an unproblematic depiction—the regression signified in Beckett's "clownish humor" also addresses a regression in Hegel's Dialectic (Adorno *ND* 362).

31. Walter Benjamin, *Illuminations*, trans. Harry Zohn, ed. Hannah Arendt (New York: Schocken, 1968), 256.

32. Consider how opposite Adorno's position is to that of the early Hegel in his scornful rejection of the Jews: "The subsequent circumstances of the jewish people up to the mean, abject, wretched circumstances in which they still are today, have all of them been simply consequences and elaborations of their original fate. By this fate—and infinite power which they set over against themselves and could never conquer—they have been maltreated and will be continually maltreated until they appease it by the spirit of beauty and so annul it by reconciliation" (*ETW* 200).

33. This position is comparable to that which Anders attributes to Didi and Gogo. He argues that the two characters invert the traditional views of desperados who leave because they have no expectations. Didi and Gogo, he argues, are the exact opposite. Since they are waiting, they believe that they have something to expect: "'Wir bleiben', scheinen sie zu sprechen, 'also warten wir'. Und: 'Wir warten, also haben wir etwas zu erwarten'" ["'We remain', they appear to say, 'so we wait'. And: 'We wait, so we expect something'"] (219).

34. *DE* 169. Judith Butler, in her analysis of dialectic of desire, offers what can easily serve as a philosophical explanation of tragic miscalculation of Jewish desire for accommodation: "Perhaps extrapolating from its experience with objects, self-consciousness naively expects that the Other will be passive like objects, and differ only insofar as it can reflect self-consciousness' structure. Apparently, this initial self-consciousness did not take seriously enough the extent to which the Other is, indeed, *like* itself, i.e., a principle of *active* negation, and so is scandalized by the independent freedom of the Other" (*Subjects of Desire* 48).

35. The dignity of contemporary art is commensurate with its ability to develop rather than attempt to reconcile "unreconciled reality" (TUE 127).

36. Bernstein describes this relegation as the reduction of art to a pseudo-praxis: "Because art's praxis has become autonomized, consigned to a realm outside the centre(s) of societal production and reproduction, its praxis is a pseudo–praxis, a praxis which transforms without external societal effects. Nonetheless, art's very restriction to an autonomous domain entails that its forms can, although harassed, provide a reminder and a clue as to what non-dominating or normatively constituted praxis might be like" (179). As far as these arguments might be related to *Waiting for Godot*, the autonomous realm of artistic praxis is reflected in Didi's and Gogo's position outside of the lordship/bondage relationship dramatized by Lucky and Pozzo.

37. This logic can be seen as a counter to the arguments Hegel formulated on the Jews:

> The Jewish desire for isolation was bound to succumb to the pressure of other peoples toward union; it was worsted again after battles made all the more frightful the more the Jews were peculiar, and when their state was subjected to a foreign power they were deeply mortified and embittered. Henceforth the Jews clung all the more obstinately to the statutory commands of their religion; they derived their legislation directly from a jealous God. An essential of their religion was the performance of a countless mass of senseless and meaningless actions, and the pedantically slavish spirit of the people had prescribed a rule for the most trivial actions of daily life and given the whole nation the look of a monastic order. Virtue and the service of God was a life filled with compulsions dictated by dead formulas. Of spirit nothing remained save obstinate pride in slavish obedience to laws not made by themselves. But this obstinacy could not hold out against the fate which was falling on them with ever increasing speed and with a weight which grew heavier from day to day. Their whole polity was dismembered once and for all. Their mania for segregation had been unable to resist political subjection and effective linkage with the foreigner *(ETW* 178).

38. If Beckett had been in Auschwitz, one survivor has claimed, he would have a creed of "trying to give men hope," instead of being so negative. Adorno rejects this argument because it relies on a structure of the mind to give hope and does not take into account that to adjust to the men who created Auschwitz—even under the banner of "giving men courage"—robs individuals a second time of their due; it reconciles them to the unreconcilable (*ND* 367–8).

39. In this respect there is an addition parallel between Schoenberg and Beckett which Eugene Lunn noted in *Marxism and Modernism*:

> Writing after the bureaucratically rationalized, administrative mass murders of the Jew by the Nazis, Adorno cited Schoenberg's wrenching and painful "Survivor of Warsaw," which refuses all sentimentalizing as containing an element of that ultimately inexpressible suffering which he held to be most characteristic of our age. Yet, even here, in the farthest reaches of an expressionistic nightmare world which is the actual waking reality, art is inadequate to those who suffer, because, as art, it contains assuaging images and sounds which, "however remotely," still have "the power to elicit enjoyment oft of it. . . . Something of its horror is removed. . . . Even the sound of despair pays its tribute to a hideous affirmation." . . . Yet, Adorno stressed that such work as Schoenberg's (and . . . Beckett's) provided some scant hope by its capacity to give even the slightest expression to the horrors of contemporary society (263).

40. "The unprotesting depiction of omnipresent regression protests against a disposition of the world which obeys the law of regression so obligingly, that a counter-notion can no longer be conceived to be held against it" (TUE 126).

41. *Phenomenology of Spirit*, trans. A. V. Miller (Oxford: Oxford University Press, 1977) 114; hereafter *PHS*.

42. Hyppolite provides a summation of Hegel's argument on the emergence of self-consciousness which is illuminating for the present discussion. Hyppolite summarizes Hegel with the statement that "I am a self-consciousness only if I gain for myself recognition from another self-consciousness and if I grant recognition to the other" (166). After Auschwitz, this dialectic of recognition becomes marred because recognition of Jews necessitates a recognition of their lack of recognition. The recognized "lack" imposes limitations on the emergence of Jewish self-consciousness because it is premised upon a recognition that no matter how far self-consciousness evolves, it is missing something it cannot obtain.

43. Samuel Beckett, *The Unnameable*, in *Three Novels* (New York: Grove, 1955), 414. On this issue Zipes's analysis of the reception of Beckett in Germany is particularly helpful: "Adorno regards Beckett's art work as exemplary for the post–Auschwitzian world because in art unreconciled reality tolerates no reconciliation with the object; realism, which does not reach the level of subjective experience, to say nothing of reaching further, merely mimics reconciliation" (157). At this point Adorno's reading of Beckett and Beckett's relation to dialectics can be placed in direct contrast to the interpretation of his contemporary, Anders, who sees the master-slave dialectic in *Godot* as the motor of history, and argues that history owes its movement to the continued antagonism of individuals which we find represented in *Godot* (229). Whereas Anders views this antagonism as positive, Adorno views its representation in Beckett as regressive and destructive.

4. The Lexicon of Music: Adorno, the Philosophy of Music and Eliot's *Four Quartets*

1. "The Music of Poetry," *On Poetry and Poets* (New York: Farrar, Strauss and Cudahy, 1957) 17–33.

2. "Language and Music: A Fragment," *Quasi Una Fantasia* [1963], trans. Rodney Livingstone, (New York: Verso, 1992) 1–8.

3. *Four Quartets* [1943] (New York: Harcourt Brace Jovanovich, 1971).

4. In his analysis of Adorno's arguments on music and language, Max Paddison calls this a composition's "rationality," which he argues is part of music's self-referential character: "The other aspect of the similarity of art works to language is their rationality, which gives to them the appearance of 'communicative language' through the logicality of the construction, along the lines of conceptual language (but which is, however, largely self-referential, even in modes of art which make use of words as their material)." See *Adorno's Aesthetics of Music* 143.

5. *Philosophy of Modern Music* [1949], trans., Anne G. Mitchell and Wesley V. Bloomster (New York: Seabury Press, 1973) 128. Hereafter *PMM*.

6. Peter Dews, *Logics of Disintegration* (New York: Verso, 1987) 226.

7. "The Four Quartets Reconsidered," *T.S. Eliot: Four Quartets*, ed. Bernard Bergonzi (London: Macmillian, 1969) 113. In a recent polemic article "Four Quartets?," W.B. Bebbington attempts to reaffirm Flint's position and draws the conclusion that the title *Four Quartets* was "at worst the result of ignorance and presumption, and at best another example of the poet's failure in 'the intolerable wrestle with words and meanings', and no more than 'a way of putting it—not very satisfactory'" (*Essays in Criticism* 39.3 (1989): 241). For Bebbington, however, "the intolerable wrestle" and the "not very satisfactory" allusion to the quartet form have nothing to do with the problems of language itself that the poems explore, but rather with Eliot's misunderstanding of music (and presumably the misunderstanding of every subsequent critic who has explored the musical dimensions of *Four Quartets*). Unfortunately, the understanding that Bebbington incorporates into his article comes solely from *The New Oxford Companion to Music*.

8. "The Music of Poetry" is not alone in its allusions to the poetic agenda of *Four Quartets*. The epigraphs to the poems themselves subtly register the tensions that the subsequent poems explore. Recently, John Paul Riquelme has examined the relation of these epigraphs to the poems' meditation on language. In his book *Harmony of Dissonances* [Baltimore: Johns Hopkins University Press, 1991], Riquelme structures his discussion of *Four Quartets* around the two epigraphs from Heraclitus that stand "at the head of 'Burnt Norton', and in some editions at the head of the entire *Four Quartets*" (200). He argues:

> part of the historical material that might help us understand Heraclitus's writings has been lost, apparently irretrievably. Not only is our evidence about Heraclitus's social and intellectual context incomplete . . . but Heraclitus's work itself survives only as fragments, most of them no longer than a sentence (Riquelme 201).

He notes furthermore that the epigraphs, since they are in Greek, are generally inaccessible to English readers for whom "the most important single word in a first encounter with the epigraphs may not be in the quotations from Heraclitus themselves but in the title of Diels's edition of the pre-Socratic philosophers, which Eliot cites as his source" (202). Hermann Diels, a German philologist, published Heraclitus's fragments in *Die Fragmente der Vorsokratiker* [Berlin: Weidmannsche Buchhandlung, 1922]. The word most immediately recognized is the German "Fragmente" whose derivation from Latin links it with the English "fragment." Riquelme argues that "the encounter with an alien, permanently fragmented part of history dislocates any sense of present self-sufficiency that assumes either a continuity with a stable past or a determinate break from such a past" (Riquelme 208). While Riquelme's discussion of the historical status of the epigraphs from Heraclitus does coincide with the meditation on history that permeates *Four Quartets*, the mediation of these fragments through German philology plays a more significant role in the poems than Riquelme acknowledges. This is largely the result of the poems' allusion to classical music and in particular to the form of the quartet. The peculiar status of the Heraclitean fragments suggests that the quartet as a form must also be subjected to the same historical scrutiny.

9. Keith Alldritt, *Eliot's Four Quartets: Poetry as Chamber Music* (Totowa, NJ: Woburn Press, 1978) 39.

10. All citations refer to the lines of the poems. BN = "Burnt Norton"; EC = "East Coker"; DS = "The Dry Salvages"; LG = "Little Gidding."

11. Hugh Kenner, *The Invisible Poet: T.S. Eliot* (London: Methuen, 1965) 251.

12. There is a sense in which the "unheard music in the shrubbery" and the "thrush's" plea to depart reproduce what for Adorno is the radical component of modern music, which, as Lucian Krukowski has observed in his article "Form and Protest in Atonal Music: A Meditation on Adorno," omits "the devices of integration properly characteristic of traditional works" and thus becomes "doomed to remain largely unheard" (106). Yet Krukowski argues that remaining "largely unheard" is partially a deliberate strategy of modern music's protest and that for Adorno the radical dimension of dodecaphonic music exists in the "particular relation between the twelve-tone row as it is constituted in the score, and the score as it is performed" (107). He maintains that "the relationship between score and performance is not one where the score is subsumable as a means to appreciation; the score, rather, is a *subject for* appreciation" and that "the inadequacy of performance in projecting the rule-governed structure of the row serves as a *reproach* to those who are content to 'merely listen'" (116–17). Inasmuch as this relation between score and performance is reproduced in the "rose-garden" experience of "Burnt Norton," the unrealized state of the "what might have been" as exemplified by the "music in the shrubbery" signifies a redeemed state that, like the musical score, is sustained only so long as it is not subjected to the inadequacies of realization or performance. For the whole of Krukowski's argument see *Bucknell Review: A Scholarly Journal of Letters, Arts and Sciences* 29.1 (1984): 105–124.

13. Harry Blamires calls this dialectic "a dominant theme in the poem" and notes that "as the poem precedes, further relationships, corresponding to that between time and eternity, are explored both abstractly and concretely—notably the relationships between movement and stillness, change and fixity, flux and pattern" (*Word Unheard* [London: Methuen, 1969] 15–16).

14. Ferenc Feher, "Negative Philosophy of Music—Positive Results," *New German Critique* 2.1 (1975): 106.

15. This lack of qualification initially appears to be at odds with the poem's earlier statement that "the dance" is located "At the still point of the turning world" (BN 62). Yet there are clear indications that "the still point" is a qualitative rather than a spacial description of "the dance," a description that denotes "the still" as unrealized potential which "the dance" sustains as an absent but assertively negative force.

16. The third movement of the poem methodically lists the inadequacies of the "Here" and highlights their incompleteness with a series of sentence fragments, which are full of particulars but never conjugated with verbs. Even the verb participles that serve as adjectives have no specified temporal status. Rhetorically, this fragmentary structure sustains distance from the "disaffection" that the movement notes in its initial description. It avoids action, speaks from the spacial dichotomy of "Neither from nor towards" and negates the temporal dichotomy of "Time before and time after." In short, by not conjugating the phrases, the poet does not place them in time.

17. Ronald Bush, *T.S. Eliot* (New York: Oxford University Press, 1983) 201.

18. Poetic "form" and "pattern" are thus seen as contrapuntal to the words themselves. Their relation to words is that of "what has been" to a "what might have been." Indeed, the redemptive function that poetic "form" and "pattern" provide the poem's content is reflected in an allusion to St. John of the Cross's explanation of "the ten steps of the mystic ladder of Divine love" in *Dark Night of the Soul*: "The detail of the pattern is movement, / As in the figure of the ten stairs" (cf. St. John of the Cross *Dark Night of the Soul* in *Complete Works*. vol. 1. trans. E. Allison Peers. [London: Burns, Oates and Washbourne, 1953] 432–441).

19. "Voices that Figure in *Four Quartets*," *The Placing of T.S. Eliot*, ed. Jewel Spears Brooker (Columbia: University of Missouri, 1991) 154.

20. Robert Schweik, "T.S. Eliot's *Four Quartets* and the Uses of 'Referred Forms'," *Cithara* 28.2 (1989): 45.

21. In its modified repetition of the images from "Burnt Norton," this convergence, as Helen Gardner has generally noted, strengthens the parallels between poetry and music in *Four Quartets*: "One is constantly reminded of music by the treatment of images, which recur with constant modifications, from their context, or from their combination with other recurring images, as a phrase recurs with modifications in music" ("The Music of *Four Quartets*," *T.S. Eliot: Four Quartets*, ed. Bernard Bergonzi [London: Macmillian, 1969] 129). In an essay that largely discounts the relevance of "The Music of Poetry" to *Four Quartets*, F.O. Matthiessen at least conceded the relevance of this same point to the poems, citing specifically that Eliot in his essay "insists . . . that 'the use of recurrent themes is as natural to poetry as to music'" ("The *Quartets*," *T.S. Eliot: Four Quartets*) 93.

22. While "the deep lane" suggests a conception of unavoidable aging and decline, it is important to note that it stands in contrast to the conception with which the poem opened. The gradual decay of the lane suggests that temporal succession is not, as the poem initially claims, as clean or smooth as a "rise and fall" of "Houses," which, when they "crumble," are "removed" (EC 2–3).

Although I have strong reservations regarding Edward Lobb's claim in "Limitation and Transcendence in 'East Coker'" that "the lane's insistence on the direction into the village is . . . an illusion . . . . [because] if you were facing the other way, it would insist just as firmly on the direction away," his interest in the image of the "closed room" in *Four Quartets* offers clear insight into the dynamics between the first and second voices of "East Coker" (*Words in Time*, ed. Edward Lobb [Ann Arbor: University of Michigan, 1993] 28). Lobb's interest in "the closed room" repeats the more general arguments of his earlier article "Chamber Music: Eliot's Closed Rooms and Difficult Women," the title of which suggests that the "houses" referred to by the first voice in "East Coker" subtly allude to a chamber. As the coming arguments will demonstrate, the central musical tensions of "East Coker" derive from the historical relation of the quartet form to dance, and in that the quartet is a form of chamber music, the allusions to "houses" by the first voice and "dancing" by the second voice foreshadow this tension.

For Lobb's article see *T.S.Eliot: Man and Poet*, vol. 1, ed. Laura Cowan (Orono: University of Maine, 1990) 167–179.

23. Recently, Maud Ellmann has argued that "The poetic 'feet' . . . regulate the measure: as if the element of earth were the embodiment of rhythm." Yet it is a peculiar sort of rhythm that clings to the feet and makes them "clumsy" (*The Poetics of Impersonality* [Brighton, Sussex: Harvester Press Limited, 1987] 117).

24. This comment typifies the attitude that Fred Dallmayr has argued Adorno had toward "one of the most objectionable features of traditional philosophy": "Desire for security was closely linked for Adorno with the strategy of 'hypostasis' or hypostatization, namely, the elevation of passing or ephemeral phenomena into invariant structures and fateful constraints. One of the most objectionable features of traditional philosophy, in his portrayal, was its preoccupation with 'permanent, unchanging' essences and, accordingly its bent to hypostatize historical experiences into timeless truths" (*Between Freiburg and Frankfurt* [Amherst: University of Massachusetts Press, 1991] 56; This is a reprint of his earlier article, "Adorno and Heidegger," *Diacritics* 19.3–4 [1989]: 91).

25. In its relation to "Burnt Norton," the old English diction of "East Coker" exposes the absolute realm of signification upon which "Burnt Norton" continues to rely even in its references to the "strain," "crack[ing]," "break[ing]," and "decay" of words (BN 149–53). Unlike the old English forms, these references remain in theoretical realms, never betraying their own historicity. The emergence of old English in "East Coker," on the other hand, radically historicizes the material substance of the poems themselves.

26. Max Paddison, *Adorno's Aesthetics of Music* 15. Critics have often noted that "East Coker" borrows the old English from Sir Thomas Elyot's *Boke named the Governour* (1531). This indebtedness is particularly significant to the parallels that *Four Quartets* draws between language and music because it stresses the intertextuality of language's aging rather than merely the aging of "a signified outside" itself. It is in this respect that "East Coker" parallels the aging of music's "lexical items."

27. It is worth noting in passing that the association of dance with a general conception of music has a long tradition in the culture of India. The sanskrit "saugita," for example, means both dance and music. See Kapila Vatsyayan, *Classical Indian Dance in Literature and the Arts* (New Delhi: Sangeet Natak Akademi, 1977) 177.

28. Adorno's comments on dance occur in his criticism of Stravinsky's neo-classicism and have particular relevance to what Steve Ellis in *The English Eliot* (New York: Routledge, 1991) describes as the classic design of *Four Quartets*. Ellis maintains that Eliot sought in the image of the dance to achieve a "classic stasis," or a "'stillness' . . . represented throughout the poem as the axial centre of the 'turning world'" (Ellis 59; 16).

29. The historical relation of dance to the quartet form is not only played out in Eliot's poetry but is in fact, as John Holloway has noted, played out in one of Beethoven's late quartets as well. "The peasant dancing" and "rustic solemnity" of "East

Coker" coincide with Beethoven's citation of "a traditional, popular peasant-dance" in "a short passage from the movement of Opus 132, which precedes the *heilige Dangesang*: or what has been termed the 'trio' from that somewhat scherzo–like movement" ("Eliot's *Four Quartets* and Beethoven's Last Quartets," *Fire and the Rose: New Essays on T.S. Eliot*, ed. Vinod Sena and Rajiva Verma (Delhi: Oxford University Press, 1992) 150–51.

30. Charles Rosen, *The Classical Style* (New York: Norton, 1972) 137.

31. Edward Said, *Musical Elaborations* (New York: Columbia University Press, 1991) 13.

32. John Booty, *Meditating on Four Quartets* (Cambridge, MA: Cowley, 1983) 26.

33. Richard Shusterman, *T. S. Eliot and the Philosophy of Criticism* (New York: Columbia University Press, 1988) 151. The citation from Shusterman is actually part of a critique that he formulates against Eliot. It derives from a section of his text that is one of the few examples of scholarship on Eliot where Adorno's critical theory is taken into account.

34. Rose Subotnik, *Developing Variations* (Minneapolis: University of Minnesota Press, 1991) 58.

35. Ferenc Feher, "Rationalized Music and its Vicissitudes (Adorno's Philosophy of Music)," *Philosophy and Social Criticism* 9.1 (1982): 56.

36. To some extent, one could argue that Eliot already sought such a parallel in "East Coker" when he adopted the archaic English of his ancestor Sir Thomas Elyot. According to Steve Ellis, for example, the archaic English "reminds us of a common root behind the modern divergence of nations; not only are the 'English' very much an admixture of the foreign, but 'foreigners' themselves can once have been English" (Ellis 26). But the poem is far less concerned with the "common root" between Britain and America than it is with the emerging disparities between European nations, in particular between Britain and Germany.

37. cf. *Dialectic of Enlightenment* pp. 32–37; 43–80. So enticing is the lure of the sirens' song that Odysseus's galleymen plug their ears for their own survival. Yet with ears plugged, they cannot contemplate their relation to the past and thus succumb to repetition. They thus perpetuate what Adorno denotes as a cyclical or stagnant course of history (DE 35). They remain consciously practical and undistracted and thus lack self-consciousness and maturity (34). Their oblivion leaves them with "no advantage over the immobility of the master" (36). Fredric Jameson's discussion of the "parable of the oarsmen" in *Late Marxism: Adorno, or, the Persistence of the Dialectic* somehow misses this sentence. He argues that labors' learning is more profound than Odysseus's aesthetic experience. For Jameson's argument see pp. 127–131.

38. Roberts also argues that beneath his analysis of Homer's *Odyssey*, Adorno harbors a "longing to escape the self-alienating compulsions of necessity." The "longing" suggests a strategy comparable to the "voice descanting" in "The Dry Salvages" (DS

147). Self-alienation is evident in the voice's lament that "you who think that you are voyaging; / You are not those who saw the harbour / Receding, or those who will disembark" (149–51).

39. Joel Whitebook, "From Schoenberg to Odysseus: Aesthetic, Psychic, and Social Synthesis in Adorno and Wellmer," *New German Critique* 58.1 (1993): 50.

40. James L. Marsh, "Adorno's Critique of Stravinsky," *New German Critique* 10.1 (1983): 151.

41. Although one must be cautious with such comparisons, Eliot's sense of the futility of art in the face of historical events finds its correspondence in Adorno's conclusion at the end of "Cultural Criticism and Society," where he asserts that "to write poetry after Auschwitz is barbaric" (*Prisms* [Cambridge MA: MIT Press, 1981] 34).

42. It is worth noting that "Little Gidding" lends credence to Russell Berman's criticism of Peter Bürger's implicit suggestion that it was only the avant-garde that rejected "the aesthetic of autonomy that had attained a privileged (but by no means ubiquitous) status in the bourgeois culture of the nineteenth century." Eliot's allusion to Little Gidding is a gesture that claims for his own position an opposition to the aesthetic autonomy of nineteenth–century bourgeois culture that Bürger attributes solely to the avant-garde, and in this respect Eliot validates Berman's correction of Bürger's myopic vision:

> In fact one might push Bürger further on this point, for homologous rejections of idealist aesthetic are evident not only in the specifically avant–garde movements (dadaism, futurism, surrealism, constructivism) but also in the literary texts and theoretical reflections of authors who might be designated as "modernist" rather than "avant-garde" (Russell Berman, *Modern Culture and Critical Theory* [Madison: University of Wisconsin Press, 1989] 49).

However, what distinguishes Eliot from the avant-garde is that while they may share opposition to "the bourgeois culture of the nineteenth century," the avant-garde was not seeking a reunification of art and daily life in the end of history that is implicit in Eliot's poetic correlation of the ruins of London with the ruins of poetry. Quite the contrary, the politics of the avant–garde evinced a faith in revolutionary progress, and, if one pursues Berman's arguments further, one would have to ally Eliot's imagery with the dawning of the postmodern. "With the end of history," Berman argues, "the aesthetic category of the new loses its relevance; instead the aesthetic debris of the past (which is no longer a past opposed to the present) reappears as immediately accessible in the historicist eclecticism of postmodernist architectural referentiality" (Berman, *Modern Culture and Critical Theory* 84).

43. Richard Shusterman, "Reactionary Meets Radical Critique: Eliot and Contemporary Cultural Criticism," *T.S. Eliot: Man and Poet*, vol. 1, ed. Laura Cowan (Orono: University of Maine, 1990) 389.

44. Harvey Gross, "Compound Ghost, Triple Devil, Terminal Books," *T.S. Eliot: Man and Poet*, vol. 1, ed. Laura Cowan (Orono: University of Maine, 1990) 121.

45. In its relation to language, Leverkühn's "invention" culminates in a composition that fulfills his promise to take back "The Ninth Symphony"—which he does by inverting Beethoven's progression from instrumental music to a climatic setting of Schiller's "Ode to Joy" (Mann, *Doctor Faustus*, trans. H.T. Lowe-Porter [New York: Vintage, 1948] 478). Contrary to his audience's expectation to hear a choral symphonic work, Leverkühn delivers a semi-poetic, rambling "confession" that culminates in a wail and his attacking the keys of his piano "in a strongly dissonant chord" (Mann 503). He regresses from word to dissonant wailing music.

5. Adorno, Ellison, and the Critique of Jazz

1. Andrew Arato and Erike Gebhardt, *Essential Franfurt School Reader* (New York: Urizen Books, 1978) 270; Jamie Owen Daniel, "Introduction to Adorno's 'On Jazz'," *Discourse* 12.1 (1989–90): 41–2.

2. Ulrich Schönherr, "Adorno and Jazz: Reflections on a Failed Encounter," *Telos* 87.1: 85; Adorno, *Dissonanzen* (Göttingen: Vandenhoeck und Ruprecht, 1962) 6; Levin, "For the Record: Adorno on Music in the Age of Its Technological Reproducibility." *October* 55.4 (1990): 28, 47.

3. The reasons for this neglect derive in part from the fact that until 1991 there had been no adequate critical examination of the socio-historical and ideological dimensions of jazz criticisms. This lack led Gary Carner, in the introduction to the special issue on jazz that *Black American Literature Forum* (25.3) published in 1991, to argue that after seventy years of jazz literature, it is finally time for some serious attempt to examine it (Carner 443). As an illustration of the state of scholarship on the question of Adorno and jazz, it is worth noting that the same year, *Telos* published a special issue on Adorno, jazz, and popular music (87.1). While Adorno receives only a passing swipe in *Black American Literature Forum*, *Telos* examines Adorno's views without a single reference to the array of scholarship *Black American Literature Forum* was exploring at the same time.

4. The importance of African-American music to this novel has often been cited, most notably by Houston Baker, Kimberly Benston, and Berndt Ostendorf. Their work will be discussed later in this essay.

5. Review of *American Jazz Music* by Wilder Hobson and of *Jazz Hot and Hybrid* by Winthrop Sargeant. *Studies in Philosophy and Social Science* 7.9 (1941): 168. Hereafter "Review."

6. Wilder Hobson, *American Jazz Music* (New York: Norton, 1938) 82–83; Gordon Craig, *Germany 1866–1945* (New York: Oxford University Press, 1978) 475.

7. Theodor W. Adorno, "On Jazz," Trans. Jamie Owen Daniel. *Discourse* 12.1 (1989–90): 49.

8. Theodor W. Adorno and Joachim-Ernst Berendt, "Für und Wider Jazz," *Merkur: Deutsche Zeitschrift für Europäisches Denken* 7.9 (1953): 892. Hereafter "Wider."

9. Adorno, "Perennial Fashion—Jazz," *Prisms*, trans. Samuel Weber and Shierry Weber (Cambridge, MA: MIT Press, 1981) 121; hereafter "Perennial"; *Introduction to the Sociology of Music*, trans. E.B. Ashton (New York: Continuum, 1989) 33–34.

10. Ralph Ellison, *Invisible Man* (New York: Vintage, 1972) 13. Hereafter *IM*.

11. Berndt Ostendorf, "Anthropology, Modernism, and Jazz," *Ralph Ellison*, ed. Harold Bloom (New York: Chelsea House Publishers, 1986) 166.

12. Grover Sales, *Jazz: America's Classical Music* (New York: De Capo, 1992) 74.

13. Ralph Ellison, *Shadow and Act* (New York: Random House, 1964) 209. Hereafter Shadow.

14. Winthrop Sargeant, *Jazz: A History* (New York: McGraw Hill, 1964) 18.

15. James Lincoln Collier, *The Making of Jazz* (Boston: Houghton Mifflin, 1978) 247. Hereafter *Making*.

16. Frank Kofsky, "Afro-American Innovation and the Folk Tradition in Jazz: Their Historical Significance," *Journal of Ethnic Studies* 7.1 (1979): 3.

17. Lee B. Brown, "The Theory of Jazz Music: 'It Don't Mean a Thing'," *Journal of Aesthetics and Art Criticism* 49.2 (1991): 117, 125–26.

18. Amiri Baraka, *Black Music* [1967]. (Westport, CN: Greenwood Press, 1980) 15.

19. Julian Cowley, "The Art of Improvisors: Jazz and Fiction in Post-Bebop America," *New Comparison* 6 (1988): 196.

20. Pancho Savery, "Ellison's Existential Blues," *Approaches to Teaching Ellison's Invisible Man* (New York: MLA, 1989) 69; Houston A. Baker Jr., *Blues, Ideology, and Afro-American Literature: A Venacular Theory* (Chicago: University of Chicago, 1984) 190; hereafter *Blues*; Ostendorf, "Anthropology, Modernism, and Jazz" 151.

21.Mare Weiner, "*Urwaldmusik* and the Borders of German Identity: Jazz in Literature of the Weimar Republic," *The German Quarterly* 64.4 (1991): 484.

22. The foundations for these arguments were first provided in Andreas Huyssen's "Adorno in Reverse: From Hollywood to Richard Wagner," which was first published in *New German Critique* 29.2–3 (1983): 3–38 and then later included in *After the Great Divide*. For Huyssen's entire argument see *After the Great Divide* pp. 16–43. It is important, however, to note that while, with regard to the effects of the culture industry, there are similarities between Adorno's critique of Wagner and of jazz, Adorno's association of Wagner with the beginning of the culture industry is in large part a

rhetorical counter to Wagner's anti-Semitism. By locating the beginning of the culture industry with Wagner, Adorno subtly rebuts Wagner's claim that Jewish financial interests are corrupting German culture. Thus a simple association of the two critiques is highly problematic. Unlike his discussion of the culture industry and jazz, Adorno's discussion of the culture industry and Wagner is inseparable from his critique of Wagner's anti-Semitism. I examine the problematic nature of this comparison in the final chapter of this book.

23. Theodor W. Adorno, "On the Fetish-Character in Music and the Regression of Listening," *The Essential Frankfurt School Reader*, ed. Andrew Arato and Eike Gebhardt (New York: Urizen Books, 1978) 276. Hereafter "Fetish."

24. Martin Jay, *The Dialectical Imagination* (Boston: Little Brown, 1973) 182.

25. Despite these general statements by Adorno, which challenge high-low cultural dichotomies, his fixation on European music demonstrates that he only made cultural concessions on a theoretical level and was unable to turn his recognition that high-low distinctions were "obsolete" into a serious consideration of the critical dimensions of "light" music. In his discussion of what he calls the "incestuous choice" of the German intellectual exiles who fled from Nazi Germany to Los Angeles, Mike Davis has implicitly provided a partial explanation for this tendency in Adorno's writings. Davis notes that "segregated from native Angelenos, the exiles composed a miniature society in a self-imposed ghetto, clinging to their old–world prejudices like cultural life–preservers" (Mike Davis, *City of Quartz* [New York: Vintage, 1992] 47). While Davis's metaphor of the "life-preserver" highlights the personal investment in Adorno's, Horkheimer's, Schoenberg's and Mann's German cultural predilections, they also saw themselves as contributing to the preservation of the culture that the Nazis were destroying.

26. Frank Kofsky, *Black Nationalism and the Revolution in Music* (New York: Pathfinder Press, 1970) 75. Hereafter *Nationalism.*

27. John Gennari, "Jazz Criticism: Its Development and Ideologies," *Black American Literature Forum* 25.3 (1991): 475.

28. Adorno began to develop this critique of jazz as far back as 1936 in his essay "On Jazz," in which he claimed that use value of jazz intensifies rather than supersedes alienation because its innovations are produced "in terms none other than its marketability" (Adorno "On Jazz" 48). He repeats the same argument in "Fetish Character of Music and the Regression of Hearing" and again in 1941 in his review of Sargeant and Wilder: jazz "cheats the masses as soon as it holds them in its grip" (Adorno "Review" 170).

29. Scott DeVeaux, "Constructing the Jazz Tradition: Jazz Historiography," *Black Literature Forum* 25.3 (1991): 528–29.

30. Cited in Mary Frances Berry and John W. Blassingame, *Long Memory: The Black Experience in America* (New York: Oxford University Press, 1982) 416.

31. James Lincoln Collier, "The Faking of Jazz," *New Republic* 18 Nov. 1985: 37; *The Reception of Jazz in America* (New York: Institute for Studies in American Music, 1988) 70–71.

32. See in particular: John Gennari, "Jazz Criticism: Its Development and Ideologies" 496–504.

33. William Lyne, "The Signifying Modernist: Ralph Ellison and the Limits of the Double Consciousness," *PMLA* 107.2 (1992): 328.

34. Mark Naison, "Communism and Harlem Intellectual in the Popular Front: anti-Fascism and the Politics of Black Culture," *Journal of Ethnic Studies* 9.1 (1981): 22.

35. Cushing Strout, "'An American Negro Idiom': *Invisible Man* and the Politics of Culture," *Approaches to Teaching Ellison's Invisible Man* (New York: MLA, 1989) 82.

36. Martin Williams, *The Jazz Tradition* (New York: Oxford University Press, 1983) 251.

37. Amiri Baraka, *Daggers and Javelins* (New York: William Morrow, 1984) 271.

38. Jerome de Romanet, "Musical Elements in *Invisible Man* with Special Reference to the Blues," *Delta* 18 (1984): 113.

39. Neil Leonard, "The Jazzman's Verbal Usage," *Black American Literature Forum* 20.1–2 (1986): 152.

40. Gunther Schuller, *Early Jazz: Its Roots and Musical Development* (New York: Oxford University Press, 1968) 100.

41. Houston A. Baker, *Afro-American Poets* (Madison: University of Wisconsin, 1988) 153.

42. Kimberly Benston, "Controlling the Dialectical Deacon: The Critique of Historicism in *Invisible Man*," Delta 18 (1984): 91. Hereafter "Historicism."

43. See also his arguments in "Performing Blackness: Re/Placing Afro-American Poetry," *Afro-American Literary Study in the 1990's*, ed. Houston A. Baker, Jr. and Patricia Redmond (Chicago: University of Chicago, 1989) 170.

44. Ajay Heble, "The Poetics of Jazz: From Symbolic to Semiotic," *Textual Practice* 2.1 (1988): 53; Robert Hullot-Kentor, "The Impossibility of Music: Adorno, Popular and Other Music," Telos 87.1 (1991): 100.

45. Amiri Baraka, *Blues People* (New York: William Morrow, 1963) 184–85.

46. Frank Kofsky, "Black Nationalism in Jazz: The Forerunners Resist Establishment Repression, 1958–1963," *Journal of Ethnic Studies* 10.2 (1982): 2.

47. Howard Koval, "Homogenization of Culture in Capitalist Society," *Popular Music and Society* 12.4 (1988): 2–3.

48. Adorno, "Jazz," *Encyclopedia of the Arts*, ed. Dagobert D. Runes and Harry G. Schrickel (New York: Philosophical Library, 1946) 512.

49. Russell A. Berman and Robert D'Amico, "Introduction: Popular Music from Adorno to Zappa," *Telos* 87.1: 73.

50. André Hodeir, *Jazz: Its Evolution and Essence*, trans. David Noakes (New York: Grove Press, 1956). 158–181.

51. Tony Tanner, "The Music of Invisibility," *Ralph Ellison*, ed. Harold Bloom (New York: Chelsea House Publishers, 1986) 49.

52. Robert B. Stepto, *From Behind the Veil: A Study of Afro-American Narrative* (Urbana: University of Illinois, 1979) 168.

53. Eric Lott, "Love and Theft: The Racial Unconscious of Blackface Minstrelsy," *Representations* 39.2 (1992): 33–37.

54. Florindo Volpacchio, "The Unhappy Marriage of Music and Emancipation," *Telos* 87.1 (1991) :120.

6. Cultural Identities, Commodities, and Myths: Adorno and Baraka on Wagner and the Flying Dutchman

1. Theodor W. Adorno, *Introduction to the Sociology of Music*, trans. E.B. Ashton (New York: Continuum, 1989) 7. Hereafter SM.

2. Theodor W. Adorno, *In Search of Wagner*, trans. Rodney Livingstone (New York: Verso, 1981) 90. Hereafter Wagner.

3. L. J. Rather, *Reading Wagner* (Baton Rouge: Louisiana State University Press, 1990) 161. Rather uses this similarity as the basis for a questionable historicized apology for Wagner's essay, an apology which casually dismisses the wider implications of Wagner's anti-Semitism and which downplays the ideological compatibility of Wagner's text with the later atrocities committed by Nazi Germany.

4. Paul Lawrence Rose, *Wagner: Race and Revolution* (New Haven: Yale University Press, 1992) 57; Jacob Katz, *The Darker Side of Genius* (Waltham, MA: Brandeis University Press, 1986) 34.

5. Theodor W. Adorno, "Wagner, Nietzsche and Hitler," *Kenyon Review* 9.1 (1947): 162.

6. Katz, who has little tolerance for even the revolutionary anti-Semitism of Marx, Bauer, Bakunin, etc., offers a general assessment which accounts for Wagner's private motivations. According to Katz, revolutionary anti-Semitism emerges only when religious anti-Semitism has been exhausted: "If the traditional theological justification for the ostracism of the Jews no longer appeared acceptable, it was necessary to adduce other religious—though undogmatic—or explicitly secular motives for their rejection" (Katz 7).

7. Richard Wagner, "Jews in Music," *Wagner on Music and Drama*, trans. Ashton Ellis, ed. Albert Goldman and Evert Sprinchorn (New York: Dutton, 1964) 53; Adorno Wagner 17.

8. Martin Jay, "Introduction to Horkheimer," *Telos* 54 (1982–83): 7.

9. As Lyotard, in a paraphrase from Hannah Arendt, has recently noted: the Jews "can only assimilate . . . if they also assimilate anti-Semitism" (Lyotard *Heidegger* 22).

10. Lyotard has formulated an almost identical argument which only through later elliptical comments shows its indebtedness to Adorno: "'The jews' are the irremissible in the West's movement of remission and pardon. They are what cannot be domesticated in the obsession to dominate, in the compulsion to control domain, in the passion for empire, recurrent ever since Hellenistic Greece and Christian Rome. 'The jews,' never at home wherever they are, cannot be integrated, converted, or expelled. They are also always away from home when they are at home, in their so-called own tradition, because it includes exodus as its beginning, excision, impropriety, and respect for the forgotten. They are required more than guided by the cloud of free energy that they desperately try to understand, even to see, storm cloud in the Sinai" (Lyotard *Heidegger* 22).

11. The eradication of European Jewry under the Nazis not only exemplifies the most brutal form of forced assimilation (the Nazis systematically eliminated Jewish difference), but it also demonstrates the violence of any social organizing principle that establishes uniformity.

12. This aspect of Wagner's work was based upon the marketability of anti-capitalistic sentiment, which "in the context of nineteenth-century German revolutionary thought," as Paul Rose has argued, implicitly indicted the Jews "as both the spirit and practice of modern bourgeois capitalism" (Rose *Race and Revolution* 69). Interestingly enough, Robert Weisbord and Arthur Stein suggest that Harold Cruse succumbs to a similar pitfall his *Crisis of the Negro Intellectual*. They argue that "Cruse presents a brand of anti-Capitalism combined with aspersions toward Jews which is readily marketable on the American Scene" (Weisbord and Stein, *Bittersweet Encounter: The Afro-American and the American Jew* [Westport, CT: Negro University Press, 1970] 116).

13. Bryan Magee, *Aspects of Wagner*, 2nd ed. (Oxford: Oxford University Press, 1988) 24–25.

14. Amiri Baraka, *Dutchman and The Slave* (New York: Morrow Quill, 1964) 6. Hereafter *Dutchman*.

15. Richard Wagner, *Der Fliegende Holländer / The Flying Dutchman* (New York: Riverrun Press, 1982) 67. Hereafter *Flying Dutchman*.

16. To speak of the limitations of jazz's representation of experience is not to single jazz out as inadequate, but rather to acknowledge that jazz is not exempt from the problems that plague all aesthetic representation.

17. John Hagopian, "Another Ride on Jones' Subway," *CLA* 21.2 (1977): 270.

18. This decision echoes Wagner's Dutchman once again. Like the Flying Dutchman's decision not to pass sentence on Senta, Clay's decision not to "bleed" Lula marks his decision to leave, a decision that for both the Dutchman and Clay ends in death.

19. Hugh Nelson, "LeRoi Jones' Dutchman: A Brief Ride on a Doomed Ship," *Educational Theatre Journal* 20.1 (1968): 55.

20. Werner Sollors has argued that "the presence of the other 'citizens' increases Lula's aggressiveness" as well "and helps to reveal that her idyllic description was an illusion" (*Amiri Baraka / LeRoi Jones: The Quest for a "Populist" Modernism* [New York: Columbia University Press, 1978] 120).

21. Sherley Anne Williams, *Give Birth to Brightness* (New York: Dial Press, 1972) 133. Hereafter Brightness.

22. Andrzej Ceynowa has argued that these provocations are in fact "appeals to Clay, a Christ figure, for release." Whether Clay actually serves as a Christ figure is subject to debate, but Ceynowa is, I think, correct in associating Lula's liberal attitudes with a need to assuage guilt ("The Dramatic Structure of Dutchman," *Black American Literature Forum* 17.1 (1983): 15).

23. Kimberly Benston, *Baraka: The Renegade and the Mask* (New Haven: Yale University Press, 1976) 166.

24. Williams *Brightness* 110; Jerome Klinkowitz, "Dutchman as Drama," *Negro American Literature Forum* 7.4 (1973): 125; Theodore R. Hudson, *From LeRoi Jones to Amiri Baraka* (Durham, NC: Duke University Press, 1973) 152.

25. These subtleties would appear to be at odds with the general course of Baraka's thought as Gerald Early has plotted its course in "The Case of LeRoi Jones / Amiri Baraka." Early argues that Baraka falls into the "philosophically absurd" in his "quest for the fictive purer self—as expressed by Baraka's fervent wish to be 'blacker' during his cultural nationalist days and to be more 'revolutionary' now during his Marxist present" (*Salmagundi* 70–71 (1986): 346).

26. Max Horkheimer, "Egoism and the Freedom Movement," *Telos* 54 (1982–83): 17.

27. Lloyd W. Brown, *Amiri Baraka* (Boston: Twayne Publishers, 1980) 146.

28. Hugh Nelson, who was the first critic to address the similarities between Wagner and Baraka, went so far as to argue that "Jones' subway car bears no more than a superficial resemblance to 'the Flying Dutchman' and its doomed crew" (54).

29. John Livingston Lowes, *The Road to Xanadu* (Boston: Houghton Mifflin, 1927) 277.

30. Fletcher S. Bassett, *Sea Phantoms* (Chicago: Morrill Higgins, 1892) 360. Bassett cites two variations of this aspect of the legend (cf. 347; 352). In *Amiri Baraka*, Lloyd W. Brown also notes that the "Flying Dutchman's" ship is reputed to be a slave-trading vessel, but Brown does not appear to have known that the Dutchman is

condemned for murdering the slaves (Brown 143). This version of the legend has some historical basis. Robert Weisbord recounts, for example, the history of the slave ship "Zong," whose Captain Collingwood cast 130 slaves—most of whom were alive—into the sea in an attempt to force the underwriters of the ship to pay compensation for "cargo" lost (Robert Weisbord, "The Case of the Slave-Ship 'Zong', 1783," *History Today* 19.8 [1969]: 562). In *Black-Jewish Relations in the United States* (Westport, CT: Greenwood Press, 1984), Lenwood Davis attributes this story to instances where Jews were slave owners or slave traders (90). More recently, Henry Louis Gates, in an editorial response to "The Secret Relationship Between Blacks and the Jew" (a publication of the Nation of Islam that suggests that Jewish involvement in the slave trade was widespread) notes that "of all the African slaves imported into the New World, American Jewish merchants accounted for less than 2 percent (Gates "Black Demagogues and Pseudo-Scholars," *New York Times*: July 20, 1992).

31. In the myth of the Flying Dutchman, Baraka stumbles upon the perfect catalyst for expressing the wider aesthetic and cultural implications of Clay's wearing a jacket and tie "from a tradition . . . [he] ought to feel oppressed by" (Baraka *Dutchman* 18). For Baraka to follow in the literary tradition of his predecessors would be tantamount to casting aside or over-board, i.e., ignoring countless brutal exclusions of Blacks, and accepting, in the name of cultural traditions, the cultural repression of the African-American experience. Hence, the task that Baraka sees before him is not one of reconciliation but of recovery and reassertion of the black aesthetic and cultural values that are inherently precluded in the system in which Clay tries to make his way.

32. Samuel Taylor Coleridge, *The Poems of Coleridge*, ed. Ernest Hartley Coleridge (New York: Oxford University Press, 1912) 193–94. The entire original stanza, which Lowes cites in *The Road to Xanadu* reads:

And are those two all, all the crew,
  That woman and her fleshless Pheere?

His bones were *black* with many a crack,
  All black and bare, I ween;
Jet-black and bare, save where with rust
Of mouldly damps and charnel crust
  They're patch'd with purple and green.

Her lips are red, her looks are free,
  Her locks are yellow as gold:
Her skin is as white as leprosy,
And she is far liker Death than he;
  Her flesh makes the still air cold.

In the 1817 version Coleridge replaces these passages with the lines:

And is that Woman all her crew?
Is that a DEATH? and are there two?
Is DEATH that woman's mate? (Coleridge 193).

Lowes notes that through these alterations Coleridge slowly forged an image of the Mariner that was a composite of Cain, the Wandering Jew and the 'Old Navigator' (cf. Lowes *The Road to Xanadu* 277–78).

33. Almost twenty years after *Dutchman* was written, Baraka himself described Clay's predicament in similar terms. *Dutchman*, he writes, "expressed the difficulty of becoming a man in America—that if you try to deal truthfully you'll be killed and if you don't, you kill yourself psychologically" ("Confessions of a Former anti-Semite," *The Village Voice* 25.50 [Dec 17–23, 1980]: 20).

34. This aspect of the Dutchman myth undermines the most dominant trend in the scholarship on Baraka's drama, viz., the association of Lula with the role of the Dutchman. The association began with Nelson's initial study of the relationship between *Dutchman* and the myth of the "Flying Dutchman," and is repeated by Hagopian and Ceynowa (Nelson 55; Hagopian 273; Ceynowa 15).

35. Erick Rappl notes that "between 1978 and 1984 the production of 'The Flying Dutchman' created by Harry Kupfer was performed 36 times at seven Bayreuth Festivals" ("A New Departure for Romantic Opera," *Der Fliegende Holländer*, dir. Harry Kupfer [Munich: UNITEL film– und Fernsehproductionasgesellschaft, 1985] 1). Although the production encountered protests, it also enjoyed lasting success.

36. Senta's rejection of Erik coincides with Lula's enticing and then denying "the sexual urge of Clay." John Lindberg has argued that the sexual tension of both pieces functions as a locus of grave threat masquerading as acceptance and security (John Lindberg, "*Dutchman* and *The Slave*: Companions in Revolution," *Imamu Amiri Baraka (LeRoi Jones)*, ed. Kimberly W. Benston [Englewood Cliffs, NJ: Prentice–Hall, 1978] 141).

37. Brian Branston, *Gods of the North* (London: Thames and Hudson, 1980) 108.

38. On this same point, it is important to recognize that the logic of Clay's identification as a poet with the music of Charlie Parker parallels the conclusion of Wagner's own earlier argument in "Jews in Music," where after arguing that Jewish composers corrupt German music, he maintains that the Jewish poet Heinrich Heine, whose *Memoirs of Herr von Schablewopski* was the source for Wagner's libretto, composed "versified lies" that were a corrupt or illegitimate form of German literature (Charles Osborne, *The Complete Operas of Richard Wagner* [North Pomfret, VT: Trafalgar Square Publishing, 1991] 69–70; Wagner "Jews in Music" 59). Both Clay as an African–American and the Dutchman as a Wandering Jew are at best illegitimate or bastard participants in the repressive normative values that Wagner ultimately defends in his opera *The Flying Dutchman.*

39. Bassett discusses the relation between the "Wandering Jew" and the "Flying Dutchman" in *Sea Phantoms* (362–63; 375). Wagner acknowledges the relation in his essay "The Flying Dutchman: Use of Myth" (*Wagner on Music and Drama*, trans. Ashton Ellis., ed. Albert Goldman and Evert Sprinchorn [New York: Dutton, 1964] 254). And Nietzsche criticizes the manner in which Wagner adapted the legend of the

"Wandering Jew" for *The Flying Dutchman* in *The Case of Wagner* (trans. Walter Kaufmann, [New York: Vintage, 1967] 160–161).

40. Historically, the image of Ahasver has often provided the forcible expulsion of Jews with an ideological cover. S. Hurwitz has noted that "even those who have but a rather narrow range of knowledge of Western history, and specifically of the history of the Jewish people, can furnish proof without difficulty that almost all Jewish migratory movements, starting with the Babylonian captivity throughout the whole of the Middle Ages to modern times, *can never be explained on the basis of inner causes*. The numerous migrations of the Jews were entirely the result of forcible mass expulsion, which resulted from the infamous accusations concerning the desecration of eucharistic wafers, ritual murders and the poisoning of wells." (S. Hurwitz, "Ahasver, The Eternal Wanderer: Psychological Aspects," *The Wandering Jew*, ed. Galit Hasan-Rokem and Alan Dundes [Bloomington: Indiana University Press, 1986] 217).

41. Lowes 259; Peter L. Thorslev, Jr., *The Byronic Hero* (Minneapolis: University of Minnesota Press, 1962) 104. In the oral traditions of Christianity in the South, Cain has served as a stereotype of African-Americans. This may in part derive from accounts suggesting that Cain's violence against his brother was a reaction to a vision given to him by a devil "of a future in which his sons and daughters are persecuted and enslaved by the children of Abel, and upon waking, while his frenzy is still on him, he commits the murder" (Thorslev 95). Hurwitz offers evidence that this peculiar reading of Cain has its origins in the Apocalypse of Moses, where Cain is referred to "as *Adiophotos*, 'the one without light,' 'the dark one,' but at the same time as *Diaphotos*, 'the enlightened' (Hurwitz 217).

42. In their book *Ku Klux Klan* (New York: Garland Publishing, 1991), Michael and Judy Newton argue that the symbol of the Burning Cross has its origin in Scottish signaling and that it did not become associated with the KKK until 1915. Though "often described as a 'religious ceremony', cross burnings . . . soon became a traditional form of KKK intimidation" (145).

43. Timothy P. Martin, "Joyce, Wagner, and the Wandering Jew," *Comparative Literature* 42.1 (1990): 55.

44. It is important to note, however, that Baraka has publicly distanced himself in recent years from his earlier anti-Semitism. I also believe that his attempt in "Confessions of an Anti-Semite" to understand the reasons for and the circumstances leading to his anti-Semitism evince a sincere effort to come to terms with it without becoming reductive.

45. Susan Sontag, "Going to Theater, etc.," *Against Interpretation* (New York: Farrar, Strauss, Giroux, 1966) 151. While in one sense Sontag may be correct about the shift in the focus of liberalism, the militancy itself was not new. When, in the nineteenth century, Wagner turned to the image of the Wandering Jew, it was already in a state of transition. Among romantic poets, Ahasuerus quickly evolved "from a sinner to an accuser" who "rebels against a punishment administered unjustly by a tyrannical deity" (Edgar Rosenberg, *From Shylock to Svengali* [Stanford: Stanford University Press, 1960] 197).

46. It is of fundamental importance to recognize that the image of the Wandering Jew is by no means a neutral reference to the Jews. In his essay "Ahasuerus the Wandering Jew," R. Edelmann argues, for example: "The figure of the Wandering Jew, which has preoccupied the Western world to such a degree for more than 350 years in literature as well as in pictorial art, in music and in the popular imagination, is, after all, a concern of Christians. He is a Christian invention. Ahasuerus, the Wandering Jew, is a Jew by postulate only, not even by name" ("Ahasuerus, The Wandering Jew: Origin and Background," *The Wandering Jew*, ed. Galit Hasan-Rokem and Alan Dundes [Bloomington: Indiana University Press, 1986] 3).

47. In *The Byronic Hero*, Thorslev notes: "Cain and Ahasuerus are obviously twin figures in legend and in literature. It is very likely, in fact, that the eternal Jew owes something of his origins to his older counterpart" (92). The historical king Ahasuerus is the same king whom the Greeks called Xerxes I and who unsuccessfully tried to conquer Greece in 481 B.C. He was later murdered in his bed chamber.

48. Jürgen Habermas, *The Philosophical Discourse of Modernity*, trans. Frederick Lawrence (Cambridge, MA: MIT Press, 1987) 107.

49. Theodor W. Adorno, "Cultural Criticism and Society," *Prisms*, trans. Samuel Weber and Shierry Weber (Cambridge, MA: MIT Press, 1981) 34; *ND* 362–63.

50. Harold Cruse, *Crisis of the Negro Intellectual* (New York: William Morrow, 1967) 197.

51. James Baldwin, "Negroes are anti-Semitic because They're anti-White," *Price of the Ticket* (New York: St. Martin's Press, 1985) 248.

52. Harold Cruse, "My Jewish Problem and Theirs," *Black Anti-Semitism and Jewish Racism*, ed. Nat Hentoff (New York: Richard W. Baron, 1969) 172.

Bibliography

Adorno, Theodor W. *Aesthetic Theory*. 1970. Trans. by C. Lenhardt. New York: Routledge & Kegan Paul, 1984.

———. *Negative Dialectics*. 1966. Trans. by E.B. Ashton. New York: Continuum, 1973.

———. "Commitment." 1965. Trans. by Francis McDonagh. *Aesthetic and Politics*. Ed. by Ronald Taylor. New York: Verso, 1977. 184–85.

———. "Progress." 1964. Trans. by Eric Krakauer. *Benjamin: Philosophy, History Aesthetics*. Ed. by Gary Smith. Chicago: University of Chicago Press, 1989.

———. "Language and Music: A Fragment." *Quasi Una Fantasia*. 1963. Trans. by Rodney Livingstone. New York: Verso, 1992. 1–8.

———. *Introduction to the Sociology of Music*. 1962. Trans. by E.B. Ashton. New York: Continuum, 1989.

———. *Dissonanzen*. Göttingen: Vandenhoeck und Ruprecht, 1962.

———. "Trying to Understand Endgame." 1961. *New German Critique* 9.2 (1982): 119–50

———. "Perennial Fashion—Jazz." *Prisms*. 1953. Trans. by Samuel Weber and Shierry Weber. Cambridge, MA: MIT Press, 1981. 119–32.

———. "Cultural Criticism and Society." Prisms. 1953. Trans. by Samuel Weber and Shierry Weber. Cambridge, MA: MIT Press, 1981. 17–34.

———. *In Search of Wagner*. 1952. Trans. by Rodney Livingstone. New York: Verso, 1981.

———. *Minima Moralia*. 1951. Trans. by E.F.N. Jephcott. New York: Verso, 1974.

———. *Philosophy of Modern Music*. 1949. New York: Continuum, 1985.

———. "Wagner, Nietzsche and Hitler." *Kenyon Review* 9.1 (1947): 155–162.

———. "Jazz." *Encyclopedia of the Arts*. Ed. by Dagobert D. Runes and Hary G. Schrickel. New York: Philosophical Library, 1946. 511–513.

———. "Theses Upon Art and Religion Today." *Kenyon Review* 7.4 (1945): 677–682.

———. *Review of American Jazz Music* by Wilder Hobson and of *Jazz Hot and Hybrid* by Winthrop Sargeant. *Studies in Philosophy and Social Science* 7.9 (1941): 167–78.

———. "On the Fetish–Character in Music and the Regression of Listening." 1938. *The Essential Frankfurt School Reader*. Ed. by Andrew Arato and Eike Gebhardt. New York: Urizen Books, 1978. 270–299.

———. "On Jazz." 1936. Trans. by Jamie Owen Daniel. *Discourse* 12.1 (1989–90): 45–69.

———. "Abschied vom Jazz." 1933. *Gesammelte Schriften*. vol. 18. Franfurt am Main: Suhrkamp, 1984. 795–799.

Adorno, Theodor W. and Max Horkheimer. *Dialectic of Enlightenment*. 1944. Trans. by John Cumming. New York: Continuum, 1991.

Adorno, Theodor W., Else Frenkel-Brunswik, Daniel J. Levison and R. Nevitt Sanford. *The Authoritarian Personality*. New York: Harper & Brothers, 1950.

Adorno, Theodor W., and Joachim-Ernst Berendt. "Für und Wider Jazz." *Merkur: Deutsche Zeitschrift für Europäisches Denken* 7.9 (1953): 887–93.

Alldritt, Keith. *Eliot's Four Quartets: Poetry as Chamber Music*. Totowa, NJ: Woburn Press, 1978.

Anders, Günter. *Die Antiquiertheit des Menschen*. München: Verlag C.H. Beck, 1956.

Arato, Andrew and Erike Gebhardt. *Essential Franfurt School Reader*. New York: Urizen Books, 1978.

Baker, Houston A., Jr. *Blues, Ideology, and Afro-American Literature: A Venacular Theory*. Chicago: University of Chicago, 1984.

———. *Afro-American Poets*. Madison: University of Wisconsin, 1988.

Baldwin, James. "Negroes are Anti-Semitic because They're Anti-White." *Price of the Ticket*. New York: St. Martin's Press, 1985. 425–433.

Bamps, Yvan and Ralph Heyndels. "*Modern Times* in the Light of Adorno and Beckett." *Charles Chaplin: His Reflection in Modern Times*. Ed. by Adolphe Nysenholc. New York: Mouton de Gruyter, 1991. 119–24.

Baraka, Imamu Amiri. [LeRoi Jones] *Blues People*. New York: William Morrow, 1963.

———. *Dutchman and The Slave*. New York: Morrow Quill, 1964.

———. *Black Music*. 1967. Westport, CN: Greenwood Press, 1980.

———. *Daggers and Javelins*. New York: William Morrow, 1984.

———. "Confessions of a Former Anti-Semite." *The Village Voice* 25.50 (Dec 17–23, 1980): 1; 19–20; 22–23.

Bassett, Fletcher S. *Sea Phantoms*. Chicago: Morrill Higgins, 1892.

Baugh, Bruce. "Left-Wing Elitism: Adorno on Popular Culture." *Philosphy and Literature* 14.1 (1990): 65–78.

Bebbington, W.B. "Four Quartets?" *Essays in Criticism* 39.3 (1989): 234–41.

Beckett, Samuel. *Waiting for Godot*. New York: Grove, 1954.

———. *The Unnameable. Three Novels*. New York: Grove, 1955.

Benjamin, Walter. *Illuminations*. Trans. by Harry Zohn. New York: Schocken Books, 1968.

Benston, Kimberly W. "Controlling the Dialectical Deacon: The Critique of Historicism in *Invisible Man*." *Delta* 18 (1984): 89–103.

———. "Performing Blackness: Re/Placing Afro-American Poetry" *Afro-American Literary Study in the 1990's*. Ed. by Houston A. Baker Jr. and Patricia Redmond. Chicago: University of Chicago, 1989. 164–185.

———. *Baraka: The Renegade and the Mask*. New Haven: Yale University Press, 1976.

Berman, Russell. *Cultural Studies of Modern Germany*. Madison: University of Wisconsin Press, 1993.

———. *Modern Culture and Critical Theory*. Madison: University of Wisconsin Press, 1989.

Berman, Russell A. and Robert D'Amico. "Introduction: Popular Music from Adorno to Zappa." *Telos* 87.1 (1991): 71–77.

Bernstein, Jay. "Philosophy's Refuge: Adorno in Beckett." *Philosopher's Poets*. Ed. by David Wood. New York: Routledge, 1990. 177–91.

———. "Art Against Enlightenment." *The Problems of Modernity*. New York: Routledge, 1989. 49–66.

Berry, Mary Frances, and John W. Blassingame. *Long Memory: The Black Experience in America*. New York: Oxford University Press, 1982.

Blamires, Harry. *Word Unheard*. London: Methuen, 1969.

Booty, John. *Meditating on Four Quartets*. Cambridge, MA: Cowley, 1983.

Branston, Brian. *Gods of the North*. London: Thames and Hudson, 1980.

Brown, Lee B. "The Theory of Jazz Music: 'It Don't Mean a Thing'." *Journal of Aesthetics and Art Criticism* 49.2 (1991): 115–127.

Brown, Lloyd W. *Amiri Baraka*. Boston: Twayne Publishers, 1980.

Buck-Morss, Susan. *The Origin of Negative Dialectics*. New York: The Free Press, 1977.

Bürger, Peter. *Theory of the Avant-Garde*. Trans. by Michael Shaw. Minneapolis: University of Minnesota Press, 1984.

———. "Adorno's Anti-Avant-Gardism," *Telos* 86 (1990–91): 49–60.

Bush, Ronald. *T.S. Eliot*. New York: Oxford University Press, 1983.

Butler, Judith. *Subjects of Desire*. New York: Columbia University Press, 1987.

Carner, Gary. "Introduction [to Special Volume on Jazz]." *Black American Literature Forum* 25.3 (1991): 441–448.

Ceynowa, Andrzej. "The Dramatic Structure of Dutchman." *Black American Literature Forum* 17.1 (1983): 15–18.

Coleridge, Samuel Taylor. *The Poems of Coleridge*. Ed. by Ernest Hartley Coleridge. New York: Oxford University Press, 1912.

Collier, James Lincoln. *The Making of Jazz*. Boston: Houghton Mifflin, 1978.

———. "The Faking of Jazz." *New Republic* 18 Nov. 1985: 33–40.

———. *The Reception of Jazz in America*. New York: Institute for Studies in American Music, 1988.

Cowley, Julian. "The Art of Improvisors: Jazz and Fiction in Post–Bebop America." *New Comparison* 6 (1988): 194–204.

Craig, Gordon. *Germany 1866–1945*. New York: Oxford University Press, 1978.

Cruse, Harold. *Crisis of the Negro Intellectual*. New York: William Morrow, 1967.

———. "My Jewish Problem and Theirs." *Black Anti-Semitism and Jewish Racism*. Ed. by Nat Hentoff. New York: Richard W. Baron, 1969. 143–188.

D'Amico, Robert. "Karl Popper and the Frankfurt School." *Telos* 86 (1990–91): 33–48.

Dallmayr, Fred. *Between Freiburg and Frankfurt*. Amherst: University of Massachusetts Press, 1991.

———. "Adorno and Heidegger." *Diacritics* 19.3–4 (1989): 82–100.

Daniel, Jamie Owen. "Introduction to Adorno's 'On Jazz'." *Discourse* 12.1 (1989–90): 39–44.

Davis, Lenwood. *Black-Jewish Relations in the United States*. Westport, CT: Greenwood Press, 1984.

Davis, Mike. *City of Quartz*. New York: Vintage, 1992.

Deleuze, Gilles, and Félix Guattari. *Kafka: Toward a Minor Literature*. Trans. by Dana Polan. Minneapolis: University of Minnesota, 1986.

DeVeaux, Scott. "Constructing the Jazz Tradition: Jazz Historiography." *Black Literature Forum* 25.3 (1991): 525–560.

Dews, Peter. "Adorno, Post-Structuralism and the Critique of Identity." *Problems of Modernity*. Ed. by Andrew Benjamin. New York: Routledge, 1989. 1–22.

———. *Logics of Disintegration*. New York: Verso, 1987.

Diels, Hermann. *Die Fragmente der Vorsokratiker*. Berlin: Weidmannsche Buchhandlung, 1922.

Early, Gerald. "The Case of LeRoi Jones / Amiri Baraka." *Salmagundi* 70–71 (1986): 343–352.

Edelmann, R. "Ahasuerus, The Wandering Jew: Origin and Background." *The Wandering Jew*. Ed. by Galit Hasan-Rokem and Alan Dundes. Bloomington: Indiana University Press, 1986. 1–10.

Eliot, T.S. "The Music of Poetry." *On Poetry and Poets*. New York: Farrar, Strauss and Cudahy, 1957. 17–33.

———. *Four Quartets*. 1943. New York: Harcourt Brace Jovanovich, 1971.

Ellis, Steve. *The English Eliot*. New York: Routledge, 1991.

Ellison, Ralph. *Invisible Man*. 1952. New York: Vintage, 1972.

———. *Shadow and Act*. New York: Random House, 1964.

Ellmann, Maud. *The Poetics of Impersonality*. Brighton, Sussex: Harvester Press Limited, 1987.

Feher, Ferenc. "Rationalized Music and its Vicissitudes (Adorno's Philosophy of Music)." *Philosophy and Social Criticism* 9.1 (1982): 41–65.

———. "Negative Philosophy of Music—Positive Results." *New German Critique* 2.1 (1975): 99–111.

Fischer, Ernst. *Art against Ideology*. London: Penguin, 1969.

Flint, R.W. "The Four Quartets Reconsidered." *T.S. Eliot: Four Quartets*. Ed. by Bernard Bergonzi. London: Macmillian, 1969. 107–18.

Gardner, Helen. "The Music of *Four Quartets*." *T.S. Eliot: Four Quartets*, Ed. by Bernard Bergonzi. London: Macmillian, 1969. 119–137.

Gates, Henry Louis Jr. "Black Demagogues and Pseudo-Scholars." *New York Times*: July 20, 1992.

Gennari, John. "Jazz Criticism: Its Development and Ideologies." *Black American Literature Forum* 25.3 (1991): 449–523.

Geulen, Eva. "A Matter of Tradition." *Telos* 89 (1991): 155–166.

Gross, Harvey. "Compound Ghost, Triple Devil, Terminal Books." *T.S. Eliot: Man and Poet*. Vol. 1. Ed. by Laura Cowan. Orono: University of Maine, 1990. 107–124.

Habermas, Jürgen. *The Philosophical Discourse of Modernity*. Trans. by Frederick Lawrence. Cambridge, MA: MIT Press, 1987.

———. "Modernity—An Incomplete Project." *The Anti-Aesthetic*. Trans. by Seyla Ben-Habib. Ed. by Hal Foster. Port Townsend, WA: Bay Press, 1983. 3–15.

Hagopian, John. "Another Ride on Jones' Subway." *CLA* 21.2 (1977): 269–274.

Heble, Ajay. "The Poetics of Jazz: From Symbolic to Semiotic." *Textual Practice* 2.1 (1988): 51–68.

Hegel, F. W. *Early Theological Writings*. Trans. by T. M. Knox. Philadelphia: University of Pennsylvania Press, 1971.

———. *Phenomenology of Spirit*. Trans. by A. V. Miller. Oxford: Oxford University Press, 1977.

Hobson, Wilder. *American Jazz Music*. New York: Norton, 1939.

Hodeir, André. *Jazz: Its Evolution and Essence*. Trans. by David Noakes. New York: Grove Press, 1956.

Hohendahl, Peter Uwe. "Adorno Criticism Today," *New German Critique* 19.2 (1992): 3–15.

———. "The Displaced Intellectual?: Adorno's American Years Revisted." *New German Critique* 19.2 (1992): 76–100.

———. *Reappraisals: The Shifting Alignments in Postwar Critical Theory*. Ithaca: Cornell University Press, 1991.

———. "Looking Back at Adorno's *Ästhetische Theorie*." *German Quarterly* 54 (1981): 133–148.

Holloway, John. "Eliot's *Four Quartets* and Beethoven's Last Quartets." *Fire and the Rose: New Essays on T.S. Eliot*. Ed. by Vinod Sena and Rajiva Verma. Delhi: Oxford University Press, 1992. 150–51.

Horkheimer, Max. "Egoism and the Freedom Movement." Trans. by David J. Parent. *Telos* 54 (1982–83): 10–60.

Hudson, Theodor R. *From LeRoi Jones to Amiri Baraka*. Durham, NC: Duke University Press, 1973.

Hullot-Kentor, Robert. "Suggested Reading: Jameson on Adorno." *Telos* 89 (1991): 167–177.

———. "The Impossibility of Music: Adorno, Popular and Other Music." *Telos* 87 (1991): 97–117.

Hurwitz, S. "Ahasver, The Eternal Wanderer: Psychological Aspects." *The Wandering Jew*. Ed. by Galit Hasan-Rokem and Alan Dundes. Bloomington: Indiana University Press, 1986. 211–226.

Huyssen, Andreas. "Adorno in Reverse: From Hollywood to Richard Wagner." *New German Critique*. 29.3–4 (1983): 8–38.

———. *After the Great Divide*. Bloomington: Indiana University Press, 1986.

Hyppolite, Jean. *Studies on Marx and Hegel*. Trans. by John O'Neill. New York: Basic Books, 1969.

———. *Genesis and Structure of Hegel's Phenomenology of Spirit*. Trans. by Samuel Cherniak and John Heckman. Evanston: Northwestern University Press, 1974.

"Introduction to Adorno," *Telos* 7 (1974): 2–6.

Jameson, Fredric. *Late Marxism: Adorno, or, the Persistence of the Dialectic*. New York: Verso, 1990.

Jay, Martin. *The Dialectical Imagination*. Boston: Little Brown, 1973.

———. "Introduction to Horkheimer." *Telos* 54 (1982–83): 5–9.

———. *Marxism and Totality*. University of California Press, 1984.

———. *Adorno*. Cambridge, MA: Harvard University Press, 1984.

———. *Permanent Exiles*. New York: Columbia University Press, 1985.

Katz, Jacob. *The Darker Side of Genius*. Hanover, NH: Brandeis University Press, 1986.

Kelly, George. "Notes on Hegel's 'Lordship and Bondage'," *Review of Metaphysics* 19 (1966): 780–802.

Kenner, Hugh. *The Invisible Poet: T.S. Eliot*. London: Methuen, 1965.

Klinkowitz, Jerome. "Dutchman as Drama." *Negro American Literature Forum* 7.4 (1973): 123–126.

Kofsky, Frank. *Black Nationalism and the Revolution in Music*. New York: Pathfinder Press, 1970.

———. "Afro-American Innovation and the Folk Tradition in Jazz: Their Historical Significance." *Journal of Ethnic Studies* 7.1 (1979): 1–12.

———. "Black Nationalism in Jazz: The Forerunners Resist Establishment Repression, 1958–1963." *Journal of Ethnic Studies* 10.2 (1982): 1–27.

Kojève, Alexandre. *Introduction to the Reading of Hegel*. Trans. by James Nichols, Jr. Ed. by Allan Bloom. Ithaca: Cornell University Press, 1980.

Koval, Howard. "Homogenization of Culture in Capitalist Society." *Popular Music and Society* 12.4 (1988): 1–16.

Krukowski, Lucian. "Form and Protest in Atonal Music: A Meditation on Adorno." *Bucknell Review: A Scholarly Journal of Letters, Arts and Sciences* 29.1 (1984): 105–124.

Kuhn, Thomas. *The Structure of Scientific Revolutions.* Chicago: University of Chicago Press, 1962.

Leonard, Neil. "The Jazzman's Verbal Usage." *Black American Literature Forum* 20.1–2 (1986): 150–160.

Levin, Thomas. "For the Record: Adorno on Music in the Age of Its Technological Reproducibility." *October* 55.4 (1990): 23–47.

Lindberg, John. "*Dutchman* and *The Slave*: Companions in Revolution." *Imamu Amiri Baraka (LeRoi Jones).* Ed. by Kimberly W. Benston. Englewood Cliffs, NJ: Prentice-Hall, 1978. 141–147.

Lobb, Edward. "Limitation and Transcendence in 'East Coker'." *Words in Time.* Ed. by Edward Lobb. Ann Arbor: University of Michigan, 1993. 20–37.

———. "Chamber Music: Eliot's Closed Rooms and Difficult Women." *T.S.Eliot: Man and Poet.* Vol. 1. Ed. by Laura Cowan. Orono: University of Maine, 1990. 167–179.

Lott, Eric. "Love and Theft: The Racial Unconscious of Blackface Minstrelsy." *Representations* 39.2 (1992): 23–50.

Lowes, John Livingston. *The Road to Xanadu.* Boston: Houghton Mifflin, 1927.

Lüdke, W. Martin. "Der Kronzeuge." *Theodor W. Adorno.* Ed. by Heinz Ludwig Arnold. 2nd Ed. by Munich: Edition Text + Kritik, 1983. 136–49.

Lunn, Eugene. *Marxism and Modernism.* Berkeley: University of California Press, 1982.

Lyne, William. "The Signifying Modernist: Ralph Ellison and the Limits of the Double Consciousness." *PMLA* 107.2 (1992): 319–330.

Lyotard, Jean-François. "Adorno as the Devil." *Telos* 7.1 (1974): 127–137.

———. *The Postmodern Condition.* Trans. by Geoff Bennington and Brian Massumi. Minneapolis: University of Minnesota Press, 1984.

———. *Heidegger and "the jews".* Trans. by Andreas Michel and Mark Roberts. Minneapolis: University of Minesota Press, 1990.

Magee, Bryan. *Aspects of Wagner.* 2nd Ed. by Oxford: Oxford University Press, 1988.

Mann, Thomas. *Doctor Faustus.* Trans. by H.T. Lowe-Porter. New York: Vintage, 1948.

Marsh, James L. "Adorno's Critique of Stravinsky," *New German Critique* 10.1 (1983): 147–69.

Martin, Timothy P. "Joyce, Wagner, and the Wandering Jew." *Comparative Literature* 42.1 (1990): 49–72.

Marx, Karl. "On the Jewish Question." *Marx-Engels Reader.* 2nd Ed. by Ed. by Robert Tucker. New York: Norton, 1978. 26–52.

———. "Thesen über Feuerbach." *Marx-Engels Werke*. vol. 3. Berlin: Dietz Verlag, 1956.

Matthiessen, F. O. "The *Quartets*." *T.S. Eliot: Four Quartets*. Ed. by Bernard Bergonzi. London: Macmillian, 1969. 88–104.

McCormack, W. J. "Seeing Darkly: Notes on T. W. Adorno and Samuel Beckett." *Hermathena: A Trinity College Dublin Review* 141.2 (1986): 22–44.

Nägele, Rainer. "The Scene of the Other: Theodor W. Adorno's *Negative Dialectic* in the Context of Poststructuralism." *Boundary 2* 11 (1982–3): 59–79.

Naison, Mark. "Communism and Harlem Intellectual in the Popular Front: Anti–Fascism and the Politics of Black Culture." *Journal of Ethnic Studies* 9.1 (1981): 1–25.

Neal, Larry. "Ellison's Zoot Suit." *Ralph Ellison: A Collection of Critical Essays*. Ed. by John Hersey. Englewood Cliffs, NJ: Prentice Hall, 1974. 58–79.

Nelson, Hugh. "LeRoi Jones' Dutchman: A Brief Ride on a Doomed Ship." *Educational Theatre Journal* 20.1 (1968): 53–59.

Newton, Michael, and Judy Ann Newton. *Ku Klux Klan* (New York: Garland Publishing, 1991).

Nicholsen, Shierry Weber. "Toward a More Adequate Reception of Adorno's *Aesthetic Theory*: Configurational Form in Adorno's Aesthetic Writings," *Cultural Critique* 18.2 (1991): 33–64.

Nietzsche, Friedrich. *The Case of Wagner*. Trans. by Walter Kaufmann. New York: Vintage, 1967.

Nye, William P. "Theodor Adorno on Jazz: A Critique of Critical Theory." *Popular Music and Society* 12.4 (1988): 69–73.

Osborne, Charles. *The Complete Operas of Richard Wagner*. North Pomfret, VT: Trafalgar Square Publishing, 1991.

Osborne, Peter. "Adorno and the Metaphysics of Modernism: The Problem of a 'Postmodern' Art." *The Problems of Modernity*. Ed. by Andrew Benjamin. New York: Routledge, 1989. 23–48.

———. "A Marxism for the Postmodern?" *New German Critique* 19.2 (1992): 171–192.

Ostendorf, Berndt. "Anthropology, Modernism, and Jazz." *Ralph Ellison*. Ed. by Harold Bloom. New York: Chelsea House Publishers, 1986. 145–172.

Paddison, Max. *Adorno's Aesthetics of Music*. New York: Cambridge University Press, 1993.

Rappl, Erich. "A New Departure for Romantic Opera." *Der Fliegende Holländer*. dir. Harry Kupfer. Munich: UNITEL film- und Fernsehproductionasgesellschaft, 1985.

Rather, L.J. *Reading Wagner*. Baton Rouge: Louisana State University Press, 1990.

Reinelt, Janelle. "Approaching the Postmodernist Threshold: Samuel Beckett and Bertolt Brecht." *The Aesthetics of the Critical Theorists*. Ed. by Ronald Roblin. Lewiston, NY: Edwin Mellen Press, 1990. 337–358.

Riquelme, John Paul. *Harmony of Dissonances*. Baltimore: Johns Hopkins University Press, 1991.

Roberts, David. *Art and Enlightenment*. Lincoln: University of Nebraska Press, 1991.

de Romanet, Jerome. "Musical Elements in *Invisible Man* with Special Reference to the Blues." *Delta* 18 (1984): 105–118.

Rose, Gillian. *The Melancholy Science*. London: Macmillian, 1978.

Rose, Paul Lawrence. *Wagner: Race and Revolution*. New Haven: Yale University Press, 1992.

Rosen, Charles. *The Classical Style*. New York: Norton, 1972.

Rosenberg, Edgar. *From Shylock to Svengali*. Stanford: Stanford University Press, 1960.

Said, Edward. *Musical Elaborations*. New York: Columbia University Press, 1991.

Sales, Grover. *Jazz: America's Classical Music*. New York: De Capo, 1992.

Sargeant, Winthrop. *Jazz: A History*. 1938. [original title: Jazz: Hot and Hybrid]. New York: McGraw Hill, 1964.

Savery, Pancho. "Ellison's Existential Blues." *Approaches to Teaching Ellison's Invisible Man*. New York: MLA, 1989. 65–74.

Schönherr, Ulrich. "Adorno and Jazz: Reflections on a Failed Encounter." *Telos* 87.1 (1991): 85–96.

Schuller, Gunther. *Early Jazz: Its Roots and Musical Development*. New York: Oxford University Press, 1968.

Schulte-Sasse, Jochen. "Theory of Modernism versus Theory of the Avant-Garde." Forward. *Theory of the Avant-Garde* by Peter Bürger. Trans. by Michael Shaw. Minneapolis: University of Minnesota Press, 1984. vii–xvii.

Schweik, Robert. "T.S. Eliot's *Four Quartets* and the Uses of 'Reffered Forms'." *Cithara* 28.2 (1989): 43–61.

Shusterman, Richard. "Reactionary Meets Radical Critique: Eliot and Contemporary Cultural Criticism." *T.S. Eliot: Man and Poet*. Vol. 1. Ed. by Laura Cowan. Orono: University of Maine, 1990. 367–393.

———. *T. S. Eliot and the Philosophy of Criticism*. New York: Columbia University Press, 1988.

Sollors, Werner. *Amiri Baraka / LeRoi Jones: The Quest for a "Populist" Modernism.* New York: Columbia University Press, 1978.

Sontag, Susan. "Going to Theater, etc." *Against Interpretation.* New York: Farrar, Strauss, Giroux, 1966. 140–162.

Starr, S. Frederick. *Red and Hot: The Fate of Jazz in the Soviet Union.* New York: Oxford University Press, 1983.

Steinberg, Michael P. "The Musical Absolute." *New German Critique* 19.2 (1992): 17–42.

Stepto, Robert B. *From Behind the Veil: A Study of Afro-American Narrative.* Urbana: University of Illinois, 1979.

Strout, Cushing. "'An American Negro Idiom': Invisible Man and the Politics of Culture." *Approaches to Teaching Ellison's Invisible Man.* New York: MLA, 1989. 79–85.

Subotnik, Rose. *Developing Variations.* Minneapolis: University of Minnesota Press, 1991.

Tanner, Tony. "The Music of Invisibility." *Ralph Ellison.* Ed. by Harold Bloom. New York: Chelsea House Publishers, 1986. 37–50.

Taylor, Ronald, et al., eds. *Aesthetics and Politics.* New York: Verso, 1977.

Thomas, Lorenzo. "'Communicating by Horns': Jazz and Redemption in the Poetry of the Beats and the Black Arts Movement." *African American Review* 26.2 (1992): 291–298.

Thorslev, Peter L. Jr. *The Byronic Hero.* Minneapolis: University of Minnesota Press, 1962.

Townsend, Peter. "Adorno on Jazz: Vienna versus the Vernacular." *Prose Studies: History, Theory, Criticism* 11.1 (1988): 69–88.

Vatsyayan, Kapila. *Classical Indian Dance in Literature and the Arts.* New Delhi: Sangeet Natak Akademi, 1977.

Volpacchio, Florindo. "The Unhappy Marriage of Music and Emancipation." *Telos* 87.1 (1991): 118–123.

Wagner, Richard. "Jews in Music." *Wagner on Music and Drama.* Trans. by Ashton Ellis. Ed. by Albert Goldman and Evert Sprinchorn. New York: Dutton, 1964. 51–59.

———. "Flying Dutchman: Use of Myth." *Wagner on Music and Drama.* Trans. by Ashton Ellis. Ed. by Albert Goldman and Evert Sprinchorn. New York: Dutton, 1964. 254–55.

———. *Der Fliegende Holländer / The Flying Dutchman.* New York: Riverrun Press, 1982.

Weiner, Marc A. "*Urwaldmusik* and the Borders of German Identity: Jazz in Literature of the Weimar Republic." *The German Quarterly* 64.4 (1991): 475–487.

Weisbord, Robert. "The Case of the Slave-Ship 'Zong', 1783." *History Today* 19.8 (1969): 561–67.

Weisbord, Robert G. and Arthur Stein. *Bittersweet Encounter: The Afro-American and the American Jew*. Westport, CT: Negro University Press, 1970.

Wellmer, Albrecht. *The Persistence of Modernity*. Trans. by David Midgley. Cambridge, MA: MIT Press, 1991.

———. "On the Dialectic of Modernism and Postmodernism." Trans. by David Roberts. *Praxis International* 4.4 (1985): 337–362.

———. "Truth, Semblance, Reconciliation: Adorno's Aesthetic Redemption of Modernity." Trans. by Maeve Cooke. *Telos* 17.4 (1984–85): 89–115.

———. "Reason, Utopia and the Dialectic of Enlightenment." *Praxis International* 3.2 (1983): 83–107.

Whitebook, Joel. "From Schoenberg to Odysseus: Aesthetic, Psychic, and Social Synthesis in Adorno and Wellmer," *New German Critique* 58.1 (1993): 45–64.

Williams, Martin. *The Jazz Tradtion*. Rev. Ed. by New York: Oxford University Press, 1983.

Williams, Sherley Anne. *Give Birth to Brightness*. New York: Dial Press, 1972.

Wright, Elizabeth. *Postmodern Brecht*. New York: Routledge, 1989.

Wright, George. "Voices that Figure in *Four Quartets*." *The Placing of T.S. Eliot*. Ed. by Jewel Spears Brooker. Columbia: University of Missouri Press, 1991. 152–162.

Zipes, Jack. "Beckett in Germany/Germany in Beckett." *New German Critique* 9.2 (1982): 151–58.

Zuidervaart, Lambert. *Adorno's Aesthetic Theory*. Cambridge, MA: MIT Press, 1991.

———. "The Social Significance of Autonomous Art: Adorno and Bürger." *Journal of Aesthetics and Art Criticism* 48 (1990): 61–77.

———. "The Artefactuality of Autonomous Art: Kant and Adorno." *The Reasons of Art*, Ed. by Peter McCormick. Ottawa: University of Ottawa Press, 1986. 256–263.

Index

Adorno, Gretel, 152n
Adorno, Theodor W.
American reception, 1, 3, 11–16
elitism, 103, 115–116
eurocentrism, 117, 146
exile, 92, 102, 110
and Hegelian dialectics, 22
ideology, 118
and jazz, 7, 108
compared with his critique of the enlightenment, 110
musicology, 6
postmodernism, 1
race, 118
works
"Abschied vom Jazz," 103
Aesthetic Theory
historical relation to *Dialectics of Enlightenment*, 37
historicization of art, 12
language of, 5
reception of, 11–16
revision of dialectics, 4, 11, 13, 16, 22, 27
rhetoric of, 4, 14, 16–17, 23
structure of, 20
translation of, 149n
writing style, 37–38
Authoritarian Personality, 102
Dialectic of Enlightenment, 1, 3, 7, 60
"Elements of Anti-Semitism," 127
forced equivalences, 29
limits of social critique, 35
and *Waiting for Godot*, 54
structure of, 118
as critique of revolutionary anti-Semitism, 124
Dissonanzen, 97
"Für und Wider Jazz," 99
Introduction to the Sociology of Music, 98, 99, 121
"Jazz," 97, 99
Minima Moralia, 3
and preclusions of history, 61
"Music and Language: A Fragment," 6, 65
Negative Dialectics, 5, 25–26
and Hegel, 26
revision of dialectics, 59
"On Jazz," 99, 115
"On the Fetish Character in Music and the Regression in Listening," 103, 115
"Perennial Fashion," 99
Philosophy of Modern Music, 5, 6, 67
relation to *Dialectic of Enlightenment*, 83
influence on *Doctor Faustus*, 92
"Review of *American Jazz Music* by Wilder Hobson and of *Jazz Hot and Hybrid* by Winthrop Sargeant," 98–99
In Search of Wagner, 7, 103
influence on *Dialectic of Enlightenment*, 126
"Theses Upon Art and Religion," 34, 40
"Trying to Understand *Endgame*," 51
Aesthetic and Politics, 155n
Alldritt, Keith, 70, 75, 79
American Writers' Congress, 106
Anders, Günter, 54, 59, 159n
anti-Semitism
and African-Americans, 8, 146
and anti-capitalism, 125
Baraka, 142

anti-Semitism (*continued*)
and dialectics, 60
Hegel, 57
Holocaust, 6, 51, 54, 63
Auschwitz, 6, 147
and Becket, 160n
Jewish assimilation, conditions of, 128
Marx, 57
non-identity, Jewish, 128
pogroms, 127
Wagner, 118
Wandering Jew, 118, 142
See also cultural identity; Flying Dutchman; Second World War
Armstrong, Louis, 98, 100
and bebop, 111
commercial exploitation of, 102
teleological structure of his music, 109
virtuosity, 102
See also Ralph Ellison
art
art work
decay of, 14, 42
autonomy of, 4, 11, 17, 27, 32
commodification of, 124
concept of, 16
contradictions of, 5
culpability of,
complicity, 42–43
discordance, 29–30
engagement, 13, 16–18, 31, 33, 42, 55
See also Brecht; music
historical dialects, 33
historical specificity of, 32
Hegelian triad, challenge to, 29
illusion,
aesthetic, 27, 30
redemption of, 30
of unity, 30
irreconcilability, 27
l'art pour l'art, 12
"law of motion," 38
mimesis, 12, 13 (*Nachbilder*)
negation, aesthetic, 15, 16–19, 25, 27–28, 31, 33–34, 38
negative dialectics, 23, 25, 29, 31
and non-identity, 12, 14, 25, 27–29, 33–34, 36, 41, 124
limits of, 44–45
origins of, 20–24, 39, 44
paradoxical task of, 30
and positivism, 17
progress, 35
relation to socio-historical context, 11, 15
counter-image, 19
social function of, 42–43
and society, 14, 17, 21, 24, 40
repressing principle (*Unheil*), 18, 34
social totality, 43
secondary function of, 34
syntheses of, 29
unities posited by, 36
See also dialectics
atomic bomb, 51
authoritarian normative values, 127, 129, 145–148

Baker, Houston, 102, 109, 122
Baldwin, James, 148
Bamps, Yvan, 158n
Baraka, Amiri, 3, 5, 176n
anti-Semitism, 142, 144, 177n
dialectic of Enlightenment, 120, 145
Dutchman, 8, 119–120
Clay, 132–134
jazz, references to, 133
Lula, 131–132, 135, 143
Parker, Charles, 133, 140, 141
recovery of myth, 137
slave trade, 137–138
Smith, Bessie, 133
on jazz, 102, 105, 110
Wagner, influence of, 130
Bassett, Fletcher, 174n
Baugh, Bruce, 112, 152n
Bebbington, W. B., 162n
Beckett, Samuel, 3, 157n, 160n
absurd, 14
and Enlightenment philosophy, 62

and scholarship on Adorno, 51
resistance
to appropriation, 56
to history, 56
works
Endgame, 6
Waiting for Godot, 5, 6, 8, 51–64
clowning, 59
critique of dialectics, 52
and dialectics, 51
lordship and bondage, 52, 57, 64
revision of, 58
senility of, 53
Jewish identity, 52
relation to *Dialectic of Enlightenment*, 54
Beethoven, Ludwig van, 80, 113
Benjamin, Walter, 51, 155n
on history, 61
Der Ursprung des Deutschen Trauerspiels, 153n
"Work of Art in the Age of Mechanical Reproduction," 97
Benston, Kimberly, 109, 135
Berendt, Joachim-Ernst, 98, 99, 102
Berg, Alban, 99
Berman, Russell, 3, 7, 112, 167n
Bernstein, Jay, 155n, 157n, 158n, 159n
Black American Literature Forum, 168n
Blamires, Harry, 163n
Block, Ernst, 51, 155n
Booty, John, 82
Brown, Lloyd W., 174n
Brecht, Bertold, 18, 51, 155n
Bürger, Peter, 11–12, 89, 151n, 167n
Buck-Morss, Susan, 156n, 157n
Bush, Ronald, 74
Butler, Judith, 63, 155n, 159n

Calloway, Cab, 106
Carner, Gary, 168n
Ceynowa, Andrzej, 174n
Chaffin, Deborah, 158n
Chaplin, Charles, 60, 158n
Charles I, 89
Coleridge, Samuel Taylor, 137
Collier, James Lincoln, 105–106
Comintern, 107
See also jazz
Cruse, Harold, 148, 173n
cultural identity
African-American, 7, 102
assimilation, 134
black nationalism, 104, 107, 108
and bebop, 110
essentialism, 135
Garveyism, 107
racism against, 146
slavery, abolition of, 136
alienation, 128
German
nationalism, 122
Jewish, 6
and anti-Semitism, 8
assimilation, 60
Auschwitz and Jewish subjectivity, 54, 62
and negative dialectics, 58
See also *Waiting for Godot*
normative values, 146
race, 118
repression of, 118
shared tradition vs. racial characteristics, 127
See also Flying Dutchman, myth of; Wagner and German cultural identity
culture
folk, 7
Adorno's skeptical view of, 107
and fascism, 104
high, 103
popular, 97
culture industry, 7, 39, 44, 98, 117, 126
anti-Semitism, 124
and consumption, 121
and fascism, 104
"perpetual sameness," 121
resistance to, 123
Wagner, 118–119, 126
See also Ellison: entertainment industry

Daily Worker, 106
Dallmayr, Fred, 165n
D'Amico, Robert, 112, 152n
Daniel, Jamie Owen, 103, 117
Davis, Mike, 170n
Davis, Miles, 100
DeVeaux, Scott, 105, 106, 115
Dews, Peter, 23
dialectics
  Adorno's revision of
    See works: *Aesthetic Theory*; *Negative Dialectics*
  and aesthetics, 4
  Aufhebung, 4, 11, 14–15, 22, 25–26, 27, 36, 80, 158n
  Auschwitz, after, 161n
  competing paradigms, 53
  concept (*Begriff*), 23
    historical continuity of, 32
  decay of, 51
  dissonance, 56, 61
  heterogeneity, 4, 24, 25, 29, 31
  lordship and bondage. *See* Beckett
  negation, 4, 15 (aesthetic)
  negative dialectics, 23, 28, 57
  non-integrable, 4
    in art, 29–33, 41
    in Adorno's writing style, 38
  regression, 60
  senility of. *See* Beckett
  subjectivity, 55
  synthesis, 29 (aesthetic)
  unity. See also *Aufhebung*
    imposed system, 1
  See also Hegel; Beckett
Diels, Herman, 162n

Early, Gerald, 174n
Edelmann, R., 178n
Eliot, T. S., 3
  language and decay, 69, 76
  redemption, 70
  works
    Four Quartets, 5, 6, 7, 65–93
      dance, 72, 73, 77
      dialectic of Enlightenment, 74
      form and content, 70, 76, 84
      Germany, 84
      Good Friday, 82
      old English, use of, 77
      Second World War, 84, 86–87
      singing, 72
    "Music of Poetry," 6, 65–69
  See also music
Ellington, Duke, 101
Ellison, Ralph, 3, 5
  "Change the Joke and Slip the Yoke," 102
  entertainment industry, 102
  Invisible Man, 7, 97, 100
    and African-American Identity, 102
    and black nationalism, 112
    and communist party, 112
    "Jack-the-Bear," 101
    Louis Armstrong, 100, 108, 110
    Marxism, 109
    representations of the left, 105–106
Ellmann, Maud, 165n
Elyot, Sir Thomas, 165n
Enlightenment
  Adorno's critique of, 55
  dialectic of, 54
  and dissonance, 61
  and myth, 136
  See also Beckett
Estes, Simon, 139

Fascism, 51
  and culture industry, 104
  folk culture, 105
  Nazi ideology, 103, 118
    and Adorno's critique of jazz, 103
  and revolutionary anti-Semitism, 125
Feher, Ferenc, 72
Ferguson, Otis, 105
Ferrar, Nicholas, 89
Flint, R. W., 68
Flying Dutchman, The myth of, 7–8, 118, 120
  anti-Semitism, 120

as black captain, 139
Cain, relation to, 142, 144, 177n
Coleridge's use of, 137
Rime of the Ancient Mariner, 139
Falkenberg, 137, 144
false unities in *The Flying Dutchman* and *Dutchman*, 137
as metaphor for jazz, 137
Old Navigator, relation to, 176n
parallel uses by Wagner and Baraka, 130, 136
slave trade, 137
specters, accompanied by, 137–138
Wandering Jew, relation to, 118, 141–143
Ahasuerus, 144–145
Nietzsche on, 143
wild huntsman, relation to, 140, 144
Zong, 175n
See also Baraka, Amiri; Wagner, Richard

Gardner, Helen, 79, 164n
Gennari, John, 104
Geulen, Eva, 149n
Gordon, Eugene, 106
Gross, Harvey, 91

Habermas, Jürgen, 2
Haggin, B. H., 105
Hammond, John, 105, 106
Hayden, Joseph, 80, 84
Heble, Ajay, 109
Hegel, G. W. F., 6, 14, 21–22, 25, 38–39, 58, 62–63, 159n
on Jews, 52, 57, 59
works
Early Theological Writings, 57, 59
Phenomenology of Spirit, 57
Herbert, George, 89
Heine, Heine, 176n
Heyndels, Ralph, 158n
Hindemith, Paul, 99
Hitler, Adolph, 102, 124
Hobson, Wilder, 98, 103
Hodeir, André, 113
Hohendahl, Peter, 3, 11, 13, 15–16, 21–22, 38, 44, 54, 150n, 153n
Holloway, John, 165n
Homer, 83–85, 166n
homo oeconomicus, 127
Horkheimer, Max, 3, 29, 40, 54, 83, 108, 118, 125, 128
"Egoism and the Freedom Movement," 136
Hughes, Langston, 102
Hullot-Kentor, Robert, 149n, 150n
Hurwitz, S., 177n
Huyssen, Andreas, 44, 117, 136, 169n
Hyppolite, Jean, 57, 155n, 161n

idealism, German, 11

Jameson, Fredric, 37, 103, 149n, 166n
Jauss, Hans Robert, 54
Jay, Martin, 61, 98, 103, 105, 117, 151n, 152n, 153n, 156n
jazz, 5, 7
and Adorno's critique of Wagner, 117
African influences, 102
appropriation of
by State Department, 105
by Comintern, 105, 107
audience, 122
bebop, 99, 110–111
critics, 104
entertainment industry, 102
history of, 98, 100
Adorno's position in, 98, 100
improvisation, 113–114, 122
"Jack-the-Bear," 101
liberation, 123
minstrelsy, 114–115
and modernism, 117
Nazi banning of, 103
production, conditions of, 123
swing, 99
tradition, 97

jazz (*continued*)
  and Wagner, 103, 120
  See also Adorno; Louis Armstrong; Miles Davis, Charles Parker
St. John of the Cross, 164

Kant, Immanuel, 13, 39
Katz, Jacob, 172n
Keats, John, 76
Kelly, George, 156n
Kenner, High, 71
Klu Klux Klan, 177n
Kofsky, Frank, 104, 111
Kojève, Alexandre, 155n
Krenek, Ernst, 67, 99
Krukowski, Lucian, 163n
Kuhn, Thomas, 54
Kupfer, Harry, 139

Levi, Herman, 143
Lindberg, John, 176n
Lobb, Edward, 164n
Lott, Eric, 115
Lowes, John Livingston, 137
Lüdke, W. Martin, 63, 156n, 158n
Lukács, Georg, 21, 51, 53, 153n, 156n
  aesthetics compared to Adorno's, 41
Lunn, Eugene, 23, 160n
Lyne, William, 106
Lyotard, Jean-François, 2, 54, 124, 156n, 173n
  "Adorno as Devil," 13

Madame Bovary, 14
Mann, Thomas, 92, 168n
Marcuse, Herbert, 61
Marx, Karl, 40
  aesthetics, Marxist, 41, 51
  Hegelian-Marxism, 38
    Adorno's critique of, 53
    Lyotard's critique of, 54
  materialism, 150n
  "On the Jewish Question," 57, 125
  revolutionary anti-Semitism, 118, 124–126
  "Thesen über Feuerbach," 150n
    See also Wagner
Matthissen, F. O., 87, 164n
McCormack, W. J., 155n, 156n
Mozart, Wolfgang A., 80
music
  absolutes, 74, 75
  civilization, 69, 82
  classical, 98
    vs. "light" music, 103
  engagement, 122
  Gebrauchsmusik, 99, 100
  and history, 66–68, 73, 121
  and language, 65–69, 83
  late romanticism, 110
  Neue Sachlichkeit, 99
  as negative experience, 72
  universality, 86
  Viennese school, 124
  See also jazz

Nägele, Rainer, 25
Nation of Islam, 175
Neal, Larry, 109
Nelson, High, 174n
Newton, Judy, 177n
Newton, Michael, 177n
Nietzsche, Friedrich, 142
Nye, William, 103

Osborne, Peter, 37, 153n
Ostendorf, Berndt, 102

Paddison, Max, 2, 149n, 161n
Parker, Charles, 100, 110
politics
  telos, 42
  See *Aesthetic Theory*: recognition of; art: *engagement*
proletariat, 53

Rappl, Eric, 176n
Rather, L. J., 172
reification, 22, 40, 120, 123, 127
Reinelt, Janelle, 157n
Roberts, David, 1, 35, 81, 84, 166n
Rose, Gillian, 152n
Rose, Paul, 173
Rosen, Charles, 80

Said, Edward, 81
Sargeant, Winthrop, 98, 101
Savery, Pancho, 102
Schoenberg, Arnold, 86, 100, 110, 124, 160n
Schönherr, Ulrich, 103, 112, 117
Schubert, Franz, 80
Schulte-Sasse, Jochen, 151n
Schweik, Robert, 77
Seiber, Mátyás, 98
Second World War, 51, 63, 69, 84, 86–87, 90, 143
Shusterman, Richard, 90, 166n
Smith, Charles Edward, 105
social totality, 4
Sollars, Werner, 136, 138, 174n
Sontag, Susan, 143, 177n
Spanish Civil War, 106
Stalin, 108, 157n
Star, Frederick, 105, 106
Stein, Arthur, 173n
Stepto, Robert B., 114
Stravinsky, Igor, 86, 99, 165n
Subotnik, Rose, 83

Telos (journal), 168
Tiedemann, Rolf, 152n
Thomas, Lorenzo, 103
Thorslev, Peter, 178n
Townsend, Peter, 103

Volpacchio, Florindo, 116

Wagner, Richard, 7, 117
  anti-capitalism, 123
    and nationalism, 125
    and plight of individual, 126
  anti-Semitism
  Bayreuth, 122
  beat, use of, 121
  The Flying Dutchman, 8, 118–119, 129
    Dutchman, 131–132
    Erik the Hunter, 140
    Senta, 130–132
    production of, by Harry Kupfer, 139
  German cultural identity, 8
  and history, 122
  and jazz, 103, 117, 120
  "Jews in Music," 118, 125
  Jews, plight of, 128
  proto-fascist tendencies, 143
  redemption
    Adorno on, 142
    Nietzsche on, 142
  revolutionary anti-Semitism, 118, 124–126
Waller, Fats, 106
Wandering Jew. *See* anti-Semitism; Flying Dutchman, the myth of
Weber, Max, 40
Weil, Kurt, 99
Weimar Republic, 103
Weiner, Marc, 103
Wellmer, Albrecht, 1, 29, 40, 42
Weisbord, Robert, 173n
Whitebook, Joel, 86
Whiteman, Paul, 103
Wright, Elizabeth, 151
Wright, George, 76

Zipes, Jack, 51, 155n, 161n
Zuidervaart, Lambert, 2, 30–31, 33, 149n, 150n, 151n, 155n